W9-CEW-139

Along the Roaring River

My Wild Ride from Mao to the Met

Hao Jiang Tian

with

Lois B. Morris

FOREWORD BY ROBERT LIPSYTE

LINCOLN CENTER for the Performing Arts

WILEY

John Wiley & Sons, Inc.

This book is printed on acid-free paper. ∞

Copyright © 2008 by Hao Jiang Tian, Lois B. Morris, and Robert Lipsyte. All rights reserved

Published by John Wiley & Sons, Inc., Hoboken, New Jersey
Published simultaneously in Canada

"Wandering Ch'ing Ling Stream in Nan-Yang," by Li Po, translated by David Hinton, from *The Selected Poems of Li Po,* © 1996 by David Hinton. Reprinted by permission of New Directions Publishing Corp. "Goodbye at the River," by Li Po, from *Five T'ang Poets: Wang Wei, Li Po, Tu Fu, Li Ho, Li Shang-yin,* translated and introduced by David Young, Oberlin College Press, © 1990. Reprinted by permission of Oberlin College Press

All photographs courtesy of Hao Jiang Tian except the following: p. 8, Tommy Ng; pp. 43, 50, Lois B. Morris; p. 222, Arnaldo Colombaroli; p. 226, Bonini; p. 274, Carol Pratt; p. 285, © Beth Bergman, 2001; p. 297, Mark Kiryluk

No part of this publication may be reproduced, stored in a retrieval system, or transmitted in any form or by any means, electronic, mechanical, photocopying, recording, scanning, or otherwise, except as permitted under Section 107 or 108 of the 1976 United States Copyright Act, without either the prior written permission of the Publisher, or authorization through payment of the appropriate per-copy fee to the Copyright Clearance Center, 222 Rosewood Drive, Danvers, MA 01923, (978) 750–8400, fax (978) 646–8600, or on the web at www.copyright.com. Requests to the Publisher for permission should be addressed to the Permissions Department, John Wiley & Sons, Inc., 111 River Street, Hoboken, NJ 07030, (201) 748–6011, fax (201) 748–6008, or online at http://www.wiley.com/go/permissions.

Limit of Liability/Disclaimer of Warranty: While the publisher and the author have used their best efforts in preparing this book, they make no representations or warranties with respect to the accuracy or completeness of the contents of this book and specifically disclaim any implied warranties of merchantability or fitness for a particular purpose. No warranty may be created or extended by sales representatives or written sales materials. The advice and strategies contained herein may not be suitable for your situation. You should consult with a professional where appropriate. Neither the publisher nor the author shall be liable for any loss of profit or any other commercial damages, including but not limited to special, incidental, consequential, or other damages.

For general information about our other products and services, please contact our Customer Care Department within the United States at (800) 762–2974, outside the United States at (317) 572–3993 or fax (317) 572–4002.

Wiley also publishes its books in a variety of electronic formats. Some content that appears in print may not be available in electronic books. For more information about Wiley products, visit our web site at www.wiley.com.

Library of Congress Cataloging-in-Publication Data:
Tian, Hao Jiang, date.
   Along the roaring river: my wild ride from Mao to the Met / Hao Jiang Tian with Lois B. Morris; foreword by Robert Lipsyte.
     p.   cm.
   Includes index.
   ISBN 978-0-470-05641-7 (cloth: alk. paper)
   1. Tian, Hao Jiang, 1954-   2. Basses (Singers)—United States—Biography.
   3. Chinese American musicians—Biography.   I. Morris, Lois B.   II. Title.
   ML420.T49A3 2008
   782.1092—dc22

   [B]

                                                  2007046849

Printed in the United States of America

10 9 8 7 6 5 4 3 2 1

For Martha

Out of respect for their privacy, we have changed the names and other identifying information about some of the people who appear in this book.

CONTENTS

FOREWORD
by Robert Lipsyte

In the summer of 2002, Lois B. Morris and I were in Shanghai following Itzhak Perlman's program for young string and piano prodigies, which we had written about for the *New York Times*. A friendly woman named Martha Liao, who was involved in the Perlman group's joint workshop with Chinese youngsters, introduced us to her husband, Tian.

Who knew this was *yuan*—what was meant to be?

We had seen Tian on posters all over town. He had a big, handsome face with soulful dark eyes and lips about to break into a mischievous smile. He was giving a recital. Our attention was elsewhere. The Itzhak Perlman–sponsored young musicians were practicing with their Chinese counterparts. While the music was grand, the culture clash was startling: the Americans were polite and respectful, but the Chinese were rude and arrogant, often text-messaging during rehearsals. Lois and I realized that our advance reading hadn't prepared us for twenty-first-century China; we reeled through the hot, wet, teeming streets of Shanghai.

And then, in the cool, hushed lobby of our hotel, we met Tian, a man of both twenty-first-century and ancient China. When those eyes sparkled and the smile broke out, the young players and their cell phones faded. And when that impossibly deep voice began to tell tales of a teenager growing up wild on the streets of Beijing during the Cultural Revolution, we were enthralled. We sat for hours in the lobby bar, oblivious to anything but the vivid saga of this lifelong rebel and Red Guard–for-a-day; this lover, smuggler, factory hand, accordion player, and dreamer, who had educated himself with stolen books and had outraged authorities by singing songs heard on Voice of America while shaking his hips like Elvis.

At first, the stories sounded like fantasies from an alternate universe. We were only two days into our first trip to China and were overwhelmed by the new sights and sounds and smells. We had no idea that Tian—we weren't yet able to pronounce his name properly—was a historical character. He was the first world-class opera singer to emerge from China.

A few days later, we found out that he was also a singer of rare and thrilling talent. Along with Itzhak and Toby Perlman and some voice and drama coaches from the Metropolitan Opera, we went to Tian's recital at the Shanghai Grand Theatre. Once again, he enthralled us. Speaking in English and Chinese, he reached out to the audience with the same intimate warmth we had felt in the lobby. He sang arias, lieder, Chinese folk songs, "Danny Boy," and "Some Enchanted Evening." This last number, with Martha at the piano, was a collaboration they would repeat two years later when Lois and I were married in New York.

Who could have imagined that a pleasant afternoon in a Shanghai hotel lobby would turn out to be the unrehearsed overture to a friendship that would open a window on the return of China to the world stage of art, business, and politics and put us on the path to this book?

Now that's *yuan*!

The sense of fate and karma, of what was meant to be, was a recurring theme as our relationship with Tian bloomed. Because he was kind and generous, he was our introduction to such Chinese artists as the composers Tan Dun and Guo Wenjing, the pianist Lang Lang, the violinist Cho-Liang (Jimmy) Lin, the film director Zhang Yimou, the novelist Ha Jin, and many others who were catalysts of their times, transforming their arts and making connections to the West. Because Tian was so modest and humble, it was a while before it became apparent that he was one of those catalysts, a transformer and a connector in his own right.

Like many other artists whose characters were tempered in the heat of the Cultural Revolution, Tian's struggle for survival eventually became a struggle to achieve a higher purpose. It was an idealistic vision that unfolded slowly, like a flower opening. First, he refined his gifts with the best teachers in China. Then he dared to think about learning from the best in the West. The dream expanded; he would be successful in the West, an inspiration to other Chinese, and a wake-up call to Americans and Europeans of the huge Asian talent pool that was ready to reinvigorate classical music.

When we met Tian, he was taking the next major step: now an American citizen, he was returning to China to develop young musicians who would compose and perform modern works melding East and West, creating a new tradition for the world.

Some task! But there is a steely purity in the idealism of those who survived the Cultural Revolution as youngsters. They saw not only the dangers of a country turning on itself and punishing its best and brightest, they also saw the resilience and passion of Chinese artists. These are men and women who place art before commerce and their heritage before themselves—they are dedicated to the possibility of bringing back China's ancient role as a cradle of creativity and innovation.

This isn't all that simple in today's China, which is reveling in its role as the emerging world power. In Xi'an, visiting the terra cotta soldiers buried with the First Emperor, we were lectured by our tour guide. "We will be number one in the world," he told us. "Maybe not today or tomorrow, but my daughter will live in a China that is number one."

In four trips to China that included Lois's visits to the villages where Tian's mother and father grew up, we came to realize that the tour guide was echoing a national sentiment. From year to year, skylines changed, old neighborhoods disappeared, new stores appeared and bulged with expensive goods. Cars were replacing bicycles in the cities. The Forbidden City had a Starbucks!

Artists were changing, too. The younger musicians we met did not have that same idealistic purity as Tian's generation. They were more like many Americans we knew, proud of their fancy apartments, their cars, their clothes, their maids.

By this time, Lois could not only pronounce Tian (T.N.), but she was beginning to understand how those tumultuous, gritty, sometimes dangerous early years were key to the emotion in his work and the passion in his drive to be better. He had gotten a late start, but he brought so much real-life experience and feeling to his roles. How else could a wild child end up on the stage of the Metropolitan Opera?

In the search for answers, Lois (by now dubbed LoLo—I was BoBo) ate hundreds of delicious handmade dumplings from Martha's kitchen and talked to Tian for hours in the United States and China. She lived with them in Beijing and Colorado, and they stayed with us on Long Island. We played with Luke, their parrot who sings opera, and their English springer spaniel, Niu Niu, which means Little Girl, who is not only very much a girl, but a diva. It was always fun, but it was also often frustrating. There is a sweet reticence to Tian that makes him a great friend but a sometimes difficult subject. His achievements are amazing, but he would rather talk about how honored he was to sing on the same stage as Luciano Pavarotti and Plácido Domingo.

Sometimes, the most telling moments were not in his telling at all.

Going back with Tian to the Beijing factory where he had worked for seven years, we spotted an American flag outside the front door. The world had changed radically since Tian cut sheets of steel there; the factory was now a joint venture of Chinese and U.S. companies. But the factory itself hadn't changed. Inside, the steel still moved perilously close overhead, and the workers still brought their metal bowls to the cafeteria for their rice lunches. The hard work that had forged Tian had not changed at all. Old factory comrades ran over to hug him, retell stories, laugh, and cry. They later came to his recital and went back to his hotel to drink and sing.

If Tian was boisterous with his old buddies, he was tender with students in his master classes. He listened to them sing, then clapped, laughed, and made gentle suggestions. He had much to give, not least of all the sense of possibility to youngsters who had never been out of China. Tian had come back to them from New York City, Milan, and Buenos Aires to say, "If I could have made it under my circumstances, you have far more of a chance now." This was no idle encouragement. When he was their age, Tian had never seen a Western opera performed. And he had no role model, as they did, of someone who had made it on the world's greatest opera stages.

The images of Tian on the factory floor and in the master classes seemed naked and endearing compared to the images of him in costume, wig, and makeup on the opera stage in typical bass roles as elderly doctor, comic old landlord, cuckolded rich husband, and tragic king, often an object of pity, scorn, or laughter. Even as a fool, he brought dignity and an intense drama to his roles. As Mephistopheles, he was fearsome.

Watching him as the general in Tan Dun's *The First Emperor*—stalwart, thwarted, and furious—I was amazed anew at his skill, knowing that underneath that actor's mask was the sweet, romantic, thoughtful, bold, daring Tian of his early swashbuckling years.

And then, in the summer of 2007, he appeared in a mountaintop opera house in Central City, Colorado, as the title character in *Poet Li Bai*—a dreamer, a lover, a rebel. For ninety minutes onstage playing China's greatest poet, this former wild child of the Beijing streets, this powerful hauler of steel, raged and wept and crooned and died. And enthralled the audience.

For those of us who had come to love Tian, seeing the reach of his dramatic and musical gifts was a visceral thrill. But we also saw something even grander—we saw his vision develop and expand; we saw him transform classical music and forge joyous connections between East and West.

Yuan

A bird does not sing because it has an answer.
It sings because it has a song.

–Chinese proverb

MY MOTHER, BORN a decade after China's last emperor forever departed the Forbidden City, marched to a new tune—in her combat boots.

She left her provincial home in 1939 when she was just thirteen years old, to repel the Japanese occupiers. She joined a military propaganda entertainment troupe, where she met my father, who was a year older. Her given name was Du Li—Li, meaning "beauty." Now, as she and my father helped to usher in a new era under Mao Zedong, in which vanity and femininity were bourgeois pursuits, she foreswore the name her parents had given her. She changed even her family name and became Lu Yuan, which together mean "big land." (In China, the family name always comes first.) My father changed his from Tian Xiaohai, the given name indicating his birth year on the lunar calendar, to Tian Yun, which means "cultivate." And thus, in 1954, Big Land was Cultivated and along came me.

They named me Roaring River. That's what Hao Jiang means. Chinese parents seek names to signify *yuan*—fate, what is meant to be—and character, to preserve a memory, to honor a national event, to embody a dream, a prayer. I have friends born in 1949 or on October 1, the year and the day of the founding of the People's Republic of China, whose parents named them Jianguo—"found a nation." My friend Jian Jun, meaning "found an army," was born on August 1, the day the Red Army was established in 1927. Many people born into old revolutionary families in the city of Yan'an, the headquarters of the Communist Party from 1936 to 1947, have "Yan" in their names, as does my friend Yansheng—"born in Yan'an."

So now you are thinking that Hao Jiang represents the Roaring River of Mao's might and power, perhaps even that it foretells the ultimately onrushing tide of contemporary Chinese commerce. If you do, you will be wrong, and you will never understand me or my parents or what they did or did not have in mind for me or how I grew up in the upside-down world of China's Cultural Revolution.

In fact, I had no real name at all until I was fourteen and my parents had to come up with one in order to register me for middle school. So they chose Hao Jiang, not to mean anything at all promising or hopeful or powerful or political, but rather because my older brother's name was Hao Qian ("big road"), and it is customary to duplicate the first part of the name for a sibling. Until then I had only a nickname, Xiao Lu, a girl's name. It means "little deer." My parents gave me this name before I was born, hoping that I would be a girl, since they already had a boy. (They called him Mimi, meaning "kitty." They had expected a girl the first time, too.) When my mother heard my first cry, and it was a loud one, she knew immediately that it was a boy again. But Little Deer I remained. A Little Deer whom the forces of destiny would toss into a raging stream.

Now, perhaps, you are beginning to perceive the sounds of my youth. Indeed, by the time of my birth my parents had become important musicians in the People's Liberation Army, where they spent their entire careers. From little lambs bleating for their nation, they ripened into dragons breathing fire-music to inspire militant and revolutionary passion. They grew powerful and well-connected, she as a composer, he as a conductor. This was the white-hot sound in which I grew up, the clamorous lullaby of my childhood.

I loathed the increasingly loud, unrelenting sameness of this music. After the incarceration of my politically questionable piano teacher, the lessons that had been forced on me stopped, and my parents gave up on me. Later, it was I who gleefully destroyed my father's one hundred musical recordings, piece by piece. Then our whole world came crashing apart, and even they, loyal musicians of the revolution, were sent away to the provinces, where they remained faithful and continued to make music, though shamed. I raised myself by myself, skirting ignominy, surviving as a wild boy on the fringes of society, indulging in the odd vestiges of privilege my parents had left behind. And I found, within that once reviled piano, now stripped of its strings, the music of my future. My name is Roaring River, and I sing grand opera.

The Beast with Eighty-Eight Teeth

1

Music Torture

THE MOOD IN the Metropolitan Opera rehearsal room was tense and frustrated. Tempers were fraying.

"I can't play it another way. I've changed it so many times already, I just cannot do it again," said the normally accommodating soprano Elizabeth Futral, in a don't-mess-with-me tone of voice.

The December 2006 world premiere of *The First Emperor* was one week away, and our collective spirit was deteriorating. Every opening of a new production is fraught; multiply that by a hundred for a brand-new opera. But this opera had even more at stake. Plácido Domingo, the biggest star currently on the opera stage, was heading this first-ever Chinese-written, Chinese-directed, Chinese-designed opera, which was also the first-ever collaboration between the Metropolitan Opera and a Chinese creative team. Composer Tan Dun, whose film scores for *Crouching Tiger, Hidden Dragon* and *Hero* were his works most familiar to American audiences, had teamed with Chinese film director Zhang Yimou, whose movies had ranged from the small and tragic, such as *Raise the Red Lantern*, to the spectacular, like *Hero*. The libretto was written in English by the prize-winning Chinese novelist Ha Jin.

For me, *The First Emperor* represented the first time in my opera career that I would sing the role of an actual Chinese character in a work about real Chinese history. By that time, I had sung King Timur in Puccini's Italian conception of a Chinese opera, *Turandot*, at least two hundred times in opera houses all over the world. But never had an opera been presented for Western ears that told an authentic Chinese story, written by a Chinese composer, with a production designed by a Chinese artist. I could bring my personal history and that of my country to bear on this work, in which I was to sing the principal role of the doomed General Wang, who also happens to have some great singing in this opera.

Publicity was everywhere in print and on the airwaves and had been growing for months. Now this opera was being billed as a breakthrough in the history of the art form and even of East-West relations. Oh, the pressure.

"Okay, let's take a twenty-minute break," sighed one of the Met's artistic staff members.

As the cast and production crew began to wander off, I sat down to let my fingers loose on the piano. I needed to lighten the mood. The tune that came to my fingers was "The East Is Red," the

Plácido Domingo (on the left) sang the title role in The First Emperor, *a Chinese-written opera by Tan Dun that had its world premiere at the Met in December 2006. I'm the general, who believes he will gain the hand of the princess once he fights the emperor's bloody battles. But the princess has a mind of her own and the centerpiece love scene is not with the general.*

omnipresent anthem from the long-gone era of the Cultural Revolution. And then, all around me, one by one, Chinese voices began to sing:

Dongfan hong, taiyang sheng,
Zhongguo chu liao ge Mao Zedong,
Ta wei renmin mou xingu,
Hu er hei you, ta shi renmin da jiu xing.

Our peals of laughter must have rolled out like a tidal wave into the hallway. The people from the Met and the non-Chinese performers, who had no idea what we were singing about, rushed back in. They were astonished to find Zhang Yimou, normally so dour, singing and raising his fist to the sky in a gesture familiar to anyone who had been alive during the Cultural Revolution. And his codirector, Wang Chaoge, who had been the most stressed out of his team, was actually dancing! Now all the singers were back in the room, and everybody was laughing, something no one had expected to experience during this rehearsal.

For the full twenty minutes we sang and sang and sang, one revolutionary song after another, plus set pieces with characteristic poses from the model operas we'd been required to attend during the Cultural Revolution. Wang Chaoge danced on, Zhang Yimou leaped about and gestured, and, as I added my own voice, I felt a rush of mixed feelings. The Cultural Revolution had been such a difficult time.

Whenever I sing "The East Is Red" now, so often I think back to an evening I spent in 1971 with a peasant farmer near my home in Beijing. The dumpling restaurant where I'd come for a cheap dinner that cold winter night was fairly crowded. I sat down at a table that had only one other customer, a very dirty man with a filthy old winter coat but no shirt on underneath. He probably wasn't as ancient as he looked, but the lines on his face were deep, not to mention dirt-caked. He quietly sang some old folk songs while nursing a cup of cheap Mongolian wine made from white yams. I'd heard many of his tunes before, since most of our revolutionary songs, including "The East Is Red," had been set to old folk melodies, but I'd never heard these lyrics, some of which were very romantic, some raunchy. Though it was a little hard to understand the man, because he had no front teeth, I got to talking with him. He told me he had just delivered a load of cabbages to the city and was now on the way back to his village. With his horse and cart, the trip in had taken him all day, and the trip back would take him all night. Because of traffic congestion, farmers with carts were allowed to come into the city only at night in those days. I asked him about his life and his songs, and for four hours I bought us both more cups of the harsh, burning, definitely intoxicating wine.

The man told me he knew all the old folk songs but wasn't so good at the new words. Back in 1966, he said, some Red Guards took offense when they heard him singing "The East Is Red" with the lyrics to the original love song. They rushed over and began to beat him. He was a counterrevolutionary, they yelled, because he had "changed the text" of an important revolutionary song, and that was a big crime. When they demanded that he sing it with the "correct" words, he was so scared he couldn't remember them. They beat him harder and threatened him more. At one point they had his head pushed down nearly to the ground as they hit him across the back of his skull. But the more they hurt him, the less he could recall the required lyrics. So they said that if he couldn't sing the song correctly, they would make sure he could no longer sing the words at all, and they smashed him with a stick directly in his mouth. Laughing as he told me this, he pointed to the empty hole where his front teeth should be. He laughed and laughed.

And here, more than thirty-five years later, in a rehearsal room at the Metropolitan Opera in New York City, were three survivors of that horrific decade, singing those songs of oppression, yet suffused with the warmth of bittersweet nostalgia. We were back in our youth, the youth in our hearts, feeling a camaraderie that lifted our transient worldly cares. I felt such a loving kinship with my Chinese colleagues. We had come through that terrible time, yet in spite of it, or perhaps because of it, we had discovered our artistic identities. And life goes on.

We wrapped up our little intermezzo in such fine spirits, with a rendition of "East Wind Blows," a popular revolutionary song from those days with lyrics from a Chairman Mao quotation: "The east wind of socialism is prevailing over the west wind of imperialism." We sang it in Chinese, so who knew? We were young again, invigorated, ready for anything.

It was good to be born in Beijing.

Ever since the Forbidden City had become home to China's ruling dynasties in the fifteenth century, the people of Beijing have believed themselves more cultured, more refined, more knowledgeable, and better-spoken than everyone else in this vast and ancient land. By the time I howled my way into the universe, Beijing was Chairman Mao's seat of power. Nanjing had been Chiang Kai-shek's center of government during the Kuomintang (KMT), or Nationalist Party, period. In 1949, after the revolution, the Communists reestablished the capital of the People's Republic of China in its historic place in the land.

Because of the *hukou* system, which confined the residence of each Chinese citizen to one particular location that was registered at birth, a person born elsewhere in China could not remain in Beijing for more than a brief period. Indeed, no one could move—even from a rural area to a nearby town—without government approval, which was hard to obtain. The system remains in effect even now, and it is especially difficult to change from a rural to a city *hukou*—although this is becoming easier to evade with all the free enterprise that is prevalent throughout China today. Nowadays, at least half of the people in Beijing were not born there, and perhaps the superior airs of those in the capital are fading. But in those days, to have a Beijing *hukou* was a huge privilege.

My parents had not been born anywhere near Beijing. Although they grew up just one mountain apart in rural Shanxi province, they did not know each other when they left their families in 1939 to fight the Japanese. In the town of Jincheng, my mother's family, named Du, had once been very influential and had owned considerable property. Their tile-roofed houses encompassed five courtyards, all connected to one another and surrounded by thick gray-brick walls. The Du family was so well-off generations ago that they had their own *si shu*, or traditional Chinese elementary school, just for their own children. There was even a separate hall in their home to preserve their ancestors' memorial tablets and the family *zupu*, the book of generations in which all names were recorded.

By the time my mother was born, however, her family's circumstances had vastly changed. Her father eventually had to leave the family in Jincheng to live far away in Beijing, where he worked as a private chef in an antique store to support his family. The Japanese, who invaded Shanxi province in 1937, captured my mother's two oldest brothers; one was never heard from again, and the other died in captivity after he broke his back doing hard labor. Two words—"Move out!"—spared her father's life. Lined up alongside other men in their village, he awaited his turn as, one by one, their throats were cut. The sword was at my grandpa's neck when the commander issued the fateful order that inadvertently saved his life.

My mother had received no education until she was ten, when she pleaded with the local teacher to allow her to study, even though she had no money to pay for it. The good woman offered to teach my mother to knit and to help her sell what she made to pay her tuition. Thus, my mother obtained three years of education— enough, in her words, "to go do Revolution."

My father was from Yangcheng, a poor farming village in the mountains. He was one of six children in the Sun family. They were so poor that his parents gave him up for adoption to a family named Tian; two of his brothers went to other families. By the time he met my mother in the entertainment unit of the 93rd Army Battalion, the Japanese had already massacred hundreds of thousands of civilians in the siege of the Chinese capital at Nanjing. The two young teens had no musical training, but they had no end of vitality and enthusiasm—and outrage. Their mission was to fill the soldiers' and the citizens' hearts and minds with courage and patriotic fervor through music, dance, and drama. It was something they would do, in one way or another, for the rest of their professional lives.

To their chagrin, their battalion soon fell into retreat, so, along with three of their friends, they simply walked away, to seek the enemy on their own. Until they saw their names painted huge on billboards as deserters to be executed when found, they had no concept of AWOL. Too late, they shed their uniforms. Military police caught up with them at a railway station. The five cried their eyes out. The senior officer took pity on them and, moved by their desire to face the foreign invader, let them escape.

Now the thirteen- and fourteen-year-old comrades made their way to the Second Anti-Enemy Performing Arts Troupe, one of ten propaganda ensembles under the aegis of the KMT. Mao Zedong and Chiang Kai-shek had agreed to abandon their civil war, to form a united front under KMT military leadership to fight the Japanese. My parents did not know at first that the Second Troupe was an underground Communist cell. It was under the leadership of Zhou Enlai, who would one day serve as premier of Communist China, but who, like everyone else in wartime, wore the KMT uniform. Soon their political sympathies leaned earnestly, if secretly, leftward. As the Japanese approached and bullets flew, they sang and danced and acted their way from town to town, encouraging soldiers and townsfolk alike to be just as strong and brave and patriotic as they were.

Soon after they joined, the Second Anti-Enemy Performing Arts Troupe was selected to perform the premiere of *The Yellow River Cantata*. Immediately, the stirring work became the symbol of Chinese defiance against the Japanese. (It remains the most famous choral work in China and is known in every Chinese community throughout the world.) As a result, the Second Troupe became famous throughout China. But the KMT leadership was growing suspicious of the political allegiance of this troupe. Why, they began to wonder, had the Second Troupe been chosen over the other nine ensembles? Was it because the performance was held in Yan'an, the headquarters of the Chinese Communist Party? Misgivings were so great by the end of the War of Resistance against Japanese Aggression that the KMT government detained a third of the troupe's members and grilled them for three months. My parents were not held, however, and although my father had joined the Communist Party in 1941, no one disclosed this or any other secret. Ultimately, the ensemble relocated to Beijing (then called Beiping), where they performed in the massive public celebration of the Chinese victory over the Japanese.

Without a common enemy, all pretense of cooperation between the KMT and the Communists disintegrated. Civil war broke out again in 1946. My father became involved with clandestine Communist activities at Beijing University, teaching sympathizers the music and politics of revolution. Beijing was occupied by the KMT, and my parents, now married, continued to wear that uniform. But when it appeared that the troupe's true leanings were finally going to be exposed and arrests were imminent, all the members made their escape in small groups and went their separate ways. My parents decided to head for Communist Party headquarters, then in central Hebei province, about two hundred miles away. Disguised in long traditional Chinese gowns and with my mother cradling their infant firstborn, my parents made the dangerous journey by train, bus, and horse cart. They had to show their false identification papers to prove their Communist loyalties at blockade after blockade.

The Communists placed my parents in the brand-new university founded by the People's Liberation Army (PLA), the new name for the Red Army, to train officials for the new China—Xin Jongguo— they were fighting for. Here, they studied music as well as politics and joined the PLA. Both studied violin; my mother also studied piano and began to compose. Here, too, they became part of the first formal philharmonic orchestra of the Communist military force. As the civil war raged on, they often studied or practiced while on the march, fleeing Nationalist bombers. In this stressful life, my mother produced no milk for my brother. The advancing force had to scout for nursing mothers in each village ahead of them, and my brother would be put to a stranger's breast until their group had marched completely through. In the next village, the process would be repeated. And so it was always said that my brother grew up drinking milk from a hundred mothers.

After the Communist victory in 1949 and Chiang Kai-shek's retreat to Taiwan (then called Formosa), the new government founded the Central Conservatory of Music in the city of Tianjin. The PLA sent twenty people, including my parents, to be part of the first class, reserved for officials with military backgrounds. Nothing in this newly proclaimed land was separate from Communist beneficence, certainly not the study of music, for on the wings of song one can control the hearts of the people.

At that time, Mao Zedong and the Party leadership were enamored of Stalinist Communism, so my parents' musical education was modeled on the Soviet system, which was rigorously classical in the Western tradition. The Central Conservatory relocated to the capital in 1950, and thus my parents moved back to Beijing. By now, my father had taken up conducting and my mother had become a composer.

In 1950 and 1951, the PLA was ready to organize its own new song and dance ensembles. They chose my father to be among the founders of the new orchestra of the People's Liberation Army Song and Dance Ensemble, under the umbrella of the Zhongzheng, the powerful political arm of the PLA. My mother became an ensemble composer. She wrote song and dance music, all with revolutionary themes. She sometimes used folk melodies and composed in a Chinese style but with the Western musical scales and the compositional technique she had learned at the conservatory. Every military branch and virtually every unit had their own such troupes; at their peak, there must have been more than a hundred of them. The PLA Zhongzheng Song and Dance Ensemble was the most influential, famous, and powerful of them all. My parents were important people.

It was the realization of their ideals and dreams. They had dedicated their youth to a cause, decimated the enemy, defended their beliefs—and now the People's Republic of China was raising them up. The Communists created an enormously complex system of rank and privilege. Among officials alone, there were twenty-four ranks. The highest officials were ranked from one to thirteen, which was my father's designation. My mother lagged a level behind; she had not joined the Party until 1949, in part, family legend has it, because she had a big mouth and did not keep all her thoughts to herself. Workers made about forty yuan a month, equivalent to about five dollars by today's valuation. Pay at the highest levels could be upward of three hundred yuan. My father made one hundred sixty, my mother one hundred twenty. They were entitled to better housing than were officials or comrades of lower levels, but not as good as people at higher levels. Likewise, they were fed from special stores of food but not the best and were entitled to different levels of hospital care. My father could travel by train first-class (called soft-bed level); my mother was entitled only to a hard bed—fortunately, they rarely traveled together—while the lowest classes were permitted only seats, no beds. The highest of the high ranks might have had the whole train car or a Soviet-made car and driver for their personal use. The first Chinese-made car, the Red Flag (Hongqi), was the pride of Mao Zedong and became the official car of the Chinese head of state. Today's Chinese leaders prefer Audis and Mercedes. You can still ride in a Red Flag; just call a car service—or buy one.

My own background was officially *geming junren*—revolutionary military. It held great prestige. I was very proud of it.

Class background—*beijing* (spelled and pronounced differently from the city name in Chinese)—was everything in New China. Where you came from and who your people were and what they had done before the Communists took power remained of greatest significance to your survival. To have a military, worker, or farmer background made you a pillar of the new society. But if your family had been in trade before 1949, then your background was bourgeoisie entrepreneur, and that was very bad. If your ancestors had been landlords, they were reactionaries and you were equally despised and poorly treated. One of the worst backgrounds was having relatives overseas, *haiwai guanxi*. It was especially bad for you if your relatives had gone to Taiwan, Hong Kong, the United States, or Europe; then you were treated like a spy. (The immediate family of my wife, Martha, had relocated to Hong Kong, for which her relatives in China suffered unspeakably.) And, of course, having been a KMT made you a counterrevolutionary, which made it difficult and sometimes impossible to find employment, education, and housing or even to maintain the right to live.

But to have a good background—and by the time I was born, there was nothing better than my parents' senior revolutionary background—meant a higher rank, a better position, a higher salary, better housing, and great prestige. Revolutionary military seniority was decided according to when you began to serve the country during the revolution. The most senior of all were those who had joined the Red Army in the late 1920s, especially those who had participated in the Long March in the early 1930s and who had fought in the anti-Japanese war.

Later, as the Cultural Revolution approached in the mid-sixties, the boundaries of bad backgrounds expanded. As Mao Zedong became an absolute ruler, the proletarian purity of class and family, stretching backward over generations, became a bloody goal. Yet even an otherwise faultless background could change overnight because of some newly apparent or implied wrongdoings by just one member of a family. Suddenly, the whole family had a bad, antirevolutionary background, and friends and extended family members would shun them as enemies. Such was the case with my family. My parents' earliest, adolescent, heartfelt fervor would come back to haunt them and to ruin me.

In 1954, though, Little Deer's universe consisted of the similarly privileged in a large military *dayuan* (residence compound). How I loved my parents' uniforms! I am still drawn to those shades of brown and green. The military uniforms in the early days of the People's Republic of China were much influenced by those of the USSR in color, style, and quality of the material, which varied depending on rank. My parents' uniforms were of very fine materials. (Later, during the Cultural Revolution, all ranks wore cotton, and the red collar and the single red star on the cap replaced the gold stars that previously differentiated the various ranks.)

All of the Zhongzheng ensemble members lived and worked together in the same buildings. My parents lived in the north building with the orchestra members. The singers and the dancers lived in

In three generations in China, how drastically things will change. My mother's father represents the old traditions. My mother wears her People's Liberation Army uniform. At age two, I have barely begun my journey from Mao to the Met—but I'll get there.

the south building. Both buildings had three upper floors each, and my parents' apartment was on the ground floor. At the end of the hallway was the infirmary. To this day, the smell of disinfectant invokes in me the memory of being in a bright, sunny, clean place with none of Beijing's otherwise inescapable dust. I often wandered into the perfectly sanitary world of the infirmary and watched the doctors and the nurses with long white robes over their uniforms. Even when there were no patients, everyone was always cleaning, mopping, and washing windows. I was crazy about the smell of disinfectant.

As a small boy, in good weather I sometimes played outside in the courtyard among the gardens and the trees. There was a green-house, tended by an old gardener who used to put potted flowers in the garden. When I was old enough, I sneaked grapes from his grapevine. I remember the rustling leaves of the *yang* trees, which

I know now as poplars. Those I must have heard in the afternoons, when young men and women performers were often outside cleaning the compound. Mornings were practice hours, and mostly what I remember hearing was a strange cacophony of sounds coming from the different windows, like a chorus, an orchestra, and a ballet forever warming up.

But these were not the daily sounds of my early life, for, unlike my brother, I did not live with my parents during those years. In the six years that separated my brother and me, our parents had become too busy traveling around the country and throughout the Soviet Union and Eastern Europe to look after their children. While my father was touring with the ensemble, my mother often went off to the minority areas and collected folk music, to provide ideas for her compositions. Sometimes my parents composed together, working the whole night. And as important in the official hierarchy as they were, they had only two rooms in the four-story building complex, one of which was their studio. The building was more a dormitory than an apartment. Everyone living there shared a common bathroom.

So when I was almost two, they hired a nanny, and I, and eventually my little sister, Lin, who's three years younger than I am, went to live with her. Hao Qian, whom we called Tian Mimi, was in boarding school. Four of us—including my nanny's daughter and, on weekends, my brother—lived in a traditional single-story Beijing walled quadrangle, or *siheyuan*, about ten minutes' walk from my parents' apartment. Formerly home to one family and now totally controlled by the Zhongzheng, the building housed four different families.

Although my sister and I might eat with our parents when they were in Beijing, most often we returned to our courtyard and to our Gugu, as we were told to call our nanny. *Gugu* means "Auntie" (specifically, "father's sister"), which made her part of the family, and she truly was to my sister and me. She was in her late thirties and so pretty. A small woman, she had smooth and delicate features. She always encouraged me to read and write, although she was illiterate. We loved her dearly. I remember once my parents teasingly asked us, "Who will you follow when you grow up—Gugu or us?"

"We'll go with Gugu!" we cried excitedly. She was the one we wanted to impress.

We had no bathroom, which was not unusual in the 1950s. (Even today, many old dwellings in China lack toilets; public facilities remain quite common.) We would proceed outside to the shared public bathroom or use a chamber pot. We bathed in public bathhouses, perhaps twice a week in winter.

Our home with our nanny was just one room, on the smaller side of the quadrangle. My sister and I shared a bed. We had no hot water; we boiled it on a stove in our room. Cabinets divided the space to provide some privacy, especially for Gugu's daughter, Gin Zelin. She was several years older than I was. Just before I reached school age, a young engineer fell in love with her. Sometimes they went out to dance. Ballroom dancing was very popular then, as it is now (like tai chi, it is often practiced outside in the parks and the streets). Even Chairman Mao loved to dance, although it was banned (as were all other "bourgeois" entertainments) during the Cultural Revolution. One day the boyfriend came looking for Gin Zelin, but only I was home. So he picked up a chair and started to practice his dancing.

"What kind of dance is with a chair?" I asked.

"A waltz," he said, "*one*-two-three, *one*-two-three, *one*-two-three."

I thought waltzing was very strange.

My wife, Martha, loves ballroom dancing, but I am not much good at it. Sometimes I think I should practice with a chair.

At seven, I entered the boarding school for the children of army officers. The school occupied the Wanshou Temple (Temple of Longevity), which had been built as a Ming dynasty Buddhist shrine. Later, it was used as an imperial residence before the overthrow of the Qing dynasty, and it currently houses the Beijing Art Museum. My classroom truly was a temple, with soaring ceilings and tall, graceful windows. On weekends, chauffeur-driven cars lined up to fetch the children of high-ranking leaders. My parents were not important enough for the use of a car and driver. (Until the early 1990s, no one could own a car privately.) I joined the rest of the children from our compound on the Zhongzheng ensemble bus. This was the military, and, of course, we children were well aware of our parents' rank. I was a little sad that my father was not a general, only a lieutenant colonel, and that my mother was but a major, one rank below him.

What I liked most was reading and drawing. I was sure I would grow up to be an artist. I wasn't much good at any of my formal school subjects, probably because I preferred to draw during my classes. My drawing teacher liked my work and predicted that I would be a painter one day. But my parents were not inclined toward such a future for me. My mother made sure to tell me stories of famous European painters who had died as paupers. I wouldn't want to be a starving artist, would I? If there were starving musicians or composers, she never mentioned them to me.

It was mostly the colors, the shapes, and the shades of light and dark in my world that attracted me. The sounds—and that included my parents' music—often bothered my ears, especially as music became the soundtrack for the increasingly strident politics of the Cultural Revolution. Then, any tones of "bourgeois" tenderness simply ceased. The practice-hour noise in the compound courtyard began to seem more pleasing, more natural than what my mother and her colleagues composed and the Zhongzheng ensemble orchestra played as my father conducted. Their music was thoroughly military, without nuance, unfailingly upbeat, relentlessly loud, and amplified on top of that. There were no differences in sound or revolutionary content from one song to the next, no soft passages, no dreamy refrains. The harmonies were boring, without variation—repeat, repeat, repeat.

My father began to take me to his rehearsals from time to time when I was only a few years old. The colors and the smells of the hall fascinated me and became the best part of the Zhongzheng ensemble. Every time I went to a rehearsal, the light in the concert hall was dim, the curtain very thick and purple, the backs of the seats deep red. I still recall the smell of the dust stirred up by the

In 1964, my father conducted Beethoven's Sixth Symphony, *the* Pastorale, *with the symphonic orchestra of the People's Liberation Army, the premier military entertainment unit in the country. This was his last concert of Western music before the Cultural Revolution.*

dancers as they rehearsed on the wooden floors. The revolutionary good-guy singers and actors appeared in bright stage light. Dimming lights foretold the approach of bad, counterrevolutionary characters. I liked to run through the hall and the rehearsal rooms, touching everything, including the bronze Russian-inspired statues in the lobby. It was all so different from what I saw, smelled, and felt in the dusty gray streets, in the grim department stores, in my parents' apartment, at school, and at home with my Gugu.

I lasted only two and a half years at boarding school. In the middle of the third year I had to leave, not because of my poor scholarship or my drawing fixation, but because I had contracted a scalp disease that affected the roots of my hair. I had to be treated in a hospital and at home for what was said at the time to be only the third case in Asia of what probably was a fungal disease. The doctors prescribed a variety of medicines to be applied directly to my scalp. When these didn't work, they tried ultraviolet light treatments. Again, no improvement. So the doctors told my parents that they would have to pull out each hair, one at a time, from the root. Thus, dutifully, night after night my parents took turns carrying out this painful process. They used music to distract me, and that's how they ended up ruining even Western music for me. They had been taught at the conservatory by Russians and East Germans in the finest Western repertoire—Beethoven, Tchaikovsky, Brahms, Chopin, Prokofiev—and had amassed a large collection of recordings, at least a hundred of them. As the hair torture began, they put one of their precious recordings on the gramophone. When they were finished for the evening, they lifted the arm of the gramophone and the music ceased. So conditioned did I become to this horrific treatment that as soon as I heard the music begin, I felt sick and woozy.

The disease still was not eradicated after months of this nightly misery. The new hair came back, the infection was still visible, and the musical plucking torture continued. I had to wear a special hat all day. The disease went away eventually, although I never returned to the boarding school. It is a miracle that I have hair today, not to mention a musical career.

I did not hear any of my parents' classical recordings again until a bittersweet moment six years later as my family was preparing for their banishment from Beijing. I certainly never heard that kind of music anywhere else. All the songs we sang at school voiced revolutionary praise of Chairman Mao, like the ubiquitous "The East Is Red":

The east is red, the sun rises.
China has brought forth a Mao Zedong.
He amasses fortune for the people,
Hu er hei yo, he is the people's liberating star.

Chairman Mao loves the people,
He is our guide,
To build a new China,
Hu er hei yo, he leads us forward!
The Communist Party is like the sun,
Wherever it shines, there is light.
Wherever there is a Communist Party,
Hu er hei yo, there the people are free!

By the mid-sixties, we had to sing this song every morning at the start of school, and along with other revolutionary songs, it blasted from speakers throughout the city all day long, beginning at sunrise. Even the bells in the belltower ding-donged its so-so-la-re/do-do-la-re tones. There was no escaping it, anywhere.

At the boarding school, the teachers, the facilities, the food, and our clothing all had been of a much higher quality than at the neighborhood public school, which I now attended six days a week. It was tough making friends at first. I was *ganbu zidi*—a child of an official. The difference in our status was instantly obvious just by the clothes we wore. I remember pleading with my mother to get me some old clothes because my new ones made me so uncomfortable around the other kids. Their families were from the old, pre-1949 Beijing. They were not the poorest, but compared with my family, they were nonmilitary and of much lower Communist status. These differences became more of a real problem for me in middle school, where I got into fights over rank and status. Now, though, in the regular world that I had just entered for the first time in my life, my classmates and I eventually warmed to one another. I was able to reconcile my pride in my revolutionary background with the revelation that it was much more fun to play at their homes after school than it was at mine. But this freedom soon came to an awful end, when I was forced to confront the big black beast with eighty-eight teeth: the dreaded *gang qin*.

2

The Little Emperor
of Destruction

LITTLE DEER HAD yet to roar, but hear him cry.

Picture my tears slipping between the keys on the prized up-right German piano—the *gang qin*—in my parents' studio.

"Practice!"

"Wrong note!"

"Stop crying!"

These words bring pain even now. Poor Xiao Lu.

I was eight when I was forced to take piano lessons and give up whatever free time I had to play, read, or draw.

The last time my mother had told me terrible tales about painters who'd starved to death in Europe, in order to steer my ambitions away from the visual arts and into music, I'd argued with her. "These were the greatest artists in the whole world," I protested.

"Only after they were dead," she said, unmoved. There was a very stern man from the Zhongzheng ensemble sitting next to her throughout this interchange. He was a piano soloist and an accompanist with the ensemble. Though I did not know it, he was there by design. The next week when my mother dragged me back to their studio for my first piano lesson, it was he who was waiting for me. His name was Jiao Shuan.

Teacher Jiao was so serious. His big eyes stared straight into mine. He seldom laughed, but when he did, I could see every tooth in his mouth. I have a special feeling for people who laugh big, but back then there was little else I could like about him. He had a twitch on the left side of his face that transfixed and horrified me at the same time. Perhaps in his mid-twenties, he was a recent graduate from the Central Conservatory. He was very straightforward and never complimented me if he did not mean it, so he never had much good to say. When we began our lessons, he did tell my parents that I would be a great pianist one day because I had big hands. Maybe that's why my hands never seemed to grow after that day. I am a big man, for a Chinese of my generation, but I have small hands. Big hands would be much better for me on stage, for more dramatic gestures.

Mostly, Teacher Jiao scolded me. "You play! If you don't play, what will you do in the future? You sit still! You play that piece another twenty times!"

My school was halfway between my parents' complex and my nanny's courtyard, about ten minutes' walk in either direction. I had

How happy my mother and I were as I practiced the piano—as long as there was a camera present. When the photo op was over, I would return to my weeping and mother to her yelling at me to stop crying and to get the notes right.

to practice every day for two hours after school before going back to Gugu for dinner. Practice was such punishment, like going to the guillotine. But because my head was never completely cut off, I had to return to see whether it could be severed the next day, and the next, and the next. I hated the constant exercises, the scales, the Hanon and the Czerny. The staff lines on the music were like bars on the prison camp windows that I'd seen in movies, like when the bad KMT captured good revolutionaries and they were staring through the bars at the end of their future. This heart-stopping vision comes back to me sometimes even now when I am preparing for a new opera and I cannot memorize a particular section: *I'm never going to get out of here!*

Most of the time, one of my parents sat next to me when I practiced, if they were not traveling with the ensemble. They corrected me constantly and chided me for not doing a good job. If they stepped away, my attention wandered and I plunked my fingers on different notes instead of following the music. Or I just stopped and stared at the clock and wondered why the hands moved so slowly.

A voice from the bedroom: "Why are you not playing, Xiao Lu?"

How I wept.

In those first years, I sometimes tried to escape from practice and run out the door. My sister remembers that once my father ran after me, shouting and waving his leather slipper at me, and that she ran after him. Lin, whom we called Meimei, was the only one of us three children who wanted to study piano. Tian Mimi had been as bad as I was, and they'd let him out of it, yet when my sister begged and begged, initially they refused.

When my parents were not around, I banged my fists on the piano or gave it a good kick. I hated it for ruining my life. Why was it that ever since I'd started studying the piano, everybody was so critical and mean to me?

I'd never really been disciplined before. My life was terrible. I was so bored.

It wasn't so different at school. The ideal was to be a model student of Chairman Mao. That meant you sat up straight, you listened to your teachers, you kept your hands down. Not me. I fidgeted, couldn't sit still, couldn't stay silent, couldn't pay attention. I drew and drew and drew—warships, horses, tanks, a cartoon of the teacher, cartoons of U.S. soldiers with their hands up, surrendering to the North Vietnamese. If you were a model student of Chairman Mao, you could be selected for the Honglingjin (Red Scarf) and become a member of the Young Pioneers. Everyone in my class except me had earned the red scarf that signified model student status. But, because of me, they couldn't achieve the greatest honor of becoming a Honglingjin class. So one day they decided to make me their class project. Four of the best-behaved girls were seated around me to control my behavior. I had to sit with both of my hands behind the back of my chair and remain in this posture for the entire class period. When I started to draw, the girl on my left whispered to me, "Xiao Lu, stop that and concentrate!" When I reached into my school bag trying to feel for something, the girl to my right immediately hissed, "Don't look down, Xiao Lu. Look at the blackboard!" At very long last, I, too, was promoted to Honglingjin status and wore the red scarf. Our class reveled in our glory, and I, too, was proud. Long live Chairman Mao.

Despite my hyperactivity, I was a shy boy. When, years later, a former colleague of my father's came to New York with a men's choir from Beijing in the early nineties, he expressed astonishment that I had become an international opera singer—that I actually could stand on the stage, open my mouth, and dare to sing and act in front of thousands of people. "When you were a child, you were so shy you walked with your back glued to the wall," he told my wife and me in Chinese.

At some point, I developed the art of appearances. I had learned that tears were no use, kicking the piano was no use, no form of overt resistance was any use at all. The result was the same: I still had to sit at the piano and practice. I began to act better toward my parents and Teacher Jiao, although I remained a terrible, distractible piano student. I just kept quiet about my inner turmoil. But I had to let out my rebellious energy somewhere, and I definitely wanted to cause trouble. One day I gathered all my friends who lived in my parents' *dayuan*, and we went to steal peaches in a near-by orchard. The trees were heavy with unripe, hairy fruit. We didn't care if they tasted sour. We got caught later, because peach fuzz was all over our clothes and bodies. The itchiness drove me nuts, and the bath schedule was such that I couldn't wash it off for a couple of days.

I started to get into fights at school. It was just too hard to be a model child of Mao. My classmates began to call me *nianhuai*, meaning that I appeared to be a quiet person on the outside, when in fact I was a naughty and mischievous child.

I was suspicious of some of the most commended kids in my class, though, especially our class prefect. This guy was always showing off how good he was in front of the teachers. We'd come back from recess and there he'd be, sweeping the floors or wiping the windows. One day I sneaked back to class early and discovered Mr. Perfect Prefect just sitting around kicking his legs. Then, just before everybody started to come back in, he jumped up and began sweeping and wiping like a madman. I found this confusing, and not just because he had acted deviously. If he was such a model student of Chairman Mao, why did he have to be noticed by the teachers at all? Why couldn't he do these tasks quietly and without need of praise? So, on another day, I walked in as he was about to start his usual phoney show-off stunt and laughed at him. I goaded him until he swung at me; that's just what I wanted him to do. He wasn't so perfect after all. We kept fighting as students filed in and took their seats. I didn't want to stop. Of course, I got scolded and had to stand in front of the class, and then, at home, I had to write out what I had done wrong. But I was still glad that I had behaved honestly and openly. I have always hated hypocrisy.

In 1963, when I was nearly nine, Chairman Mao started the Learn from Comrade Lei Feng campaign. All children were supposed to help each other and go out and do good deeds for needy people. Supposedly, Lei Feng, who had been born in 1940, had been orphaned after the Japanese killed his father, and his mother killed herself after being raped by her boss. The Communist Party took charge of him, and by studying the works of Chairman Mao, he learned how to lead a frugal, unselfish (*wusi*, that was the word we heard over and over again) life dedicated to the revolution. Or so we were told. He joined the People's Liberation Army (PLA), where he washed his comrades' feet after long marches, and when they arrived back, they found their clothes washed "anonymously." He gave away his small savings to the needy parents of a fellow soldier. His humble, self-sacrificing good deeds were almost beyond belief, which perhaps they were. He died in an accident at age twenty-four and left behind a diary, which we were told to study.

Most of all, we were supposed to try to be like him. So all the kids began to rush around trying to be good and helpful to others—assisting old people to cross the street, giving up our bus seats to them, sweeping the streets. It was almost a competition. Helping workers to push their groaning wooden carts, loaded with charcoal, up the steep hill near our school was particularly laudable. Day after day, through the school public address system, the principal praised kids by name who'd performed such selfless acts. I wanted to hear my name, too. So one day I decided I would help a worker inch his heavy, loaded cart up that hill. But all the while I kept wondering how the principal would find out I'd done this. Should I tell the man to write a letter and to mention my name? At the top of the hill, he just went on. I was disgusted with myself over my ulterior motive—I actually thought I was going to throw up. I never told anybody. And I never tried to prove myself like this again.

I was just a kid, and I wanted to be like other kids and be a good model student of Chairman Mao. But I also wanted to be myself. I didn't know much about politics. I did begin to notice at some point when I was about ten or eleven that the music that we heard from speakers outside and inside the school had become more and more dramatic, more military, and oh so much louder. Yet at my parents' complex, oddly, there seemed to be less music and sounds of practicing coming through the windows. Later I found out why: all the members of the ensemble were required to attend increasingly frequent political studies, in which people were being accused of political crimes.

The upside-down, inside-out time that was the Cultural Revolution had started. Even as a boy, I read the newspapers and saw headlines and articles that attacked a lot of movies and plays and artworks as being bad for our society. More and more, in the papers, in school, and on big-character posters called *dazibao*, I became familiar with terms like *bourgeoisie, reactionary, counterrevolutionary, capitalist roader, imperialist,* and *class enemy.* These were very bad words, I understood. They were aimed at writers, artists, teachers, scholars, and intellectuals—even conductors and composers.

Suspicions spread through the complex like bad smells. I sensed them, though I was still too young to understand much of what they meant. Every organization throughout China, even the schools, had a political department (they still do) that was responsible for adherence to official policy. No one wanted to have a so-called counterrevolutionary in their midst, or they would be tarred with the same brush. And, human relationships being what they are, people also had found a potent tool to get revenge on their enemies, those with whom they were competing for higher rank and privilege—or others whom they wanted to bring down. People were encouraged to criticize themselves as well, something I was familiar with, since we now had to do this in school two or three times a week. We always had to find something to say, whether we believed it or not— like, "I didn't want to clean the classroom yesterday because I was too tired. That wasn't right, because Chairman Mao has taught us that we should love working to benefit other people. I am sorry. I will be better next time."

My parents were very tense. Like everybody else, they were under pressure to *jiefa*—expose—their colleagues, but, with one exception some time later, they never did. Some people made it all too easy for their neighbors to turn them in, by sharing their opinions, by talking about politics, or by criticizing something about the ever-changing official policy that they didn't like or that made no sense to them. For me, although not for my parents, this had a good side. Teacher Jiao talked too much. Someone turned him in.

In 1964 I finally earned my red scarf and become a member of the Young Pioneers—the last one in my class to do so. My sister, Lin, whom we called Meimei, was always better behaved in school and at the piano. Now she is a very busy piano teacher in Denver.

One day in 1966, just before the beginning of what was officially called the Great Proletarian Cultural Revolution, I went to my parents' studio for my usual wretched lesson. But Teacher Jiao wasn't there. In the residence complex, through the loudspeakers, came the announcement: "Jiao Shuan has been exposed for dangerous thought and talk. He is stepping to the counterrevolutionary side because his brother and his father are counterrevolutionaries. He should step away from his brother and his father, but he hasn't. You cannot sympathize with your enemy. Please report what he told you, or you will have to take responsibility, too. We should help him to stand on the right side and to expose his brother and his father. From today, we will put him to study—*xuexiban*."

This was a scary word. It meant that he would be put in solitary confinement in a special room in our complex and wouldn't be allowed out, perhaps for years. On the other hand, the longer they kept him in there, the better for me. I ran out to the courtyard and raced around again and again. "No more lessons! No more practice!" I was dizzy with joy. "Long live Chairman Mao! Long live Chairman Mao!"

This was the best day of my whole life, all eleven years of it.

I did not know—or want to know—that Teacher Jiao had been as outspoken in his criticisms of political policy as he was of my piano technique. He had been walking on thin ice to begin with since his background was officially bourgeoisie, which he had overcome somewhat by being in the military. But he compounded these problems by often commenting on how poorly his parents and his brother had been treated. By not learning to keep his mouth shut, Teacher Jiao became an easy target, through whom others could prove their dedication to the revolution. He was totally stripped of his freedom and confined to one small room in which all the windows were locked and covered by newspaper. All day long he had to write confessions and self-criticisms. Accompanied by a guard, he could go out of the room only to eat at his own table in the ensemble's dining hall; no one was permitted to speak to him. He was also dragged out of the complex periodically for public criticism sessions, where he had to stand and hang his head, wearing a heavy blackboard from his neck that read, "I'm so sorry," or that listed his various "crimes." He no longer received a salary.

Immediately, big-character posters appeared attacking Teacher Jiao. My parents felt very bad for him but did not dare say anything in his support. In fact, they were urged to *jiefa* him themselves and report incriminating things that he had said to them. All I cared about was that *I* was free.

My parents never again insisted that I study or practice piano. They had other things on their minds, and with the mass craziness that had begun, kids like me were not attended to as closely as before. In my own childish self-preoccupation, it did not occur to me that what had happened to Teacher Jiao could happen to them.

Since I wasn't around my parents' place so much after my piano lessons stopped, I was not aware for a while that my father was reviewing everything he had ever written, to ascertain what others might use to criticize him. This, as it turned out, was the result of the new campaign to "smash the Four Olds"—old ideas, culture, customs, and habits. We were learning about this in school, where our education was now totally political. The point was to purify the revolution, to redirect the people, who, under the influence of intellectuals and artists and academics, had detoured off the correct path since the Liberation in 1949. We must resume class struggle! We must root out all old and bourgeois customs! I was still in elementary school, but I knew that in the middle schools the idealistic kids whom Chairman Mao had empowered to do the smashing, who called themselves Red Guards, were taking it upon themselves to break into "bad" people's homes and take away anything that they felt represented an "Old." They would march right into their living spaces and search for any possession to take away as "evidence," from photos to papers to books to antiques to traditional and religious paintings and sculptures, cash, and jewelry. The Red Guards called these home invasions *chao jia*, which meant literally to turn a home inside out. They pulled up floorboards and pushed through walls. Because we lived in military housing, I don't remember being afraid that this would happen to us. I do remember going to a *chao jia* exhibition in a huge hall in Beijing where the Red Guards put on display the amazing amount of loot they had collected from these home invasions.

One day when I came to my parents' apartment, I noticed that almost all of my parents' records, which were mainly Western music, had been removed from the shelves and were piled up on the floor, with a note on top in my father's handwriting: "To be disposed of." Since the hair-plucking torture years earlier, I hadn't remembered hearing any of this music. Sometimes after practicing the piano, when I might stay for dinner, I would occasionally notice my father very carefully placing one of the records onto the shelf, so these were obviously valuable belongings. I do remember that some of these records had a red center label with a dog and a big gramophone speaker. I liked that picture. I also liked the smell of the thick plastic discs.

I didn't comment on the stacked-up records, but some days later, my father asked me to go get a cart and sell all of the records to the recycling center. I asked why. He said, *"Si jiu"*—Four Olds. These records were "old stuff" and did not contain "healthy" music.

I grabbed my sister's old bamboo baby stroller. Since my parents' rooms were on the ground floor, it wasn't so difficult to load the records into the cart, but it was some job to push everything to the recycling station. It was summer and very hot. The man in charge was busy and testy and looked sideways at the load I was trying to sell to him. He snorted that I'd have to break all the records into pieces before he would consider taking them. I found a good-sized rock on the street. I removed each of the large black discs from its paper sleeve and broke it in halves or quarters. When I was just about finished, the man came back again and snapped, "Not such big pieces!" So I began to smash these Olds into shards. It took a long time, but the more time I spent at it, the more I reveled in this act of annihilation. I loved the sounds of smashing and crashing. The smaller the pieces became, the greater my joy. In return, I got less than one yuan (less than ten cents) for all that, but I went home a very happy boy.

I never apologized to my father for the devastation he had asked of me. If my parents regretted the destruction of their record collection, they showed no sign. They were faithful Communists. If Chairman Mao and the Central Cultural Revolution Committee, which included Mao's wife, Jiang Qing, were about to formally ban Western music, art, ideas, and all institutions, such as the Central Conservatory and libraries, that promoted such "elitism"—well, as my parents saw it, that's the way it had to be. No matter what horrors befell them, they believed in the revolution, in the masses, in their leaders. By the time I realized the import of what I had done to my parents, we were far away from one another, and my father and I were on difficult terms.

As for Teacher Jiao, I later found out that his punishment lasted three years, the same length of time I'd been sentenced to his piano lessons. I did not see him again for thirty-five years, not until I returned to Beijing for a visit with my mother. With my first voice teacher, we all went out to dinner together. I confessed to Jiao Shuan that the worst day in his life had been the happiest of my childhood. "I did not realize your suffering," I said. "I really want to apologize to you."

His eyes filled with tears. "I understand," he said. "Sometimes I was so tired of you because you were not a good student and you cried so much. I tried everything except hitting you." The laughter of the others at the table had a bitter note. I think it was so hard, so sad, for them to think back to what had happened to their generation in those awful years. I felt such pain for my once-reviled teacher, and for my nanny, too.

Gugu's deceptions began to come to light during the terrible famine—resulting from Mao's failed policies during the Great Leap Forward program—that afflicted China in the late fifties and early sixties. My own family, provisioned by the army, wasn't as seriously affected by the food shortages as were the workers and the farmers. Only my brother's stomach rumbled, since his boarding school fed the students so little. As my mother later told me, Tian Mimi would come home on weekends so hungry that they would forego some of their own food rations so that he could fill up one day a week. In the countryside, however, Gugu's mother was starving. Apparently, Gugu began to water down the milk meant for my baby sister and me in order to save some to take to her mother. She also took some of our rice ration, adding extra water in its place, so that we were eating rice soup. Since we didn't live with our parents, it was a while before my mother found out. When she did, she was furious, but, as she told me much later, of course she understood what drove Gugu to such desperation. So many millions of people died during this awful time—I wouldn't know just how many until I was nearly thirty years old.

My parents probably also understood why Gugu had lied to us about her husband. That story finally came out in 1966—not from Gugu, but from a local political association—and my parents had to fire her on the spot. She had told them before she was hired that her husband had died of illness at the end of the civil war. But now the word was out that, in fact, he had been a low-ranking official who worked in a KMT prison. When the Communists took over in 1949, they began to take revenge on the prison officials, whom they believed had tortured the Communist prisoners. Gugu's husband had been jailed and "suppressed"—in other words, executed—by the new Communist government.

How I remember the day she left us. My mother warned us in a low voice not to ask why Gugu was leaving, not to beg her to stay, and not to show any sympathy. So we just stood there, shocked and dumbfounded, while she gathered her belongings from our courtyard lodgings and wept, turning to look at my sister and me, time and again, with tears streaming down her face.

Her sudden flight from my life at last began to alert me to the darkness descending on my world. Gradually, my parents explained to us why Gugu had to leave. A revolutionary family like ours could not have a counterrevolutionary's wife working in their home. No matter that he was dead. And who knew what else she hadn't told my parents that could endanger all of us? My sister and I did sneak off once to find her. We discovered that she had gone to live with her daughter, who was now married and a worker in Beijing. Gugu cried and threw open her arms when she saw us, then cooked us some delicious food. But we dared not go to her again. As the Red Guards ran roughshod over more and more of the city, it began to sink in what kind of trouble we'd be in if we associated with "that kind" of person.

Gugu tried to find us after our family moved into a brand-new military *dayuan*. She stood outside the large complex for hours, in hopes of spotting us. That's what she told me when I saw her again ten years later, after the Cultural Revolution was over and I was a worker myself, in much-reduced circumstances. She died in 2000. My mother had given her money as a pension for all the years she had taken care of us, to which I contributed.

I never knew her real name. She'll always be my Gugu. Hers was the first deep loss I had ever suffered.

In that summer of 1966, when Gugu left us, the Cultural Revolution was raging across China like a fire burning into every corner.

In China, every citizen has a record—a *dangan*—that follows him all the footsteps of his life, from school to job, from one job to another, from city to countryside, from province to province, out of the country and back again. Every gold star and black mark in your life is on this confidential dossier, contained within a large brown kraft-paper envelope. Whether you were a faithful employee at this work unit or had a bad attitude at that one, everything ended up in this secret, unchangeable, and ever-thickening file. On my parents' *dangan*, of course, was their history of service in the Second Anti-Enemy Performing Arts Troupe, a KMT unit. As the Cultural Revolution gained momentum, they were questioned again and again about these youthful years of their history. The problem was that no records existed to prove that the Second Troupe was a Communist cell. So my parents always had a questionable stain on their background, as did many people in the ensembles throughout the country who had once belonged to a wartime KMT unit. My parents were continually questioned and criticized.

"Why did you wear a Nationalist uniform?"

"Everybody wore that uniform at that time. The whole Second Troupe was secretly affiliated with the Communist Party." No one accepted this answer.

"If you are a true Communist, you do not wear a Nationalist uniform. Maybe you pretended to be a Communist and you were a traitor and a spy."

A question that often came up was why they had performed for Chiang Kai-shek's birthday. Their answer was twofold: first, Chiang Kai-shek was the official leader of the war against the Japanese, in which they had participated. Second, it was not their decision where or why they performed.

Answer unacceptable.

Although my father was an emotionally reticent man, certainly with me, I could hardly ignore the stress at home, now that my sister and I were once again living with our parents. (My brother was in naval officers' training school.) Many of their colleagues from the Second Troupe who had not continued in military careers were being arrested and taken away. The only saving grace for my parents was that they had joined the PLA during the War for Liberation. In 1966, although Chairman Mao believed his power was being threatened by other influences within the party (a principal reason that he implemented the Cultural Revolution), he remained confident in the loyalty of the military, over which he maintained complete control. He had always said that the military was the central force of communism. Therefore, those who belonged to it were protected from the worst excesses of those times. But the continual investigations into my parents' background did not bode well.

It is right to rebel, Mao said. In middle schools (the equivalent of American junior high and high schools), the impassioned Red Guards began to interrogate, torture, and kill teachers, administrators, and even some parents. The school violence began in that first summer of the Cultural Revolution in 1966. Terrible things happened at the Second Middle School attached to Beijing Normal University, which I later attended. It would be some time before I got the details, but apparently the students ordered the principal, Gao Yun, a friend of my parents, to stand outside in the blazing sun, pushed thumbtacks into his forehead, and may have poured boiling water over his head. Although Gao Yun nearly died, he somehow survived. The school's Party secretary, Mr. Jiang, died, though. The students forced him to kneel down, poured ink over his head, beat him, and left him to starve in a locked room for several days. When blood began to ooze from under the door, the students found him dead, either from suicide or from the beating and starvation. That same summer they killed a literature teacher and even one student's mother.

I'd like to think I would never have done such things. I'm lucky that I was just a little too young to be challenged to find out how far I would go. I later read that teachers were sometimes forced to beat one another or to beat the corpses of other teachers. Students shaved one side of the heads of female teachers. They held teachers and administrators captive for days or months in a school jail they constructed. They made some teachers sing the "Song of Ox-Ghosts and Snake-Demons" several times a day. We all eventually knew this song:

I am an ox-ghost and snake-demon.
I am an ox-ghost and snake-demon.
I am guilty. I am guilty.
I committed crimes against the people.
So the people take me as the object of the dictatorship.
I have to lower my head and admit to my guilt.
I must be obedient. I am not allowed to speak or act
    incorrectly.
If I speak or act incorrectly,
May you beat me and smash me,
Beat me and smash me.

Among us younger students, though, in the few months that our elementary school remained open, our revolt against our teachers did not turn violent. Even before the Cultural Revolution, we were learning that our educational system had guided China's children in the wrong direction. But now we were being encouraged to criticize our teachers openly. I didn't understand why, but since I'd always been the most punished student in class, I looked forward to redressing my teachers and even the principal. Other students followed my example. I remember one day criticizing the principal for "pushing us to learn only schoolwork, not politics," as if I really cared.

One day I leaped up and criticized Teacher Ren for wearing clothes with a flowery pattern. "We are told that we must all take our hardships, wear simple clothes, and serve the revolution. Beautiful clothes are bourgeois. That's a crime!" I declared indignantly.

My teacher replied humbly, "I will make sure that I wear plain clothes from now on."

Another day, one of my classmates stood up and reminded us all of an incident in which our physical education teacher had come into our class to borrow Teacher Ren's bicycle. My classmate insisted that by lending him the key, she had interrupted our lessons and done us great harm. Also, he added, she had smiled at the phys-ed teacher—very bad, very bad.

Although the teachers were not supposed to defend themselves, instead of hanging her head and taking her punishment, this time Teacher Ren replied that she was not to blame. The student should criticize the physical education teacher, not her, she said indignantly. Now this confused me. We all knew that she and the phys-ed teacher were in love and planning to get married. So why would she turn around and put the blame on him?

What was true? What was natural? What was right? What was beautiful?

What made sense?

I needed answers urgently.

3

Mama Nature Sings

THE BIG BRIGHT-GREEN bug with bent skinny legs—ladies and gentlemen, that is a grasshopper! Fireflies, I don't mind telling you, really do light up!

Imagine me, a twelve-year-old boy from Beijing who had rarely seen such miracles before, outside of picture books.

I had just arrived at my mother's brother's family home, just outside Jincheng, her old hometown in northern China. This was the Shanxi province town from which she had marched off in all her teenage glory to fight the Japanese. How her fortunes had waxed and waned in the years since. She and my father—and all three hundred or so Zhongzheng ensemble members—were at that moment ensconced in a military academy outside Beijing, forced to remold their ideology and to confess their "problems." The reeducation, which lasted nearly a year, wasn't exactly detention, but they were rarely permitted to leave.

So, with our nanny gone and our older brother in naval training, there was no one to take care of my sister and me. My mother appealed to her brother's wife, my aunt, my *jiuma*. Auntie arrived with the youngest two of her five children to take care of us in Beijing. But after all classes were suspended in the summer of 1966, my parents thought that we should not stay in the city, and anyway Auntie had her own family to take care of. To Jincheng we went. This was my first trip ever outside of Beijing. It was a time when the "educated youth"—meaning anyone in middle school or university—in the cities were being encouraged to spread the true values of the Cultural Revolution by working alongside the peasants or the factory workers in the countryside and also to learn from them, as per Chairman Mao's order to "establish revolutionary ties." Within a few years, graduates would actually be ordered to relocate to the country-side or the frontiers. Many were happy to do Mao's bidding, at least at first, but the living conditions could be extremely harsh for them. Food and money were limited, and the labor was very hard. The peasants were not so welcoming, and for many, there was little leadership. Conditions were especially terrible at the frontiers. I heard so many stories later about the bad life they discovered, and how their revolutionary ardor cooled. It took many of them years to get back to the cities, and some never did. Yet here I was in 1966, running free and embracing a natu-ral life in the bosom of my loving extended family. My mother's

In 2006 I returned to Jincheng to give a concert. I visited my auntie and her family in the same courtyard residence they had lived in when I stayed with them as a little farmworker.
Rummaging around my old room on the top of a rickety stairway, I found my old lunch pail in which my meal was brought to me in the fields.

firm guidance was at a remove, but I discovered that I had a Mama Nature, and she knew how to nurture me.

Did you know that water buffaloes have four stomachs? I didn't, until I asked about the scrawny old beast that was constantly chewing, chewing, chewing. I didn't spend one day in school the seven months I was there, but I certainly got an education. Far and near were large and small hills, streams, and fields of light green and yellow. What I liked most was putting my face close to the ground to watch the movements of the insects and see the beads of dew on the grasses. The sounds of nature—the breezes, the songbirds, the croaks and chirps and buzzes—mesmerized me. Everything was alive here in the country: the flocks of birds in the wide sky; the jumping, crawling, wriggling insects; the crops in the fields. I did not miss the city at all, with its soot, rotten smells, noises, crowds, and gray buildings with their rows of windows, like eyes staring at me. I drank cold water from clear streams and watched the tadpoles wriggling. I was glad to be rid of my city clothes and wear the simple cloth shoes and pants and coat my auntie made for me.

Jincheng, which is now a city of more than half a million people—two million, including the extended metropolitan area—had a population of fifty thousand at that time. The town had been occupied by the Japanese during the anti-Japanese war. The extended courtyards of the Du family (my mother's original family name) had been on the outskirts of town. To erect walls that would protect the town from attack by the Chinese military, the occupiers took apart many of these courtyard houses. They even removed the bricks, the tiles, and the wooden roof beams of the Du family ancestral hall. Family records spanning the generations were lost for good. Later, after the Liberation in 1949, the county built its government offices next to the remaining Du houses. When the officials decided that they needed more room, they simply erected a wall in the middle of one house and claimed the space for themselves. (The wall came down and the Du family reclaimed their whole building once more in the mid-1990s, after pressuring the government for years.)

When I arrived in the fall of 1966, although I saw painted political slogans in big red letters all over town—"Study Chairman Mao's Works Well," "Take Part in the Cultural Revolution Actively"—no loudspeakers shrieked political messages or bombarded us with revolutionary music. So the sounds and the strains of that movement seemed far away. In any case, I didn't live in the heart of town. I was at the edge, in the countryside, where it seemed so quiet. I felt no pressures, no worry at all.

Most of my uncle's family were categorized as farmers in the *hukou* residence registration system. Even today, the *hukou* system has two tiers, urban and rural, although enforcement, as I mentioned earlier, is not so rigorous these days, and the system does seem to be in the process of change. Back then, though, members of the same family could have a different *hukou* if they lived only a mile or two apart. My uncle was a shoe salesman in a store in town, so his *hukou* stated that he must live in town. But his son and three daughters had a rural *hukou*, and they could do only farm work on the people's communes. As for me, living and farming with my cousins was fine with me, although in fact I shouldn't have been there, with my urban *hukou*.

The farmers didn't really know how to deal with the new little farmhand in their midst. I was from Beijing, the capital, which was Heaven to them. They didn't know how to treat a boy from Heaven. They called me Little Beijing.

I couldn't wait for the bell to clang at sunrise, to gather the workers to the fields. I'd toss on my clothes, throw the tools on my back, grab a bite of anything at all, and hurry off to the fields with my cousins. I did the weeding. We grew corn, sorghum, wheat, millet, potatoes, yams, and tomatoes. Later, I'd haul drinking water from the village well, one of my favorite chores. The older kids could bring back two buckets of water at a time. But try as I might, I could carry only half a bucket, and still the water spilled over the sides. I was very impressed by this well. I stared down at the surface and saw my round face peering up at me, sometimes making faces. I screamed into the deep pit and laughed as my voice echoed, amplified many times over. I played as long as I could this way until

I finally raised the pulley with the half-filled bucket and carried it home.

In front of every house in the village stood a big urn of the *cu*—vinegar—that Shanxi province was famous for. I lifted up the lid as I passed by each house. Like the well water, the vinegar was my personal mirror, and there was my face once again, urn after urn, house after house. Vinegar of Shanxi is very thick and dark and extremely pungent. For a long time, I put *cu* (pronounced "tzu") on everything I ate. And if I got sick, the townspeople told me, "Go drink some vinegar."

Everybody agreed that I was different from the kids who grew up in the countryside, but they didn't hold it against me. My auntie served my sister and me better food than she did her own children. There were strict food rations in those days, and she always fed her kids first, giving them perhaps one meatball a piece if there was any meat to go around. Afterward, she fed my sister and me two meatballs each, which her children never realized. She had practiced this favoritism even when taking care of us in our own home in Beijing. Her rationale, to this day, was that we were weaker, and she was more concerned for our health. But I think that she, too, thought we were "special" and higher in the Du family hierarchy.

Even so, we did not have enough to eat. I stole tomatoes and yams.

The farmers always laughed at my questions and my curious, if not strange, behavior, including my obsession with the horses. These animals were so obedient and hardworking. They walked, stopped, and worked according to their owners' instructions. They never seemed to complain. Why were they so kind to human beings? They didn't seem to mistrust one another, the way everybody did back in Beijing before I'd left. They did not have complicated expressions like those on the faces of kids at school, who were always ready to criticize the teachers or one another. I began to feel that the most honest living things were wildflowers, grass, birds, buffaloes, and horses, especially horses. Although they were quiet, they understood me better than anybody. Perhaps this made sense since I was born in the year of the horse, so, of course, we shared a special bond. I spoke to them, and the farmers chuckled.

The farmers loved to tease me. One day I was standing near the compost lot, where the buffalo and horse droppings were spread out and mixed with dry leaves and hay and left to decompose, until they were ready to be used as fertilizer.

"Little Beijing," one of the farmers called out to me, "do you know how to tell when the droppings are ready to be used as fertilizer?"

"No," I answered, interested.

"It's very easy. Just test it with your finger. If it tastes salty, then it is ready."

"Is that true?" I asked warily.

"Try it and you'll see," he said very seriously.

So, stupid me, I stuck my finger into the muck and tasted it. "It's not salty," I said. "So I guess it's not ready?"

The farmer doubled over in laughter. "What a naive boy you are!" he roared.

I became the village laughingstock after that, but I laughed, too. I really didn't mind at all having tasted the fermenting horse manure.

Harvest time came not long after I began my farmer's life. I helped to dig up the yams and cut off the ears of corn. Sometimes I bit into the fresh corn and felt the sweet juice dripping from my mouth. I wanted to be a part of everything, especially *kanchang*. After the harvest, the farmers threshed the wheat by hand so that the seeds would fall. They left them to dry, along with corn kernels—seeds for the next year's planting—on a flat parcel of land in the center of a field. From a mud hut with a simple built-in bed, the older boys guarded the seeds all night long from animals and thieves. This is what we called *kanchang*. They let Little Beijing tag along. We gathered together and told ghost stories. We filched corn and yams to barbecue. The older boys talked about girls. We did this many times, and it was such good fun, although my auntie was horrified that I stayed out all night and exposed my precious self to danger. She chased me round and round her little house with a stick the first time I said I was going to kanchang. The next morning, I came back with a basket of stolen yams as a peace offering.

My favorite sleeping place during *kanchang* was atop one of the towering haystacks, as tall as three men. The sky was so wide, the air so fresh, the stars so extraordinary. One night I lay out there quite late, after midnight, munching on a yam and drifting off to sleep, when I heard a man's voice singing the same line over and over: "Meimei, my heart is so happy. Meimei, my heart is so happy." Lovers in China always call each other Gege and Meimei, meaning "older brother," "younger sister," "man," "woman." The sound began from far away, growing louder and closer, then drifted off in the distance, accompanied by the wind and the rustling of leaves. Sometimes the man broke into laughter before resuming his one-line song. In the dark, his singing felt bright. I pictured his smiling eyes. I prayed that his singing would never stop. Then he and his song were gone. I had never before heard anything so sweet or touching. I had never heard music directly from a man's heart before. It was nothing like the revolutionary music I was used to, and it did not mention Chairman Mao!

This was the first time that music ever touched me, touched my soul. I began to think that maybe everyone should sing this kind of song with feelings like this. Maybe, I thought, if I could find that place in myself from which to sing, it would make me happy and others around me, too. That is the place that I sing from now, but, of course, I had no thought of becoming a singer then. At that moment, I wanted to be a farmer. Yet I began to pay attention to folk songs. The sounds were simple and natural. All music should come from this natural sound and natural feeling, I thought. I'm still thinking about it, about the time I was first moved by singing. It felt almost like the cry from the blood of my ancestors thousands of years ago. Sung that harvest night, it enlightened my senses. I am grateful for this man's song to this day. I do not know who he was or why he sang. Perhaps he'd made love to his *meimei* and was returning home afterward. Perhaps if you have to know why someone sings, then you'll lose the beauty of the singing.

A door had opened for me, and it was waiting for me to be ready to walk through.

The sounds of the Cultural Revolution began to make their way to our village. The bell that roused us to our chores turned into a loudspeaker blaring quotations from Chairman Mao and the Central Communist Party. Political editorials and decisions from revolutionary committees filled the local newspapers. Soon after that, my aunt warned me not to talk to the man next door. He was a counterrevolutionary, a murderer, she said. He was made to wear black clothes with a piece of white cloth over the front bearing the words "Counterrevolutionary murderer" and his name crossed out with big red slash marks. Once or twice a week he was dragged out of his house, surrounded by a crowd, for public criticism. I cannot forget the look on his face. It was so sad and so angry all at once. Every time I left my aunt's house, I rushed away. The man's angry-sad face and the big words on his chest frightened me.

A few months later, Auntie took my sister and me back to Beijing. It was becoming unsafe in Jincheng, and my parents were due to return to Beijing within a few months. I felt reluctant to enter the courtyard in my farmers' clothes and cloth shoes, not because I was ashamed of my appearance, but because I did not feel as if I belonged here in this military *dayuan* anymore. The kids in the complex laughed at my outfit, especially at my cloth shoes, and soon enough I did revert to my city wardrobe. But I missed the country. Our new building, which housed high-ranking military personnel, not just Zhongzheng ensemble members, seemed luxurious. It had three bedrooms, a kitchen, and even a bathroom. The piano was in the room where my brother slept when he was home on leave. By now, it was just a piece of furniture and no threat to me. My sister had taken the pressure off me. Our parents had finally given in to her pleas for piano lessons, and Meimei quickly became the young musician in the family. She had even begun to study in the elementary school run by the Central Conservatory of Music, but now this was closed and would remain so for years.

Here are my mother (left) and my auntie, her sister-in-law, in 2006 during our trip to Jincheng, my mother's old village. Auntie, although she had five children of her own, took such good care of me and my sister in 1966, the first time our parents were sent away.

I hadn't been feeling well toward the end of my stay on the farm. I remember most how tired I was all the time. The vinegar cure didn't help at all. My parents still hadn't returned from the military academy by the time I started to turn yellow and to run a high fever. I had never felt this ill. My auntie, who could not read and did not know where to turn, rushed to our neighbor next door. The neighbor in turn hustled me off to Military Hospital 305, where they told her that if she'd come three days later, I'd be dead. I had hepatitis—perhaps from eating the not-so-salty manure. I remained in the hospital for six months. Although I began to feel better soon enough, the lengthy rest cure was how they treated liver disease in China in the sixties. The timing couldn't have been better. I spent the most violent period of the Cultural Revolution in Beijing in a hospital bed.

In those days, every place all over China was constantly splintering into political cliques and blocs—every city, village, factory, farm commune, and residential unit. The sides would begin to argue; their rhetoric would magnify. There would be one side supporting the local government, another side wanting to overthrow it. One side would be supported by the army, another by students. Just after my sister and I left Jincheng with our auntie, tanks moved in there. The revolutionary call for *wudou*—armed struggle—went out all over China, and the violence got extreme. Throughout Shanxi province alone, thousands of people died.

My parents lost contact with my brother for months. Newspapers reported *wudou* in the area where he was living at the naval academy, and we were all so worried. Eventually, Tian Mimi told us that the academy had divided into two armed groups, and each side had supporters from outside. One day on his way to eat in the commissary, he nearly stumbled on a man lying on the ground and pointing a machine gun directly at him. He kicked dirt in the man's face and ran. At one point, he said, the whole school was surrounded, and an armed group broke into his dormitory. A friend of his jumped on a bed and pointed his machine gun at the invaders, daring them to start shooting, because if they did he would, too, and they'd all die together. Nobody wanted to take the first shot, and the incident fizzled out.

The craziest thing was that people on all sides of these conflicts professed to believe in Chairman Mao—and accused the other side of being anti-Mao.

As with everywhere else, our hospital, too, split into factions; doctors, nurses, and patients all took sides. One side was for the administration, the other side against it. Both sides used quotations from Chairman Mao to criticize the other in the political meetings. The young patients took sides with the doctors and the nurses whom we liked. We yelled with them and supported them. This was my participation in the Cultural Revolution, and I did not really know what was going on. Our butts paid the price. There were three of us in the room. If the nurse with the needle was on our side, she would gently administer the injections. But if she was from the opposition—watch out! I'd see her coming and I'd start to shake. She'd come at me with that needle weapon and stab me in the backside. My butt would swell and ache for days.

Patients fought one another, too, of course, although not physically. This was an infectious-disease hospital, so nobody wanted to touch anybody else. Spitting was the worst we'd do to one another, and then whoever was the target would race back to the room and wash off the noxious stuff. When hundreds of patients started yelling and screaming at one another, which happened often enough, to their credit the staff stepped in. "Don't be mad at each other! It's not good for your health!" After these encounters and heated political study sessions, for those of us with hepatitis, our liver enzymes invariably went up. Days of enforced bed rest would follow. This was the rhythm of my days during the peak of the Cultural Revolution. I was twelve. To tell you the truth, it was fun for me.

After my parents returned to Beijing, my mother came to see me in the hospital several times. My father never did. Probably, he was under more pressure to attend political meetings. Although the hospital was near Beijing, the transportation system was in chaos. The buses had no schedules and no predictable stops anymore. One day I was expecting a visit from my mother, but she didn't show up. Many hours later, she dragged in. She had walked all the way, carrying two watermelons. Watermelons were believed to be especially good for liver disease. She found me in my hospital gown, holding a bucket of flour and water and a brush, with which I was helping to paste accusatory political posters on the hospital wall. She was appalled. But I was so moved. She had marched for many hours with her healing burden and would have to return on foot again, just for her boy. Just for Little Deer.

4

So Long, Beijing

PICTURE THIS: it is early in the morning. We are just out of bed. My parents gather my sister and me, then open our front door about halfway. The four of us stand in front of Mao's picture, holding a copy of his Little Red Book—*Quotations from Chairman Mao*—out from our hearts, loud enough for the neighbors to hear: "Beloved Chairman Mao, we wish you long life, long life, long life!" Next we read one of Mao's quotations. Today we also sing "The Great Helmsman," a song almost as popular as "The East Is Red."

When I came home from my fun and games in the hospital, this was our new reality. The morning and evening Mao-worship ritual had been instituted in every farm, factory, and barracks, but to me the intrusion into our homes was intolerable. I wasn't about to complain, but I guess my attitude wasn't what my parents expected.

"Xiao Lu, stand up straight! You're slouching! Stop squirming!"

My parents were caught in a vise. As committed Party members, they wanted to contribute to the Cultural Revolution. My father fretted that he needed to prove he was faithful by writing *dazibao* accusations, exposing questionable activities in his colleagues' background as so many others in the ensemble were doing. So he did. On a poster he exposed that one of the leaders of the ensemble—whom he greatly respected—had years earlier worked with a high-ranking officer who had since been accused of being a counterrevolutionary and died in jail. The ensemble leader must tell everyone what he knew about that man, wrote my father. The leader was subsequently criticized for not having revealed this previous tie, but he did not hold this against my father. Yet my father never forgave himself. This is something I only recently found out from my mother; my father almost never revealed his human side to me. My mother also told me, warming to the subject, that my father had deeply regretted signing papers that sent away one of his orchestral players; although the decision had not been his, he hated having ruined the man's career.

The other side of the vise that was now closing on them was the intensifying pressure to *jiefa* their old Second Troupe colleagues and, of course, to criticize themselves for their own "crimes" during that period. Under intensive questioning about the troupe's activities of two decades earlier, they had to be certain that their dates, times, and places of specific occurrences were precise and did not contradict what anyone else might report. But because people under a cloud were afraid to associate with one another, my parents could not compare notes or even find out how their colleagues were. Whenever my parents heard that somebody from those days was in trouble, they even went so far as to cut that person's face out of old group photos.

My parents made it my job to scout the accusatory posters on walls all over the city and report back about anyone we knew. With schools still closed, I had nothing else to do. I was excited with my new assignment, but my apprehension grew. My parents had drummed it into my head to be careful, to run if I saw anybody watching me, and never to tell anyone our names. They wanted a word-by-word accounting of what I read, but I was afraid to be seen taking notes so I tried to commit it all to memory, at which I was hopeless. I forgot much of it and garbled the rest, which made them angry and upset with me. My sister, if it was dark enough out, would spit at any accusations against our friends. Once my father told me to go to Beijing University and scout for posters that might be accusing him because of his propaganda activities there in 1949, while he still wore the KMT uniform. I'd never been there, and when guards stopped me from entering, I got so scared I turned and ran away.

For decades, my parents had remained especially close to the three people with whom they'd gone AWOL back in 1939. We called them Uncle Shi, Auntie Fang, and Uncle Zhang. They'd all known one another so long that they even looked and talked alike. Shi, who was married to Fang, was my favorite "uncle." Since I'd been away in Jincheng and then in the hospital, I hadn't seen any of them for quite a long time. One day I went to the courtyard in Uncle Shi's complex to play with some classmates. A manhole cover that was being lifted up from underneath caught my attention. I saw two men dressed as plumbers and carrying wrenches climb out of the sewage drain. I recognized the first man as a then famous actor and the second man as Uncle Shi. I ran to him, thrilled, crying, "Uncle Shi! Uncle Shi!"

He ignored me as if I didn't exist and walked away. I was crushed and humiliated. I brooded for a while but continued to play with my friends. Later that afternoon, though, as I was leaving for home, I spotted a man with a bicycle partially obscured by some bushes.

"Xiao Lu, Xiao Lu! Come over here!" he whispered. It was Uncle Shi. "How are your parents?" I told him they were okay. "Let your parents know that we are fine and that they don't have to worry about us. Tell them to take care of themselves." I watched him get on his bike and ride away. I returned home with warmth in my heart, and sadness, too. It was obvious that life had become very hard for Uncle Shi, yet all that he cared about was reassuring my parents.

My parents explained to me later that because Uncle Shi and other people in the arts were in trouble with the revolutionary political committees, they were working in the sewers to show that they were willing to literally lower themselves to the level of workers, the heroes of the Cultural Revolution.

But Uncle Shi's and Auntie Fang's fortunes continued to darken. At the movie studio where Uncle Shi worked as a director, his interrogators, frustrated with his stubbornness, pulled his earlobe so hard that it tore almost completely from his head. He was sent away to a labor "school" for five years.

Auntie Fang's experience, before she went with him to the "school," was even more horrible. She was the principal soprano with the Central Opera. In the fifties, she'd been the first Chinese woman to sing Violetta, the tragic heroine in Verdi's *La Traviata*. Now, revolutionary interrogators ordered her to run around the Central Opera courtyard while they chased and whipped her. While she had her hands up to protect her face, the whip hit her watch so hard that it shattered.

Somehow Uncle Shi and Auntie Fang came through it all. Uncle Shi became famous directing movies once more after the Cultural Revolution, but Auntie Fang never sang again. When the opera company asked her to come back, she told them that her heart was frozen over now and she could not sing. She did agree to be a director, though.

Too many people did not survive. Some died after vicious and repeated beatings, others were executed, still others succumbed to the harsh conditions they were made to suffer. Many chose suicide. This I learned firsthand on a drizzly late-summer day just after the start of the Cultural Revolution a year earlier. I was playing with three friends at Taiping Hu (Peace Lake) on the outskirts of the city. Along the lakefront ahead of us at some distance, we saw a man on the ground, soaking wet, his faced covered with mud. When two men standing alongside saw us approaching, they blocked our way. The man was dead, a suicide; we shouldn't look. We left but came back the next day. What we saw now was a big poster hanging from the nearest tree: "Counterrevolutionary writer Lao She has used his death to defy our Party." The poor man had been criticized for killing himself. Later, the facts came out that this man was the renowned writer Lao She, sixty-seven years old. I knew about his famous play, *The Teahouse*. Attacked as a reactionary intellectual, he had been beaten repeatedly with belts and fists the day before he died. He was supposed to report for further humiliation the next morning but drowned himself instead.

I've found myself reflecting from time to time that this beloved artist, once declared a "People's Artist," chose to put an end to his cares in Peace Lake. Such were the commonplace events of those years.

From left, me, my mother, my sister (front), my brother, and my father, in a photo taken at the Beihai Park (then called Workers Peasants Soldiers Park) in 1968 when my brother, a naval officer, was home on leave. It was the height of the Cultural Revolution, and this was our last family photo before my parents were sent away from Beijing a year later.

The next summer, on another scorching day, I was playing by myself in the Summer Palace, once the traditional summering grounds of the imperial family. It was just before my thirteenth birthday. The huge park, with its lakes, temples, and gardens, was crowded with people trying to take their minds off the dreadful heat and humidity. I was wandering around aimlessly near one of the tall pagodas when I heard a loud thump, like something hitting the ground nearby, followed by lots of screaming. A crowd had gathered, and I couldn't see what they were looking at until

I inched my way through. There lay a man, maybe thirty years old, face up, so very pale, his body twitching and convulsing. He wore a light-color shirt and torn dark pants through which something protruded—I suddenly realized it was a broken bone. I don't remember seeing any blood. The crowd hushed, until whispers of "Suicide!" broke the silence. Apparently, he had jumped from the tower.

Nobody there seemed to know him, and nobody came forward to help. Coming to the aid of a counterrevolutionary—after all, he was a suicide—would probably be a bad thing to do. I could see on the faces of many of these onlookers that they did not feel sorry for this dying man at all. But he didn't look like a bad guy to me. In the movies, the enemies of our society always had horrible facial expressions and evil eyes. But this man looked like a scholar. His face seemed composed and calm, and there was a very slight smile on his lips, of that I was sure. Soon, park workers with red bands on their left arms pushed us all away. They flung the man on a flat-bed pushcart. He didn't move at all. Perhaps he was already dead.

I took off and ran home. The man's pale face and his suggestion of a smile would not leave my mind. It never will. And though I could do nothing to help this man in his final moments in 1967 in Beijing, remarkably he came to my rescue in 1995 in Bonn, where I was performing in Mozart's *Don Giovanni* for the first time and dying—in more ways than one—in a staging rehearsal. The Italian director, famous in theater but never before having worked in opera, marched onto the stage briskly. "*Buon giorno!*" he called, then flipped a chair around, sat down, stuck a pipe in his mouth, and puffed a big cloud of smoke. I was singing the role of the Commendatore, who is murdered by Don Giovanni in the first scene of the first act. (He comes back singing in the final scene, though, to drag Don Giovanni, aka Don Juan, off to hell.) I hadn't a clue how to act this part, so I was eager to hear the kind of guidance I'd come to expect in opera: where to stand, what to do, how to appear.

"Okay, let's start." That's all he said. This was the first time I'd worked with a director who didn't direct!

I was on my own. What was I to do? I die in this very first scene at the hands of the proud, boastful man who has tried to have his way with my daughter, whose honor I'm now trying to defend. But how? Then it came to me, that pale face, that sweet almost-smile from the poor man dying in the Summer Palace. He whispered to me, "I am hurt. I am dying, but I am relieved of pain." I thought, I am hurt, and I am dying, but I know I have given my life for my daughter's honor and I die in peace, relieved of my pain. So almost in slow motion I slumped to the stage, peacefully, with relief, and with the suggestion of a smile.

"Bravo!" called the director, jumping from his chair and running to me as I stood back up. He grabbed me by the shoulders and insisted I tell him how I came up with that move. So I told him about that summer day in the Summer Palace nearly thirty years earlier when the man jumped to his death. The director was silent. When the pipe smoke cleared around his face, he looked sad. Then a big smile spread over his face.

"You understand me," he said. Turning to the rest of the cast, he said, "That's what I'm looking for. Find what works for you, and if I like it, we'll go with that."

I blessed that man in the Summer Palace whose name I never knew but whose death, I hoped, I had found some way to honor.

In the summer of 1968, Teacher Ren from my old elementary school appeared at our door. "I haven't seen you for almost two years," she said, smiling benevolently. I squirmed with guilt. The last time I'd spoken to her, I was having a grand time leading the criticism against her. Yet as if none of this had ever happened, she told me and my parents that Chairman Mao had ordered that we "resume classes and do revolution." She presented two choices. I could finish the final year of elementary school or enter Second Middle School attached to Beijing Normal University, which was in my neighborhood. Skip a year of school? You bet! Yet I was surprised that this excellent middle school, run by the teachers' university and usually available only to highest-achieving students, would accept me. My grades in math, abacus calculation, and history were dismal.

I needn't have worried. There was little regular education to speak of when classes began again in September. Most of our time was spent on political studies. English class consisted of memorizing revolutionary sentences, including "Long live Chairman Mao," which we had to recite for visiting bigwigs from socialist and third-world countries. The teachers behaved tentatively with the students. This was the school where the former principal, Gao Yun, had been tortured with hot water and thumbtacks, and the Party secretary, a literature teacher, and a student's mother had been tortured and killed.

My first day at this school, I saw a tall, heavy man working hard to clean the dirt and paste from the *dazibao* that had been peeled from the windows. I was stunned to realize it was Mr. Gao. "Uncle Gao Yun," I called out, "how are you?" He turned around, looking frightened. Obviously, he didn't recognize me.

"Who are you?" he asked in a hushed voice.

"I'm the son of Tian Yun and Lu Yuan."

"Oh, Xiao Er" (Little Second, meaning "second child"), he said, now smiling. "How are your parents?" I told him they were okay. "Tell your parents I'm okay, too. I can't talk now." He turned back to his scrubbing.

For his "crimes," Mr. Gao had been sentenced to do menial labor in the school he once led, where he remained under surveillance.

It was a fateful encounter. Mr. Gao would eventually become my savior when I desperately needed one and would play that role for my sister as well. He believed that he owed his life—the first time his life was threatened, in 1945—to my parents and the other members of the Second Anti-Enemy Performing Arts Troupe. The troupe had been in Beijing to perform for the victory over the Japanese, when Mr. Gao, then in his twenties, rushed backstage pleading for help. "I have no place to hide. The KMT spies are coming after me!" he cried. KMT officials, who were still in charge in Beijing, had recognized him as a Communist activist. The troupe members hurried to provide him with a costume and pushed him onto the stage with the other players. Nobody professed to know anything about the man the KMT was seeking when they burst in a short while later. So Mr. Gao became a de facto member of the Second Troupe, where he remained until after the Communist victory. Then he went into education, only to be set upon for the political beliefs he had nearly died for in the first place.

While I was in Jincheng in 1966, Red Guards from the regular Second Middle School had literally made themselves the fashion police for the new standards: no pants with narrow legs, no high heels, no "feudal" long braids. Some of the students had rushed out to forcibly cut off braids and cut off pant legs and high heels. All of this, and so many other zealous adolescent deeds, had been in response to Chairman Mao's call to smash the Four Olds. By the time I came to that school, most of those excesses had receded. Still, we were a bunch of lawless teenagers. My seat was next to a window that was often open. Whenever I felt like it, I jumped out the window and ran to the playground. My parents had finally given me my name, Hao Jiang. Now the whole school could hear me roar.

A lot of us were from military families and we wore our parents' old uniforms, which set us apart from the kids from families who had worked in the "old" trades, running small stores and businesses. Our parents were revolutionary military officers; we were the proud successors of the revolutionary course. It became the height of high fashion to wear their old silk or wool uniforms (dark brown for army) underneath the current green cotton-for-all Cultural Revolution issue. Fights often broke out between these unofficial ranks of students. I did not often participate, but I did not try to stop them, either. The teachers never intervened. One day, a dozen students in their parents' uniforms stormed into my classroom and attacked one of the regular students with chairs and sticks. The teacher just stood there. The student was my friend. One of the attackers cast an awful look at me as I helped my friend wipe the blood off his face.

Later I went home with him to show my sympathy. His home was so different from mine. In an old, rundown courtyard occupied by many households, my friend's home was dark, dirty, and crowded with people but with almost no furniture. When his younger brother started to cry, his mother slapped the child's face. "What are you crying about? You are born in a poor family with this poor fate. You shameless little thing!" She kept cursing the little boy, while glancing sideways at me. Then I understood she was aiming at me. I had marched my official army family background into these poor people's house—my clean uniform, my leather shoes, both a luxury for ordinary people. I felt my face burning. I said a hasty good-bye. I felt her curses and the child's cries trailing me. This was the first and last time that I visited my friend at home.

The Zhongzheng Song and Dance Ensemble had ceased having concerts. Instead, the members participated in political studies and public accusation meetings and wrote and pasted *dazibao*. My parents weren't invited to the meetings anymore, because nobody could figure out whether they were criminals or just had a "historical problem." For nearly a year, they spent their days studying the writings of Marx, Lenin, and Mao; reading newspapers; and attempting to lower themselves to glorify the worker, while they waited to see what would happen to them. Along with others in the ensemble, my father stood for hours up to his hips in the icy cold river washing the stage curtain and the costumes of the ballet dancers by hand. He expressed no anger or humiliation, but he forever after believed that the pain in his leg, which became lifelong, dated from that experience.

Children were so empowered in those days that we could turn in our parents or someone else's in criticism sessions in school. As the oft-repeated saying went, "Mother is close, father is close, but neither is as close as Chairman Mao." Our sole allegiance was supposed to be to you-know-who. If you didn't have a good family background, you'd have to say, "I was born in a black family. I don't want to be their children. I will help them to clean their minds." I wasn't a political person—I didn't want to be a student leader—but like everybody else I wanted to follow what Chairman Mao said. Sometimes I even prayed to his picture. I wanted to believe that if I were facing death, like a true hero my last thought would be of Mao. And I believed the best way for me to show my loyalty was to join the Red Guards.

By the time the schools reopened, the Red Guards had been deprived of their former power and were now more like the Young Pioneers from my elementary school days. (Other groups carried on the violence, outside of school.) The Red Guards still wore red bands on their arms, and I really wanted one. After entering the school, as soon as I could, I handed in an application. I wrote that I wanted to join the Red Guards to protect Chairman Mao and the Communist Party and to take an active part in the Cultural Revolution. I went on to explain that my parents were under examination for their membership in the Second Anti-Enemy Performing Arts Troupe before the Liberation. I promised that if they were found guilty, "I will make a complete break with them." I preened with pride as my teacher praised my application in class: "The writing was fluent in language, and the feeling was touching and real."

The verdict was crushing. "Your parents are under examination, so your family background is not clean and clear."

As for making a clean break with them, that brash promise never came to the test. In early 1969, when my parents were banished for good, they took me with them.

Picture this: We have only one week to pack and go. I am helping my parents to bundle our things. It is late afternoon and the sun is low, sending a golden light into the room. The complex is so quiet. I find an old dusty record that has fallen behind the old gramophone and thus escaped my destructive blows two years ago. I call my father and show it to him. He takes it in his hand. He is silent. Then to my surprise he says, "Let's play it." His tone of voice is surprisingly, uncharacteristically soft.

I wipe the dust from the big machine. I crank the handle and place the arm and needle on the record. It is Beethoven's *Sixth Symphony*, the "Pastorale," the label says. Despite the additional danger we face if anyone hears these decadent sounds, my habitually stiff and remote father transforms before my eyes. In fourteen years of life, I have never seen his face so human and tender or heard such emotion in his voice. Talking as if to himself, he begins to explain that this is the last Western work he conducted, in 1964. "This is an interlude," he sighs after a certain passage of music. "That is the first theme." Then again, "Here the theme is developed, and now can you hear the second theme?"

My attention jumps from my father to the music to my father to the music back to my father. Never before have I heard these sounds or seen this man. His eyes are so bright! He is looking inward, I think, or toward a world I cannot see. "Can you hear," he asks, "that this is the sound of the creek singing? And now, do you hear a bird?" Never have I ever heard anybody talk about pictures in music. I concentrate. I hear them! The dust all around us rises like spun gold in the magical atmosphere of this afternoon.

I don't remember whether we let the recording play to the end or even whether we destroyed it afterward. I like to think that my father had hidden it behind the gramophone the day I smashed to bits all of his other precious music. Thus, when the time came, he could show me how such music could bring his heart to his face and tears to his eyes. The image of him transformed merged in my mind with the tune from atop a haystack on a summer's night. I walked through the door that had swung open while I lay on that haystack years before. So silently that I didn't know it happened, the same door closed behind me.

Nobody talked much on the bus to the train station the night we left. My parents, who had had to resign from the Zhongzheng, appeared sad, especially my mother. My father had packed all his feelings back inside. The day before, my mother had managed to say good-bye to Teacher Jiao in the dining hall by sitting at a table next to where he was forced to eat in solitary silence; in a very loud voice she told a woman at her table that we were leaving. I went with my parents to say good-bye to Auntie Hu Zhitao, a special lady who had been badly beaten by the girl Red Guards in the middle school where she was the vice principal. My parents were so afraid of being seen visiting her that we went at midnight. When Auntie opened the door and saw us, right away she covered her mouth so that no one could hear her cry out. During our brief visit, she never turned on the lights.

Through the bus window I looked around the city as if I had never seen it before, at the streets, the lights, the buildings, Tiananmen Square.

Zaijian. Good-bye, Beijing.

5

Embracing the Beast

COUNT NOT WHAT is lost but what is left, as the Chinese saying goes. My parents were not beaten to death. They weren't forced to hang self-accusatory political placards from their necks. They weren't separated from each other. They weren't forced to stand for hours during meetings in *zuo feiji*—airplane—style, with heads lowered, bodies bent downward, arms raised backward. They were still Communist Party members. They remained in the People's Liberation Army and on the payroll, earning three times as much as regular workers. They could still wear their uniforms with the red star on the cap.

But there's another Chinese saying: Be not disturbed at being misunderstood; be disturbed at not understanding. Why were they encamped with two of their children at a military hotel in Zhengzhou, the capital of Henan province, ten hours by train from Beijing? Nobody really knew, least of all my parents or those who now had charge of them. Along with us, there were about twenty high-ranking officers, many with families, from the various Zhongzheng departments. Everybody was under some kind of cloud. They couldn't be treated as leaders. Then again, they weren't really enemies. So they were reassigned to the Henan branch of the military, stripped of everything they had been trained for. They sat around the hotel with nowhere to go and nothing to do but wait.

My parents' political problems fell most heavily on my brother. The family's disgrace led to his immediate expulsion from the navy—never mind that they were allowed to remain in the army. Tian Mimi, who'd been sent to learn Vietnamese in preparation to aid the North Vietnamese, had been on the brink of a brilliant career. Now he had joined the sorry ranks of relatives of people with a bad background who had to, as the expression went, *bei hei guo*—carry a black wok—for the rest of their lives. (Black was a bad color. Red was the color of the revolution.) My brother never recovered his momentum in life. Now Tian Mimi was working in a factory as a laborer, which was quite a comedown. Perhaps that was why he procrastinated in completing an important chore: returning to the police the Beijing residence permits issued at birth for me and my sister, which my parents had failed to relinquish before our sudden departure. My parents, in the military, were not assigned to any permanent place. Banished from the capital, my sister and I were no longer entitled to our Beijing *hukou*. Yet no matter how much my parents nagged Tian Mimi from afar, he simply left the permits to languish in a drawer, where they lay until I made my way back to Beijing and reclaimed them.

One by one, all the other people at the military hotel had been assigned to unimportant duties in various places throughout Henan province until, after three months, my family was the only one left. My parents decided that I might as well try to get back to Beijing, since, thanks to my brother, I was technically still a resident there. Supposedly, he would look after me, and later our sister would follow. If the scheme worked, we'd go back to school and rejoin our parents when they were more settled.

They dropped me at the Zhengzhou train station and told me just to wait until a train came. Nobody knew when it would arrive since everything was so disorganized in those days. I grew hungry and bought a bowl of noodles. I sat down at a big square table, picked up my chopsticks, and was about to dig in when a tall, dirty man sat down close to me and deliberately jostled me.

"Hey, don't eat everything, okay? Leave something for me!"

His severe face scared me. I'd never seen a beggar before, since begging was not allowed in Beijing. "Here take it!" I ran away, leaving him the whole thing. This was not an auspicious beginning for me in learning to manage my resources—not that I had any idea that day how much self-management was ahead of me.

After five hours, the train came. I'd taken buses by myself, but I'd never been on a train alone before. I'd certainly never made a journey like this without my parents or my auntie. Really, I'd never spent much time alone at all. Despite all the troubles my parents had been going through, until this moment I had been a pretty care-free kid, trusting adults to look after me and never having to take much responsibility for myself. The filthy train was packed. People had even crammed themselves into the luggage racks to sleep, and some lay precariously atop the narrow ledges that attached the backward- and forward-facing benches. I stood.

Once back at our building in Beijing, I was shocked to see how much had changed in the three months since we'd been forced to leave. The apartments had all been carved up. Another family now lived in two of our three bedrooms. We shared the bathroom and the kitchen. My brother had the other room. I stayed in a small room off the common hallway, which I shared with my old neme-sis, the piano, that beast. It turned out that Tian Mimi was living in the factory dorm six days a week. He was twenty, and I was four-teen. Once a week he came back and yelled at me, "Why is this room such a pigsty?" If I was lucky, he took me out to dinner. At least he let me try to play his guitar, which was not considered a healthy instrument but which he'd learned to play from a Vietnam-ese officer before being forced out of the service.

At first, I thought this was the life for me. I went to school dur-ing the day. Other than that, I was completely free. My parents sent me fifteen yuan, less than two dollars, every month. It seemed like a lot of money since I'd never had to pay for myself before. I cooked simple meals, some noodles or rice with a little meat and vegetables, or I bought my meals in the building dining hall. I loved to invite my classmates over to my little room and feed them. I learned within the first month that fifteen yuan wouldn't nourish my little army, much less me. But being fourteen and being prudent didn't go well together, so that by the end of the month I was usu-ally skipping some meals.

Freedom had other limits, I discovered. Maybe I was free to do whatever I wanted, but there wasn't so much to do during the Cultural Revolution besides show your devotion to Chairman Mao. That's mostly what we did in school all day long and what the progressives—the devoted political types—did after school; they met in study groups and exposed people. No one had money, and thus we had little in the way of material desires. All entertainment was strictly controlled by Comrade Jiang Qing, Mao's wife, who was now in charge of culture and propaganda. Any movie, play, opera, dance, or even art exhibit that was deemed counterrevolutionary—and everything except those she developed herself fell into that category—was banned. Love songs were forbidden. Only Chairman Mao and the revolution could be glorified.

Within a short time I grew restless and lonely. I was full of energy. I needed to be rowdy, to make noise. One day, out of boredom, I ran my hands along the piano keys. Then I banged on them. Then I attacked them with chopsticks. Then I sat on a chair and kicked my heels on the keys. I had to wallop the beast in this tall, black, heavily carved, German behemoth. Over the next few days, I pounded, I hit, I banged, I kicked the demons out of it—or out of me. One day it dawned on me: *this* is freedom, to create my own sounds, loud or soft, any time I wanted, no exercises, no practice. Whatever noise I made was pure me. I became possessed, obsessed with the sounds of freedom. I invited my friends over to make noise with me. At last, my fingers began to caress the keyboard with tenderness. Whatever I was playing sounded like the most beautiful music in the world to me. But not, of course, to my neighbors. I was driving them insane.

The piano, along with most of the furniture we had had, belonged to the ensemble, to which complaints were made. Because the Zhongzheng ensemble was not really functioning during this period, it took them a few months to deal with me. One day a man who'd been an ensemble piano tuner before the Cultural Revolution appeared at the door to my little room. I recognized him, and I knew that he was someone to fear for his sneakiness.

"Play something for me," he said, smiling. I didn't trust him, but I banged on the keys in my characteristic style.

"Very good," he said, "but I think there's something wrong with the piano. I'd better fix it." He proceeded to remove all the hammers, telling me that he would return them as soon as he made them sound better. Now there was only silence when I pressed the keys. I ran home from school every day waiting for the man to return. Once when I bumped into him, he reassured me. "I'm still working on it. It's a big job."

He never came back. I missed the sound so much that I started to play even more than I had before. I touched or hit the keys and played the most extraordinary music, all in my head. I was gifted! I was great! Then I discovered that I could pluck the strings like a harp. I fell in love with that sound. I invited my friends over to hear.

"You are cheating!" they laughed.

"That's the way the best pianists play," I claimed. "You don't understand music."

At age fourteen, I was a musician, born.

Then one day when I came home from school, the piano was gone. The Zhongzheng ensemble had reclaimed it. I knew they would never give it back to me. Now I really understood what it meant to be alone. Whenever I found myself in someone's home with a piano, I immediately sat down and played. I don't know whether it sounded good to anyone else, but it was music to my ears. My brother gave me a couple of lessons on his guitar, which helped me to keep my noise-making fingers busy, but it did not replace the piano for me.

Somebody in the building who'd heard the racket I'd been making mentioned me to the head of our school's Mao Zedong Thought Propaganda Team. This was an amateur version of what my parents usually did for their living: using song and dance to promote revolutionary values. And there was no other purpose for art. Revolutionary literature and art should serve the workers (*gong*), the peasants (*nong*), and the soldiers (*bing*), Mao instructed. There must have been thousands of these Thought Propaganda Teams in every

I was fourteen when I became an accordionist in my middle school Mao Zedong Thought Propaganda Team. I'm the smiling guy on the left in the second row. Most of the others are playing traditional Chinese instruments, including the two-stringed erhu, *played with a bow; the plucked* ruan; *the zither we call* yangqin; *and the* sheng, *a reed instrument with vertical pipes.*

school, work unit, and locality throughout the country. Our school's team needed someone to play the accordion. I really hadn't a clue how to do that, but I showed up for the audition and did manage to pick out the tune to "The East Is Red" on its pianolike keys. The ensemble head got so excited. "You're a big talent!" He gave me a school accordion to use, which now replaced the piano as the object of my obsession. I got a how-to book and practiced happily and constantly. I don't recall anybody in the building complaining, but I do remember the knock on my door after months of this teach-yourself-to-play-accordion activity.

"You have a good touch," said the man standing at the door. "May I teach you?" He turned out to be a professional accordionist from the Air Force Song and Dance Ensemble. He gave me periodic instruction, for free, over the next few years.

Being a member of the Mao Zedong Thought Propaganda Team turned out to have a number of advantages. We performed on all major holidays, such as National Day on October 1, International Laborers' Day on May 1, and many others. We had to rehearse all the time, which left little time for our so-called classes.

The biggest boon was the girls—*nü hai*. Girls, girls, girls, girls, girls.

I was a teenager. It goes without saying that I was getting interested in girls. But during the Cultural Revolution, everything that was natural became unnatural and everything unnatural was de rigueur, or so it seemed. Boys and girls were permitted little familiarity with one another. Although we had classes together in my school, it was important to observe proper *zuofeng*, which meant moral integrity but in the Cultural Revolution came to have a sexual connotation. We could criticize and torture our teachers—that was progressive—but we mustn't have bad *zuofeng*, even in our fantasies. All we were supposed to dream about was healthy revolutionary ideals. That was not where my mind was one summer day when the most beautiful girl in our class stepped into the classroom while a bunch of boys were playing and goofing around before the lessons began. We pretended not to notice her, but I saw how she lifted her skirt so as not to sit on it as she lowered herself onto her chair. When she got up and left later, I saw the definite outline of her butt and even her underwear embedded in the dust on the chair. My heart beat wildly and I could not tear my eyes away, which some of the other boys noticed. One of them shoved me from behind, demanding to know what I was doing. Then he looked down at the chair and saw what I saw. "Come on, look at this!" he called to the other boys. Everybody laughed and guffawed, while I retreated to a corner, listening to my heart pound, feeling my whole body burning, imagining the girl's beautiful anatomy. Bad *zuofeng*.

In the Thought Propaganda Team, we were required to be with girls, sing and dance together to celebrate our great leader. We never touched, but the proximity was ever so appealing. And then one day that same gorgeous girl who left the shape of her behind on my fourteen-year-old heart joined the team and became a dancer. I lived for the opportunity to escort her home after rehearsal. If we worked into the evening, the teacher sometimes asked a boy to see the girls home safely. Since we weren't allowed to be alone with a girl, we asked other boys to come along. The girls walked in front. We boys would sing or joke to try to get the girls' attention. I hoped that I would stand out in front of this girl, whose chair outline has stayed in my mind so much longer than her name.

I dared to write this girl my first love letter, when she joined the army about a year later. This was the biggest step I'd ever taken to get close to a girl. These words were penned with the blood of my passion: "You are joining the army. Hopefully you will become Chairman Mao's good soldier and a revolutionary successor." It was like spitting into a river. After I handed her the note, she blinked, turned, and walked away.

Zuofeng was no joke. Even a small mistake—if you got caught— would put an end to a glorious revolutionary future. When a couple of Red Guard leaders in my school were found holding hands one evening, they were immediately removed from their positions and disgraced in the eyes of their peers. Even worse was to be labeled a hooligan or a degenerate. Love—*ai*—was a forbidden topic.

You can imagine how naive we were. We couldn't talk or learn about love or physical intimacy. We couldn't even see love in the movies, which at best featured Chinese maidens dancing with their rifles. Books, plays, poems, and dances never had love scenes or even showed couples together, and single people never mentioned having a love interest. Marriage was not permitted until we were in our mid-twenties. A friend told me a story he had heard about a wedding of a man and a woman who had met when they'd been sent away to live and work in a remote border area. Wedding guests read from Mao's Little Red Book, and they sang revolutionary songs, congratulating the couple on becoming revolutionary companions in order to help each other along their progressive road. After candies were handed out—the only sweet moment of the marriage ceremony—the couple, holding red flowers to their chests, bowed in front of Chairman Mao's portrait. After the guests departed, the couple continued to read quotations to each other into the night. Some hours later, the people in the commune were startled awake by a woman's piercing scream: "Rape! Rape!"

Or so my friend told me.

Was this story supposed to be a joke? People behaved so against their nature during these years that it's hard to know, even in retrospect, what was funny. Imagine, for example, picking up the phone in Beijing and the telephone operator saying, "Criticize selfishness," to which you would have to respond with the next part of the quotation—"Denounce revisionism"—before she'd put the call through. This was real.

We learned about what was "right" and what was "wrong" through political decree. We learned about our own natural appetites through confusing experiences and banned books, which I didn't manage to get my hands on for a few more years.

But for these two years left of my schooling, I had my music and my self-importance. I was a key member of the Thought Propaganda Team. After all, I was from a military family and wore a better-quality uniform, and with my accordion skills and the revolutionary tunes I was beginning to write, I was such a *shuai* guy—so cool. And I had a life filled with girls. Sometimes, if our rehearsals ran really late, we all slept in the classroom, boys and girls separated by a row of chairs. I imagined their body parts and dreamed of crossing over.

Many kids like me, whose parents had been taken away, turned to music and art as our best friend. Art became our way to distract ourselves from the pressures of being so suddenly deprived of our life supports and sense of justice. It was an antidote to our dark, violent, and now unpredictable lives. And so—as would become evident years later—a generation of artists developed that would distill meaning and beauty from the unsupervised insanity of that period. At the time, though, I dreamed of little that didn't take the shape of a girl; my accordion would seduce her and we would . . . oh yes, we would. . . . Very bad *zuofeng*.

After several months in the military hotel, my parents had been reassigned to a small 5/7 Cadre School outside the little coal-mining town of Jiaozuo in Henan province. The school was one of many throughout the country that had been hastily put together after May 7, 1968—hence their name. At that time, Mao gave a speech announcing the creation of labor schools for officials and intellectuals who had unclear backgrounds, where they could study the new teachings of the Cultural Revolution and work in the fields. My parents remained at the school for two years; my sister stayed with them. My father labored in the fields, while my mother worked as a secretary in the office.

No hope remained of us living together as a family, and indeed we never did. Briefly, I thought about returning to them in Henan province and then joining the army through their unit. Even my sister, Meimei, though not yet twelve years old, wanted to join the military. Many kids of high-ranking officials, including about 80 percent of my friends, were signing up since their parents could pull the appropriate strings. These young soldiers were much   admired, not least because their future was brighter, for they wouldn't have to be sent to labor as peasants for Chairman Mao and sacrifice all hopes of a decent future. Into my adolescent sense of the endless present had come the creeping awareness that if your parents couldn't use their connections on your behalf, you would be sent far, far away at the end of your schooling. Now that I could play the accordion, I thought, maybe I could become a performing soldier like my parents.

Part of it was a uniform thing. Sure, there was the navy-blue Mao suit that everybody wore, maybe with a long woolen scarf in the winter, plus the white mask to cover your nose and mouth to keep the sand, the dust, or smells out. That was the look. But to sport a green uniform, with a red star on your cap and the red patches on your collar, to fly around Beijing on a bicycle and impress all the girls, now that was prestige. But this fantasy fizzled since there wasn't a chance that I'd be stationed in Beijing, where my parents could no longer pull strings. I'd have to switch to a Jiaozuo *hukou*, with which I would never be able to move back to Beijing. And who really knew that my parents' current circumstances provided any influence anyway?

And then there was the issue of my extreme nearsightedness. I'd been going for acupuncture treatments to cure this, having needles inserted around my eyes and forehead once a week. My vision improved for a few days, but that was it. The black and purple splotches that resulted lasted much longer. My friends shrieked with laughter as they called me *xiongmao*—"panda." So I quit the treatments.

No military for me.

By early 1970, to our immeasurable relief, Chairman Mao suddenly abandoned the policy of sending the educated youths to the countryside or the remote border areas. Instead, everybody would be assigned to work in factories, since the working class needed new blood. What a luxury! What an honor! As the Chairman said, "The working class is the leading class!" And best of all, I would be able to stay in Beijing.

But as my June graduation approached, the demons that had beset our family took a long, hard look at me. True, all middle-school graduates who weren't going into the military would work in the factories—except for those with family-history problems, who would be sent to the countryside. We all knew how bad a life that was from the once-idealistic volunteers who'd returned, as well as from letters written by unwilling conscripts, many of whom the government had all but abandoned out there.

June 14, 1970, was graduation day. Hundreds of us sat crowded together on the school playground, surrounded by huge red flags, all waving in the wind. A massive portrait of Chairman Mao stood on the temporary stage. Now that we had officially finished our education, we waited to hear what our government had in store for us. The factory assignments began, site by site, punctuated with cheers from students who were overjoyed that they would remain near their homes. I sat there in dread, barely hearing the endless drone of names, names, names.

"Tian Hao Jiang." Silence. I turned to the boy sitting next to me. "Did you hear my name? Who called my name?" I kept asking, not believing my ears, as I felt waves of shivers travel up and down my spine.

I was one of the hundred graduates of my school assigned to the Beijing Boiler Factory! How could this be? I was from a problem family. It was Mr. Gao, I found out years later, who had made sure my name got on the list. He was the disgraced survivor of Red Guard torture whom I had encountered doing janitor work on my first day in the school. He had been rehabilitated and returned to school administration duties. Now his title was vice president of the Second Middle School attached to Beijing Normal University—in effect, the principal. As he later told my parents, he had vowed to help the children of the members of the Second Troupe who had saved his life in 1945.

The Beijing Boiler Factory! It sounded like the celestial kingdom.

My day offered one more miracle.

The leader of our school's Red Guards went up onstage and announced, "Tomorrow you are all going on to your new revolutionary posts. Now I want to make a formal announcement. We will recruit our last member from this class. Because he contributed to our Mao Zedong Thought Propaganda Team and studied very hard in his time here, we have decided to accept Tian Hao Jiang as an honored soldier of the Red Guard. Tian Hao Jiang, please come up onstage and accept this title and this armband."

I floated up to the stage and held out my left arm as our Red Guard leader put the shiny red band with the gold Chinese characters on my arm and slid it up my white sleeve. Eye-catching, I

Here I am in 1970 with Mr. Gao, vice-president of my middle school. By this time, he had recovered from being tortured by his Red Guard students. He was a longtime friend of my parents, and although I didn't know it at the time, he helped to make sure that I was sent to work in a factory in Beijing rather than on a farm far away.

thought the next morning, admiring my festooned arm as I sat crammed in the back of the big old truck that rumbled through the city that fine summer morning on its way to the western suburbs of Beijing.

"Take that off!" ordered Master Worker Wang. With a broad face and thick arms, my new master at the Beijing Boiler Factory stood a head shorter than me, but there was no disputing his strength or his authority. After less than a full day as a Red Guard in good standing, I removed the armband and stuffed it in my pocket. I was a worker now. At fifteen, my childhood was at an end.

I found that armband in a dusty box not long ago, when my wife and I were cleaning out the basement of a house we own in Denver. All those feelings—the sorrow, the fear, the horrors, the hopes and aspirations, the cruel realities, and yet the magical discoveries and the sheer wonderment of childhood—beset me all at once. I brought the armband back to New York with me. Perhaps it is my most prized possession, for all that it brings up in me. Maybe one day I'll put on a long-sleeved white shirt, like the one I wore to my graduation and to my first day at the factory. I'll roll that now-dulled red band back up my arm and sing a Chairman Mao quotation song composed by my mother, conducted by my father, when the system they so fervently believed in also believed in them. Call those the good old days.

CHAPTER

6

What Was I Thinking?

IN THE LATE summer of 2004, I returned to Beijing to celebrate my fiftieth birthday. My octogenarian mother, long a widow, along-with ten of her old army cronies from the Second Troupe and about a thousand other people, thronged the concert hall where I sang my first solo recital ever in Beijing. It was broadcast nationwide on Chinese TV and radio and was a glorious homecoming, reuniting me with friends and colleagues from my youth, including some from the Beijing Boiler Factory. I visited the factory the next day after an absence of almost a quarter-century. At the first view from the entrance gates, the place seemed eerily unchanged. I had arrived at this same spot, day after interminable day, six days a week for nearly seven years, stepping off the old company bus after the two-hour commute to this western suburb of Beijing. The low buildings flanking the long roadway that led from the gate were the same, if older. So, too, my comrades from those days, some of whom were still there. They were the same, only worn, the way a life of physical labor reveals its history on the body.

Look again. See those flags on either side of the entrance gate? One is the Chinese red and gold, with one large gold star flanked by a crescent of four smaller ones on a bright red field. But the other, could that be Old Glory? Indeed it was, and although I was now a U.S. citizen, I assure you that the presence of that red-white-and-blue had nothing to do with me. This factory—cranking out the same boilers—was now a Chinese-U.S. joint venture. A quarter-century ago, one could have been jailed or sent away for even conceiving of such a thing.

Truly, despite illusions of nothing having changed, the whole world had transformed around us.

And here I was, arriving in a chauffeur-driven, sleek, black Mercedes Benz. The head of the factory and the Party officials came out to greet our group personally and to invite us for tea around the massive boardroom table. Obviously, these relatively young executives had no knowledge of what a problem I had been for those in their position in days gone by. I grew almost dizzy with then-and-now thoughts during the ritual greeting. But as we walked back to the building, to the very machine where I had labored cutting steel sheets for all those years, my spirits lifted, just as they had on my very first day there.

The convoy of trucks had just disgorged hundreds of 1970 graduates of Beijing's middle schools into our new life. We were workers. Workers were the leading class—Chairman Mao said so. And I felt like one high-class kind of guy as I waited in line to be assigned a job. The master workers walked up and down, looking us over. They chose the bigger boys for the heavier work. I was tall, but I guess they didn't see that under my white shirt with the red armband my arms were like chopsticks. I was officially assigned to the steel-frame workshop.

The boilers we made at the Beijing Boiler Factory were for generating electricity. When put in place, they were several stories high, although I never saw one in its finished form. Our workshop assembled the steel frames for these huge boilers, which would eventually be filled with water and fired by coal to make steam to generate electricity. My job was to man the steel-cutting machine. It was one story high, with a huge gear wheel that made a deafening noise when operating. A row of square steel posts like teeth lowered to hold the steel sheets, some of them an inch thick, after which I guided the blade to turn this way and that, while it sliced the sheets—sometimes six at a time—into various shapes. Afterward, I had to flatten the cut sheets with large, heavy hammers that I held in both hands; then I used small hammers for the small pieces. We wore no ear plugs. I wonder how I can still hear.

That first day I was so excited by all of this and so eager to do my part. I was Master Worker Wang's apprentice now, but one day I would become his successor and take China to new heights as a leader of the working class. That's what I believed for maybe a year or two. The work grew boring pretty fast, though, and at first it was too hard for a boy who was not yet fully grown and wasn't strong to begin with. I got home exhausted, fell into my bed, and then, after too little time to recuperate, I had to be up and out to take an hour-long ride on a city bus, then switch to the factory bus for another hour. The twice daily two-hour commutes sandwiched an eight- to nine-hour workday, which also included required political studies. We had one day off a week. This assignment was for life. Although the universities had reopened, preparing for a better life through education would never be possible for me; only students with the cleanest *gong nong bing*—worker, peasant, soldier—backgrounds were admitted to universities. (*Gong nong bing* was more important than talent or aptitude, even in the music conservatory when it reopened.)

As soon as I could, I joined the factory's Mao Zedong Thought Propaganda Team, which welcomed my accordion skills and lifted my spirits. The team promised to offer some of the same benefits as the Thought Propaganda Team in middle school, including time off for rehearsing, which I looked forward to as my first weeks at the factory dragged by. I began to compose some simple songs to take my mind off the monotonous work at the steel-cutting machine. "What are you *thinking?*" became Master Worker Wang's constant refrain. Of course, I didn't tell him what was occupying my mind, but I did sincerely try to please him. When he was sick, I went to his apartment and made tea for him or went to the canteen to fetch food. One day he said to me, with such disappointment, "I like you a lot, Xiao Tian, but I don't think you're a good worker."

I liked him as well and could hardly disagree with his evaluation. Yet I could not accept him as my model for someone who lived the ideal revolutionary life. My master—deemed a member of China's leading class—could not even read. A leader should be able to impart more knowledge, shouldn't he? Of the three thousand workers at the factory, two thousand were educated youths like myself. Of the remaining one thousand older workers, who included our bosses, about a third could not read or write and knew little or nothing of history, literature, science, or art. Once again, in sincerely trying to follow what society decreed was the right path, I felt stymied.

"What are you *thinking?*"

It wasn't long before my on-the-job distraction had consequences. Before I had completed a month at the factory, I dropped one of the steel sheets and crushed my right foot. At the hospital, I was put into a supposed walking cast, although every time I bore weight on it I howled. They would not give me crutches but only told me to go home and stay there for a month until the bones healed. Once back in my little room, I felt completely helpless, and, for the first time since I had been on my own in life, I recognized how alone I really was.

I wanted to go home to my family, but I had no home with a family in it. I did not even have a telephone number for my parents. All I knew was the mailing address for their 5/7 Cadre School in Jiaozuo in northwest Henan province, hundreds of miles from Beijing. Instead of writing to tell them of my plight, I took a bus to the train station and caught a train for Jiaozuo. The pain was horrid, but my desperation to be cared for by my family overrode it.

I remember getting off the train in the early evening. I asked the driver of a bicycle rickshaw where the 5/7 Cadre School was. He said he had a vague idea, but he didn't want to take me there. I pointed at my foot and grimaced and groaned until he agreed to take me at least partway in the general direction. He pedaled for hours. It must have been about ten o'clock when he dropped me in a village and told me this was as far as he would go. A man there told me I still had ten *li* (about three and a half miles) to go. He waved in the direction I should proceed and walked away. So I hobbled on in the pitch-black night, passing darkened villages on the side of the road and taking turns onto dirt roads for no known reason. I was some kind of wounded, possessed homing pigeon.

Just before dawn, instinct told me to take another turn in the road, where an early-rising old woman I encountered told me I was in the right place. She pointed the way to my father's house. I collapsed at the door, now overcome with pain. I could not control my emotions and I wept. My mother opened the door and shrieked to find me there. Tears came to her eyes. My father and my sister awoke. There wasn't much reaction from my father, but I knew he was happy to see me. My sister was ecstatic. By the time I fell peacefully to sleep, the sun was up, my parents had gone to work, and my sister had left for school. It was the most beautiful sleep, with no worries.

My family's house consisted of two little rooms, with bars on an open screened window that had no glass; the house was very simply furnished. Still, I was so happy to be "home." My parents assigned me a chore, to look after the chickens in the small yard out back. I gave every chicken a name and talked to each one of them. Naturally, they laid huge beautiful eggs because of me. I managed to stretch out my convalescence to two months. My foot hadn't healed, with all my crazy walking. Sometimes it hurts me still.

I returned with a limp to Master Worker Wang and the steel-cutting machine. I had learned to be more attentive, but I directed all of my enthusiasm to the propaganda ensemble, which I now began to conduct as well. Our troupe consisted of about twenty workers, and although few of us had any real training, we played all sorts of instruments, including traditional Chinese ones—the two-stringed *erhu*, the mandolinlike *pipa*, the bamboo flute we called a *dizi*, tiny brass cymbals, drums, and the plucked *yangqin*, which is like a zither. Some of my comrades could even manage the French horn, the clarinet, and the violin, and, of course, I was the resident accordionist. I wrote lots of compositions that included all of these instruments. It was my own early earnest attempt at East-West fusion, although it would be decades before I ever heard that term. We performed at the Beijing Workers' Arts Festival that first year, and the audience was almost as enthusiastic as we were.

And I wrote songs, so many songs, for my friends, full of yearning for glory and using lyrics that we were permitted. One was called "Our Lives Are Full of Sunshine." These are the lyrics my friend wrote for my tune:

Our lives are full of sunshine
and we are full of enthusiasm
as the bugle calls for battle
and we martyrs set the example.

We sang this song over and over and over. On that trip back to Beijing a generation later, I went out for a banquet one night with five of my closest buddies from the factory. Most of them had moved on to other jobs and fields of endeavor over the years. We ate and toasted one another in the Chinese fashion from six in the evening until midnight, when we began to sing the songs we

My factory pals and I took off for the mountains outside Beijing to behave wildly as often as we could. We camped out, stole chickens, swam naked, fought with other guys, drank too much, smoked too much, and sang our lungs out. I am on the left.

remembered from the old days, including "Our Lives Are Full of Sunshine." We kept coming back to it again and again, with tears spilling from our eyes, until we finally dispersed at five in the morning.

What had there been to hope for? Those years of our youth should have been a time to plan our futures, but for our abandoned generation, although we had our dreams and passions, reality offered no opportunities. So we pretended that our lives were so full of the light of day and our hearts were full of revolutionary fervor, while denying the depression that we felt but could not ever talk about, just as we could not legally sing about anything besides the revolution. We didn't have any material needs, for there was nothing to want. But we did need to escape the heavy political situation of the time. Whenever we could, we went to the mountains outside Beijing to sing at the top of our lungs and behave badly. We captured frogs from the ravines and stole chickens from unwary farmers. We roasted these tasty delights on a wood fire and washed them all down with too much beer and liquor, while smoking too many cigarettes. We whooped and hollered and splashed naked in mountain streams. We fought with other kids we encountered there. And we sang and sang and sang, releasing our depression in a rush—in a rage—of boyish energy. I wasn't a singer any more than anyone else was, but I needed to sing as much as they did, to let the sounds travel between the stony mountains, into the valleys, up to the clouds. What or who would hear our urgent yearning for beauty, our striving for purpose, for meaning?

I was a leader of our band of brothers, as well as the accompanist, on the accordion or the guitar, which I was beginning to learn. It was the same one my brother had learned to play at the naval academy. Sometimes, on the rare occasions when I saw him, Tian Mimi and I sang together. There were some North Vietnamese engineers and technicians at our factory, since some of our generators were manufactured for their country. An interpreter who came with them taught me how to play guitar. (The guitar was very popular in Vietnam, introduced there years earlier by the French.) I also became friends with one of the Vietnamese engineers, until he lied to me about not tearing out the pictures of girls in bikinis and lingerie from a catalogue I'd surreptitiously passed on to him. This was our illicit entertainment, which we shared like good brothers.

If we had to resort to sales catalogues for sex thrills, we were obviously starved for reading material, with or without sex. We were smart kids without any education, after years in a school system that was nothing more than a propaganda machine. We were hungry for wisdom, literature, philosophy, history, knowledge of the world as revealed in books, all of which, especially anything Western or in any way traditional Chinese, were forbidden. Except for libraries that specialized in revolutionary material, all of the others had been closed since the beginning of the Cultural Revolution in 1966. If anyone managed to get hold of a book, we passed it on from one to another until it became so worn and dirty, it was almost unreadable. We tried hard to treat books carefully, though; they were the most precious goods. Some kids even resorted to copying out books by hand. Whenever I got my hands on a book, I stayed up all night with my treasure.

In 1971, with two of my friends from the Zhongzheng ensemble, I began to plot how to break into a library and steal some books. It turned out to be not so difficult. We found a small library near where I lived where neighbors said the books hadn't been burned or confiscated—just sealed up inside the locked and boarded-up building. After midnight one night we put our plan into action, donning dark clothes and tiptoeing to the library door with small flashlights, screwdrivers, pliers, and crowbars. Inside, books were everywhere, on the shelves, the desks, the chairs, and underfoot. All were covered with a layer of dust that, in the moonlight that streamed in through the window, looked like short, soft fur. Book stacks on the floor appeared to be sculptures when we shined our flashlights on them. It was hard to keep from coughing and sneezing as we sifted through the books and harder still to refrain from giggling, guffawing, or, in my case, cheering when I found a book I'd heard of, often because of political attacks on it or its author that I'd read in the newspapers.

We were so occupied that we suddenly realized that hours had passed and we'd better get out of there. We decided to divvy up the books we'd separately put aside. One of the fellows proved to be too timid to follow through with a major theft and took only a few picture books. I was greedy, grabbing one stack under my right arm, another under my left, and scurrying home before returning twice for more booty, until I had amassed more than eighty books. We tried to cover our tracks through the dust by sweeping with a broom, as we'd seen bad guys do in movies. We replaced the hinges on the door that we had yanked off and placed it back in the jamb so that it looked untouched.

This was really breaking the law, but it did not feel terribly criminal. What was the law anyway? During the Cultural Revolution, only Chairman Mao's words and instructions from the Central Party Committee were taken as law. But just how to interpret these so-called laws—which changed so frequently—depended on how you could twist your tongue. For example, Chairman Mao had said, "It is right to rebel." So if I broke down a door of a building that contained bad books and snatched them, well, that's rebellion, right? Ha! I sure felt good that night.

Actually, I wasn't sure which was worse for me, being in possession of "bad" books or being in possession of stolen ones. I decided that I had better get rid of all the red library seals on them. I tore out the first and end pages, then sanded off the markings on the edges. They looked pretty awful by the time I was done, but the words on the pages were all there and ready to lead me on a great journey. Most of the books that I had taken were Chinese translations of the world's great novels and included Victor Hugo's *Les Misérables* and *Ninety-Three; Jean-Christophe* by Romain Rolland; *Pride and Prejudice* by Jane Austen; Stendhal's *The Red and the Black*; and Flaubert's *Madame Bovary*. There were books by Hemingway, Jack London, Leo Tolstoy, Prosper Merimée, Somerset Maugham, and art books—books, books, books! Whenever I read something very dramatic or emotional, my whole body trembled (this still happens). I read like a starved man stumbling on a table of rich food. My voracious appetite had to be held in check at work, of course, but as soon as I returned home, I went right to the book I was currently reading and continued all night long. I told myself, Slow down! Slow down! Savor this pleasure! But I couldn't. I had to read it all here and now, fill myself up with these beautiful words and stories, these pictures of times and places and realities so different from ours. At work, my eyes were red and my brain seemed to be filled with air. One day I ended up hammering my left hand instead of the piece of steel.

"Good! Do that a hundred times and maybe you'll finally become a good worker," scolded Master Worker Wang. But I didn't care if I ever mastered the use of the hammer. I would smash my hand every time if that's what I had to do to read books. Fortunately, it wasn't.

My contraband collection enhanced my popularity. Young people had already been dropping into my room to hear me play my instruments and to sing along. Now I had my own lending library, and I exchanged my books for others. (My brother was not at all pleased, especially since he had moved into my tiny room once my sister returned and took over his room.) By day, I was a revolutionary worker. By night, I mingled with Spanish nobles and the French upper classes, shivered in the wilds of Alaska, and gazed upward with awe in grand cathedrals. And oh, the tangled, torrid love affairs I had, with the grandest and the basest of women! Because there were some juicy sex scenes in *Bel Ami*, the novel by Guy de Maupassant, I was reluctant to lend it out, for fear it would never wend its way back to me. So I did the formerly unthinkable: I tore out these steamy pages and kept them just for myself.

It wasn't long before the boundaries between reality and my reading life began to blur. I nearly killed one of my coworkers after he insulted Marguerite Gautier, the heroine of *La Dame aux Camélias* by Alexandre Dumas and one of my favorite characters. To me, she was a great tragic figure, a courtesan who sacrificed her love for the one man she had ever cared for in order to do the right thing for his family. When one of my comrades in the factory sneered that she was just a prostitute—a *jinü*—and deserved to die destitute and diseased, I grabbed his neck and began to strangle him. His eyes were rolling back in his head when another guy dragged me away. How operatic of me. I didn't know then about the great Verdi opera *La Traviata*, which was based on this Dumas story. Of course, I never would have imagined that I would sing the bass role (Dr. Grenvil) in it at the Met, much less that I would specialize in the Italian bel canto tradition epitomized by Verdi, or even that I would ever sing opera. I was just a worker in a factory who read books that took me places where my life could never lead.

For those who couldn't read or didn't dare, I began to recount the stories of these novels. At work, I traded tales for cigarettes. I remember how big the workers' eyes grew with wonder as these illiterate people listened to tales of far-off worlds.

My stories even held my father's attention, briefly, although my music didn't.

After two years at the 5/7 Cadre School, my parents had been assigned to the Wuhan military region, in the province of Hubei, which was even farther away from Beijing. Once more, they were working in a military song-and-dance ensemble, but because their "problems" had never been resolved, their former status was not restored. For the first seven of the years that they remained there and worked diligently, they received no promotions and little respect. They felt used. They composed music and dance pieces, but they were under close supervision and their work was restricted. I visited them once a year for two weeks at a time. For my first visit to Wuhan, I compiled a whole book of my music compositions to show my parents. Of course, in retrospect, I knew nothing about chords or harmony or structure; I simply expressed my feelings musically. But I wanted my parents, particularly my father, to take notice of the musician I was becoming.

I handed my father the book almost as soon as I arrived on the overnight train from Beijing. The first composition in the book was "Grenade," a song about something that is quiet during peacetime but explosive when thrown at the enemy during wartime. After he finished this first song, he closed the book and mumbled something like, "Okay, okay, let's talk about this later." We never did. I'm not sure what I had expected from him. Praise would have been out of character. Chinese fathers traditionally are very stern. They don't praise their children because they don't want them to have big heads. So maybe I expected that he would at least take me seriously enough to criticize my compositions.

My father was always work, work, work. With his students, he was always correcting, always educating. That's how he treated me when I was a small boy suffering at the piano. At least, he'd paid attention then. But now, when I finally showed him that I had returned to music, he didn't even say that I was bad at composition. He didn't offer to teach me. He didn't say anything at all. Nothing! I was his son, but I wasn't due the respect that he gave his students. Before the Cultural Revolution and afterward, he always tried to help young musicians from his ensemble. If he thought they were talented, he would try to arrange a recital, or he'd send them to conservatory. In my memory, he never helped my career.

Years later, when I confided to mother how painful that visit had been for me, she told me that my father had been very depressed and frustrated at that time. He felt that all his life he had worked so hard, and look what had happened to him. He was not being treated fairly. My mother said that he didn't want his children to suffer the way he and she had in their music career. I had already entered the working class, where he felt I would be better off. I didn't point out to her that both of them encouraged Meimei in her piano studies and now wanted nothing but a music career for her. Maybe my father thought that I was too much of a troublemaker to have such a career, especially in a military ensemble, which was what I came to want.

Reflecting now, from the point of view of a man who has grown older than my father was then, I feel certain that he must have been depressed and dispirited in those days. My father never expressed his feelings, which must have gnawed at him inwardly. What I experienced as stern and unfeeling perhaps was his barrier against showing pain and anger. Such a thought never would have occurred to me in 1972.

I remember picking a fight with him the next day about something trivial. I must have wounded him, for a decade later he still remembered what I'd said to him afterward: "You People's Liberation Army, you don't care about us ordinary people. You may be PLA, but we are the working class, the leaders of the people."

Yet he listened to the stories I told, did not ask where I learned them, and did not inquire of me, or I of him, "What are you thinking?"

7

Yellow Hair Blues

WE CALLED HER Yellow Hair Chic. She had light brown hair and fair skin, and all the boys liked her. We played war games as kids in the compound; she always played the spy. We chased one another with toy guns and made bang-bang-bang sounds. Just like in revolutionary movies, we always caught the spy. I was the policeman and subjected her to intense interrogation. "Where are you from? Who sent you here?" But she always played stubborn and refused to confess, which frustrated me. Since I was a revolutionary cop, though, controlled by ideal party discipline, I wouldn't torture her.

So I suppose the strands of the scandal that enveloped us, broke our hearts, and crushed her stretched all the way back to those sweet days of our childhood.

By the time I saw Yellow Hair Chic—Huang Mao Ya Tou—again, she was a tall girl swimming gracefully in the large pool where my friends and I liked to hang out in summer. At first, I did not recognize that this ripe young woman was my old playmate, whose name was Ding Ying. She had come with an equally attractive friend. We boys kept trying to swim up close to them to get their attention, as they effortlessly shifted from backstroke to breaststroke to freestyle. But once they realized what we were up to, they hurriedly left the pool. She was dressed in an army uniform when I spotted her at the exit.

Every chance we had, we went back to the pool to look for these girls. Finally, three or four weeks later, there they were again. This time I realized that the girl in the uniform looked familiar. That light hair, that fair skin. But as soon as I approached her to find out her name, the girls grabbed each other's hands and ran away. Just as they were about to jump on their bikes, I called out, "Ding Ying!" She turned her head sharply toward me.

We became friends again, then more.

Ding Ying worked in the army hospital. Sometimes she visited patients in their apartments in our compound to give them medicine, or she served in our infirmary. When she was on the premises, she often made her way to my little room and crowded in with the others to sing while I played the accordion or the guitar. By the time I began to teach her the accordion, we were madly in love—which was forbidden.

Marriage was not permitted before age twenty-four. Soldiers and students were not allowed to date until they were over twenty-one. We were seventeen. Any show of intimacy outside of marriage was not permissible, especially for soldiers. Thus, the risk for Ding Ying was much greater than it was for me. My friends and I were just a bunch of unsupervised young workers drifting around the edges of society. None of us was a Party member, so we didn't care about living up to its ultra-high standards. Indeed, we weren't involved in politics at all. We weren't the dregs of society either—counterrevolutionaries, imperialist spies, landlords, or capitalists. But we were rebellious, cynical, maybe a little wild, a little loud. We gathered in groups that mixed boys and girls, which raised some eyebrows but did not result in official censure.

Meimei had returned to Beijing from Wuhan by herself and was now living in my brother's room; my brother shared mine with me. Meimei had studied piano in the elementary school run by the music conservatory before our family—and Western music—had been banished. Now, even though Second Middle School attached to Beijing Normal University no longer drew students from our neighborhood, Meimei and many kids from the Zhongzheng ensemble had been admitted there, thanks to the string-pulling of our good Mr. Gao. He looked out for her in school, knowing that she was away from her parents and made sure that she always had a hot meal. I was supposed to be supervising her until my brother got home on his one day off, but I guess I left her alone more than I should have, and she was lonely. On payday, I always tried to buy a roasted chicken and fresh fruit and had a little feast with her. As an apprentice, my pay was very low, thirteen yuan a month (less than two dollars) the first year, which increased to sixteen the second year and nineteen the third. I always spent too much of my pay too fast. I didn't have much money to spend on anything besides food, but if I was circumspect—which I rarely was—it would last me the month in the factory cafeteria. Sometimes I asked my sister for money to get me through to the next payday.

I was much more careful to protect Meimei's reputation than I was my own or Ding Ying's. It was not safe for a girl in middle school to attract the boys' attention. One day my sister told me that some boy had announced to her that she would become his girl-friend. "Don't worry, I'll hit him!" I declared with teenage brava-do. With some of my friends, I marched off to his house and demanded that he come out. We just warned him off, no rough stuff. Meimei was grateful this time. A few years later, when she was living and studying at the conservatory after it had reopened, and I tried to provoke a fight with the French horn player she was in love with, she threatened never to forgive me. I didn't think he was good enough for her. She thought I was trying to control her life. (When, ultimately, she married a different French horn player, I didn't interfere.)

When Ding Ying and I went out on a date, we went in a group, often bicycling en masse to Jingshan Park behind the Forbidden City. Then one day, when I got off the factory bus on my way back home, I was surprised to find Ding Ying and her friend Ling, the same one from the swimming pool, waiting for me at the Tianan-men Square stop where I usually transferred to a municipal bus. Ding Ying was not in uniform. Ling whispered conspiratorially, "We wanted to meet you. Can we go into Tiananmen Square?" I was rather shocked at what seemed to be afoot.

Ling left us in front of the Chinese Revolutionary History Mu-seum on the east side of Tiananmen Square. Ding Ying and I walked into the vast square and sat under a pine tree. We chatted for a while, then ran out of words. Our eagerness for love was vague and awkward. We didn't know how to love. Finally, we kissed, although we really had no idea how to do this. *Kiss* was a word from books. No Chinese movies had kissing or hugging or anything intimate. At that time, Chinese parents never kissed in front of the children, and no one ever showed affection in public. All we knew was that kissing was something we were not supposed to do, yet here we were doing it. We were lip to lip all night long under that tree. Only when the sky began to grow light did we realize how long we'd been there. We grew frightened when we heard the footsteps of museum guards nearby, but no one bothered us.

My lips were so swollen, but I had to go right back to work. That morning the air seemed remarkably fresh to me, the sky a shade of blue I had never noticed before. When I stepped up to my machine at the factory, out of my mouth popped, "My heart is so happy," the song that had so moved me as I lay atop the haystack in the countryside five years earlier. Now I completely understood what that nameless, faceless young man had felt that night. I was filled with joy. I was enlightened.

I worked like a muscleman that day. Every task, no matter how difficult it usually was for me, seemed effortless. I worked eagerly all day, humming. My fellow workers were curious. "What did you eat?" one older man asked me.

"Nothing to do with food," I answered. "So what were you doing when you were seventeen?" I asked coyly.

He proceeded to explain, in detail, how he had worked with his father making matchboxes out of materials his father brought back from work, which he would sell to make extra money.

"Were you in love?" I asked more directly.

"Love? Oh, no. To release all that energy, I practiced martial arts." And he went on to tell me how he had learned to break bricks by hand and to turn somersaults.

I understood that I was much happier than he had been at my age.

Ding Ying brightened my life. I was intoxicated by her smell— that same wonderful scent of clinic disinfectant I had grown to love as a little boy. Our needs were not luxurious. We were happy if we had one or two yuan to spend in a restaurant with some friends. Our favorite spot—if we and our friends could pool enough money—was the Moscow Restaurant, built by the Soviets in the fifties in their monumental Russian style. It had high ceilings and tall carved columns inside and out. Inside, too, were statues of workers with hammers, farmers with sickles, soldiers with guns. It was the most luxurious restaurant in Beijing, so our visits were rare. We'd have some borscht, chicken Kiev, and beef Stroganoff, plus a bottle of red wine, and would forego all but the most basic food for the rest of the month.

We swam in the summer and skated in the winter, or at least we looked as if we intended to skate. The boys would strut into Shishahai skate rink with their hockey sticks; their skates, tied together, hung from their shoulders. The girls had figure skates. You could barely tell who anybody was by their faces, since we

During the Cultural Revolution, we all wanted to join the military, which was the height of prestige. Because of my parents' "unclear" background, I was turned down many times. We all wore uniforms in those days, although those who weren't in the service did not sport the official red star on the cap and red patches on the lapels. Even so, I attached them and faked military status sometimes when I went out with friends, as I did in this picture.

all wore big white gauze masks under our heavy winter hats, with only our eyes peeking out. It was rowdy there, a gathering place for delinquent youths, with police and workers' militia patrolling. The boys came to pick up girls, smoke, or fight with their enemies. Of course, a lot of fights began over girls, especially girls in uniform like Ding Ying. Sometimes a herd of people rushed outside for a fistfight or even threatened one another with their skates in their hands, but mostly these scuffles came to nothing because others from the same gangs or residential regions interceded to break them up.

Because it was such a rough place, I never dared to go by myself, and certainly not alone with Ding Ying. We got together a group of ten, even twenty, people. I was such a bad skater that most of the time I stood around shivering, so my friends started to call me North Wind Blowing—Bei Feng Chui—which happened to be the opening words to a revolutionary song that frequently blasted from the loudspeakers. I never did get into any fights myself, although I did boo and hoot. Because I played music, I was considered a gentle and civilized person, too thin, pale, and nearsighted for these wild and tough kids to bother to compete with. They used me to pass along their threats to other guys.

Mostly, I was a good-enough kid who could hold his own among bad boys, enjoying a free life with a girlfriend and staying as far away as I could from the realities of the Cultural Revolution. But I had to make it seem as if I was participating in political studies at the factory. In the morning we had to gather for the ritual of asking instruction from Chairman Mao, and we bowed to him in the evening, read his political works and attended meetings for public criticism. I loved Chairman Mao's poems, which were cheerful, colorful, and rich. At my parents' urging I had tried to read his political texts, but I could never concentrate on things that held no interest for me. We all had to recite his sayings from his Little Red Book, but devoting myself to long political tracts was impossible. I instantly grew sleepy. "Recently there has been a falling off in ideological and political work among students and intellectuals, and some unhealthy tendencies have appeared. Some people seem to think that there is no longer any need to concern oneself with politics or with the future of the motherland and the ideals of mankind. It seems as if Marxism was once all the rage but is currently not so much in fashion. To counter these tendencies, we must . . . " Zzzzzzzzzzzz . . .

Because we often had to study in groups in the factory, I developed the skill of falling into a light sleep with my eyes open.

Maybe, too, my relationship with Ding Ying was a way of falling asleep with my eyes open. Although we never went out alone after that first time in Tiananmen Square, our obvious closeness had to have been noticed by someone, with all the prying and spying and reporting of people that went on in those days.

It happened about a month after we found ourselves madly in love with each other. I knew Ding Ying had had another boyfriend, a military officer who was away in the provinces. She told me not to worry about him, even when he returned to Beijing on holiday and got in touch with her. I was so jealous and upset. She said she would explain everything to him. They went to Tiananmen Square. It was the longest day of my life. By ten o'clock that night she still hadn't come to my room, where we had agreed to meet, along with my close friend Su Xiaoming, who lived in the same building complex. I was bereft, without hope. I had already smoked so many cigarettes—two packs in two hours—that my tongue burned. Xiaoming was trying to comfort me, and together we went out to buy more cigarettes. But Ding Ying wasn't there when we came back before eleven, or at midnight. It was absolutely the end of my life.

Finally, there was a knock at my door. It was Ding Ying! Xiaoming was so happy and relieved that she hugged Ding Ying for the longest time. Then she left, and we fell into each other's arms. She did not leave until morning.

We stayed together three years, perhaps more out of loyalty in the end than out of love. And then someone alerted her unit about our relationship. We already knew we were being watched. It became a scandal, and the strain and pressure on us were terrible. Finally, her unit asked her to resign. During the period that she was looking for another job, I heard that she had fallen in love with a man who had promised to help her even though she and I were still supposedly together. My heart broke, and my pride was mortally wounded. I gathered all of her letters and photos and pedaled my bike madly to her home. I threw the letters and the pictures at her feet, then jumped back on my bike and sped away.

That was 1975. Eighteen years passed before I heard from Ding Ying again. I had recently been married to Martha, and we were living in New York in Battery Park City, just across from the World Trade Center.

The phone rang at three in the morning. "Hi, it's Ding Ying. Remember me? Are you still mad at me?" She said she'd gotten my number from my mother in Beijing. She did not seem happy. I suppose she was nostalgic about the happier days of our time together, when life for both us really was wonderful, and love was brand new.

She gave me her address and phone number, but I did not write them down.

The old grandfather in our shared apartment, who thought I was such an ill-behaved boy—because of my bad *zuofeng*—had mostly forgiven me by 1975. I won him over after inviting him and his grandchildren to join me and my friends on a two-day camping trip to a mountain valley to gather wild roses. The next time my sister saw him, he told her that I was a very smart boy and a leader and would no doubt become a wonderful man. He even began to cook for me. But he did grumble about the music that came out of my room, for I was singing about love, not about revolution. I had won and lost Yellow Hair Chic. My heart had been so happy, but now I was so blue.

8

My Mother and the
White-Boned Demon

TRADITIONAL CHINESE OPERA had thrived in many forms for hundreds of years in the land of my birth. Chinese string and percussion instruments, invented thousands of years ago, accompany the acting and the singing, complete with stock gestures and dance movements, which were usually based on traditional or historic themes. Yet by the time Jiang Qing—aka Madame Mao—took complete control of culture and art, anyone associated with either these traditional forms of entertainment or the increasingly popular Western-style diversions was persecuted as capitalist bourgeoisie. This despite Jiang Qing's well-known love for Western arts and movies; rumor had it that she was crazy for *Love Story.*

The eight model operas, which were the only permitted cultural entertainment for an entire decade, were all created under Jiang Qing's direct control, and, of course, they glorified class struggle. The most popular ones were *The Legend of the Red Lantern, Shajiabang, Red Azalea,* and *Red Detachment of Women.* They played from morning to night, day after day—in theaters and movie houses, on the radio and on television, and through public loudspeakers. (Amplifying music beyond a comfortable or appropriate level continues to this day in China, even for classical music and opera.) We went to see them because there was nothing else to see or because our work units organized our attendance. Millions and millions of

Chinese alive today, all over the world, still sing these songs and arias in their sleep.

In those days, the performers in the sanctioned forms of entertainment were big stars, known by everyone. They were fully supported by the government. Even their clothes and shoes were tailored for them to resemble army uniforms. In addition to their salaries, they received big cash bonuses, the best food, enormous benefits, and huge admiration. All this thanks to Comrade Jiang Qing, once an actress herself, before she met Mao Zedong and became his fourth wife.

I had a love-hate relationship with Jiang Qing. She looked like my mother, with her long face, short hair, and glasses, especially when she was in uniform. The first human figure I ever drew as a boy was of her—a side view, in her military cap. Although Jiang Qing's growing power would squeeze the air out of all of us before her downfall, it's also true that Jiang Qing—with my mother's last-minute emergency assistance—would be unwittingly responsible for turning me into a professional performer. That happened in 1976, after I and my countrymen came to hate Jiang Qing completely.

I found my voice in the summer of 1975.

It was a sunny day off, and I decided to go look for my friend who lived on the other side of Beijing. Nobody had private phones, so I bicycled all the way over to his building. It was very hot, and I was too tired after that ride to climb up to the fifth floor to see whether he was home. The huge courtyard at his complex was very quiet—it was around one o'clock, Chinese nap time—so I yelled up, again and again. My voice echoed off the buildings. When it ceased, all that I heard were the summer cicadas. No answer. One more try, louder. This time, from the fourth floor, a man stuck his head out the window.

"Who are you?" he called.
"Why do you want to know?"
"Are you a singer?"
What a strange question. "No."
"You have a big voice, you know."

It is 1976, just after I have begun my singing lessons. I am standing proudly in the fashionable clothing of the ganbu zidi *(child of a military official) along the beach in Beidaihe, on one of my many "sick" leaves from the Beijing Boiler Factory, where I cut steel sheets under the supervision of my illiterate master.*

"So?"

He laughed. "Come up here and talk to me."

I made the climb. He turned out to be a professional singer, perhaps about forty, and although I don't remember his name or his face, the five minutes I spent with him changed my life.

"You have a special voice. You should find a teacher," he told me. I had never thought of myself as a professional singer. On the bike ride home, I thought a lot about his suggestion. It was a very depressing time for me. All I could think about was how to get out of the factory. There were only three ways out. One was to apply to university, but I couldn't do that because of the *gong nong bing* (worker, peasant, soldier) requirements for admission. Similarly, my family's current status would keep me out of the military. Even so, I'd already auditioned for at least ten military propaganda ensembles with my accordion, to no avail. The only other possibility was a civilian song-and-dance ensemble, but I'd tried this approach without success. Usually, I tried out with my friend Su Xiaoming; she sang and I accompanied her. I loaded my accordion on the back of my bike and we pedaled over. At that time, workers were supposed to present permission from their work units in order to audition. I'd received the necessary paperwork five or six times already before they got tired of my asking, since I'd never been accepted, and I was developing a reputation for finding ways to avoid work. But Xiaoming and I discovered that if we showed up for the auditions and pleaded to be heard, they usually let us try. Although nothing ever came of our joint attempts, she was eventually accepted by a navy propaganda ensemble.

I'd also tried once to be admitted as a composition student to the Central Conservatory. The factory would not give me permission to audition for this either. On one of my mother's increasingly frequent trips to Beijing to try to wheedle permission for my father and her to be reassigned there, she agreed to come to the conservatory to help get me permission, since she and my father were conservatory graduates. The composition judges, all of whom had been her teachers or classmates, were happy to see her and were going to let me try out, until somebody from the political department stepped in to stop it because I lacked the required workplace permission.

There seemed to be no way out for me. My mood continually bounced from hope to despair. But hope came again with my newly discovered natural instrument, which in fact I'd been using all my life. Finding a good teacher was as easy as asking my parents, who arranged for me to study with the most sought-after voice teacher in Beijing, Fan Yin Xuan.

Back in 1973, the culture ministry had issued an order signed by Jiang Qing to recruit ninety young musicians from all over the country for the revolution, in three groups of thirty over the next six years. They were to be trained by the Central Conservatory for the sake of the Central Philharmonic Society. The Central Philharmonic Society was the foremost state-sponsored performing group in China, equivalent to the Royal Philharmonic in the United Kingdom. The first group of thirty was already in place when, late in 1975, the auditions for the second all-China class of thirty students were announced. Thirteen places were reserved for instrumental students, seventeen for vocalists. By this time I was thoroughly absorbed in my voice lessons, and all I wanted to do was sing, sing, sing every day. But with my daily four-hour commute, my eight-hour workday, required political studies, and just one day off, I had little opportunity to practice. I needed to become far more proficient if I was to have a chance to compete against the best voices in China. The audition was scheduled for July, still eight months away. But how would I find the time?

I already had a reputation for being a reluctant worker. Now I began to feign diarrhea, so that I could go to the bathroom for fifteen minutes—and sneak out the back door and run into the fields to vocalize. Friends shared with me their tips for finagling a day or two of sick leave. One strategy was to go to the company doctor and complain of high blood pressure. As he was pumping up the cuff, I'd force my big toe hard against the floor to drive my blood pressure up. It worked. Once I complained of bowel troubles and brought a stool sample in which I'd dripped blood from pricking my finger. I was too scared to swallow ink to blacken the stool, which one person had recommended. Other people suggested drinking extra-hot tea right before coming in to have my temperature taken, but since they cautioned that if I wasn't careful, the temperature would go too high, I decided not to try that trick. I did become friendly with one of the factory doctors, Dr. Wu, and sometimes after I hadn't shown up for work for a few days, he wrote me a note saying I'd been sick.

I'm not naturally deceitful, and I was uncomfortable with this behavior, but I didn't see any other way to get the time I needed to prepare. Maybe that's why, although I didn't have high blood pressure then, I do now. And probably that's why the factory bosses became suspicious of my absences and decided to investigate. They grilled the doctors who had excused me from work. I was under tremendous pressure and really scared. They needed me for the propaganda performing team, but they started to reduce my salary because of my bad attitude and work habits. I was notorious. The workers liked me, but the leaders hated me.

Yet I had Jiang Qing's music training program as a goal and hope in my heart, which was so new. Even the political situation seemed more hopeful. Mao was old and ill, and some of our political leaders had been trying to rectify some of the errors of the Cultural Revolution. It even seemed that Jiang Qing's iron-fisted

My brother (second from left) and I (third from left) and two friends from our building complex had just finished a huge meal at the most expensive restaurant in Beijing when this photo was taken in 1975. I paid for the meal with the money my mother had sent to fix the leaky pipes in our kitchen. This was the first of three days of dining, drinking, smoking, and dreaming before settling down to teach ourselves French to improve ourselves, which we never did.

control of the arts and literature might begin to loosen. Then, in January 1976, our beloved Premier Zhou Enlai died. As happened in China in those days, and indeed can happen still, the political tide turned against us suddenly and fiercely.

Although Zhou Enlai had been involved with setting all of the Central Committee's policies and he carried out Chairman Mao's instructions to the letter, nevertheless we loved our premier as a kind and humble man. We had heard that he had protected the old, maligned cadres from the abuses of the Cultural Revolution and that he showed concern for the ordinary people, always being sure to take care of even the lowest-ranked members of his staff. He seemed to us to lead a simple life, wearing very old shoes and worn shirts and carrying patched suitcases. We saw him as an honest, upright, moral man, contrary to our image of Jiang Qing. Premier Zhou had also been the chief political rival of Jiang Qing and her clique and was next in line for control of the country once Mao died.

Jiang Qing, through her control of the media with her cronies, tried to limit the public expression of grief for Zhou Enlai, and she provided little information about his funeral. Even so, the Monument to the People's Heroes in Tiananmen Square soon overflowed with mourning wreaths of paper flowers strung along pine boughs, an extraordinary and unprecedented outpouring. After Zhou's funeral, although the route had not been announced, a crowd of more than a half-million people, myself included, gathered to watch the hearse travel along Chang'an Avenue from Tiananmen Square to Babaoshan Revolutionary Cemetery, where revolutionary heroes and high government officials were cremated and buried. Most of us carried white paper flowers, a traditional way to honor the dead. Some people tied the flowers to trees. It was a very cold day, with everyone bundled up in dark, heavy coats. It was so very quiet but for our weeping as the hearse, trailed by white flowers, went by very slowly, followed by a long line of official cars.

We had all seen Zhou Enlai as our last hope, which was now gone for good. We were so exhausted by the Cultural Revolution, so bitter. The sense of loss kept simmering. In late March crowds began to gather spontaneously at Tiananmen Square to continue to mourn him. Because Mao was still too sacred and godlike to attack, anger swelled toward Jiang Qing and her clique, who were now jockeying for the power of the premiership and attempting to devalue Premier Zhou in the people's hearts. Remarkably, messages of hate toward Jiang Qing began to appear on the square.

The boiling point came on April 5, 1976, in Tiananmen Square, although few outside China knew of the situation, unlike the student uprising that would capture the world's attention thirteen years later.

It was the day after the Qingming Festival, when the Chinese people traditionally sweep their ancestors' graves and mourn their dead. Since Liberation, though, the graves of revolutionary martyrs had become the focus of the ritual. Babaoshan Revolutionary Cemetery had been closed for weeks to prevent a mass demonstration at Zhou Enlai's grave. In the days leading up to Qingming, some one million people gathered in and around the vast square to leave wreaths and recite poems of mourning and love for the departed premier. But the more the Party tried to convince people not to go to Tiananmen Square and not to place wreaths, the uglier the mood grew, and posters appeared calling for Jiang Qing's ouster in slightly veiled language. Instead of using her name, we called her White-Boned Demon—Bai Gu Jing—the fiend in Chinese mythology who transforms, in looks only, into a beautiful woman. Plainclothes policemen in white gauze masks snapped pictures of protesters—no doubt about it, we were openly protesting against those in power—and hauled away posters and pamphlets. Some people, in response, began to attach their banners with wire to the base of the monument, to make it more difficult for the security officers to remove them.

The night of April 4, five of my friends from the factory and I left a wreath with a banner on which we had written some slogans of our own. We walked around briefly, reading the articles people had left and copying some of the poems. We stood in silent tribute for a minute; then, because the atmosphere was so tense, we dispersed in different directions. When we gathered again later, our banner was gone and we were scared that we'd been watched. We started to talk about what to do if the situation exploded, as everyone felt it would.

I spent the whole next day in Tiananmen Square. April 5 was a cold day. I was wearing a big fur hat and a thick cotton overcoat. When I arrived, all the posters and poems and wreaths from the previous day were gone, and crowds were clamoring to have them returned. I came prepared with my workers' militia armband in my pocket, just in case. (The workers' militias trained at our workplaces; we were allowed to carry weapons in the event of an invasion by the Russians or some incident provoked by Taiwan.) New wreaths and even more incendiary pamphlets had appeared. I walked around reading them. I had brought my camera and snapped a lot of photos. I ran into many people I knew. We didn't exchange words, only greeted each other with our eyes.

At nightfall, suddenly the loudspeakers in the square began to blare: "Comrades! A handful of bad people used the Qingming festival to trump up political cases. We should grasp the reactionary nature of this political issue, expose the plot, enhance our vigilance, and not be fooled. Today some bad individuals are creating disturbances and committing reactionary sabotage in Tiananmen Square. You revolutionary comrades should leave the square immediately and not be fooled by them." So the crowds began to disperse. There were perhaps a couple thousand of us left when, all of a sudden, all the lights on the square went off. When they went back on a few minutes later, hundreds of men with weapons (but no firearms) were rushing in from all sides. Were they militia? Plainclothes police? Nobody knew. They all wore militia armbands, but that could have been a ruse. They started to arrest anyone in sight, young and old, women and men, and beat them bloody if they struggled. Often two or three went after somebody and attacked the person with wood sticks like maces that had iron wire and nails protruding from the ends, like truncheons. The screams and the curses and the moans were horrifying. In the chaos, I put on my red armband and ran. I was running in the direction of the Chinese Revolutionary History Museum when I noticed that the attackers were dragging their bloody victims in the same direction, piling their bodies under a pine tree. Three guys pulled a man by his hair, his eyeball hanging out of its socket, and threw him atop the others. I suddenly realized that this was the very tree where Yellow Hair Chic and I had kissed that long, wonderful night. My love tree had become a death tree. I ran for my life.

All the blood was gone from the square the next day; it had been hosed away. But the police continued to make arrests for days, and in the end the people's movement was violently suppressed. It wasn't safe to go to work or to return from work. One guy I knew was beaten severely, his face smashed, as he bicycled past Tiananmen Square on his way home from the night shift. He was locked up in the Great Hall of the People for two days until the authorities

This picture was taken on April 4, 1976, in Tiananmen Square. Over a million people gathered there in protest against Mao's wife, Jiang Qing, and her gang, after the death of our respected premier, Zhou Enlai. I'm standing second from left, holding Zhou Enlai's picture. I was there the next day when the violence broke out but escaped without injury.

admitted their error. The cops went to all the factories and work-places, mine included, to match their pictures against those in our personnel records. I stayed home from work "sick" for several days.

A couple of days after the incident, the door to my room suddenly swung open and there stood Su Xiaoming, in her navy uniform. I hadn't seen her in two or three months, since she'd joined the ensemble. She wasn't looking particularly friendly. "Did you go to Tiananmen Square on April fifth?" she demanded to know.

"Of course," I said.

"Did you take photographs?" No smile.

I said I did and mentioned that I'd developed and printed some—my hobby of the moment.

"Show me!"

So I pulled the film and the prints out from under my mattress, where I'd hidden them. She promptly tossed them into a water basin, set them on fire, bolted the door, and threw open the window to vent the black smoke and the foul smell. We both watched my record of what eventually became known as the Tiananmen Square Incident turn to ashes. Her face was tense and her voice nervous. She explained that her mother had rushed home to tell her that my name had come up at the neighborhood committee meeting and had been put on a list of people to be watched. Xiaoming had come over as soon as she could to make sure I wouldn't get in trouble.

I was upset to lose the pictures, my record of the outrages inflicted on the people, but I understood the act of friendship that had inspired it. Su Xiaoming and her mother had suffered so much in recent years. They were just trying to spare me.

Long divorced from Xiaoming's father, a celebrated playwright, her mother had been a senior revolutionary Communist from Yan'an, the Party's headquarters from the mid-1930s to 1947. Both of Xiaoming's parents had been leaders of the Zhongzheng ensemble, although her mom brought up the five girls on her own. Xiaoming was number five; when we were kids, we called her Black Five—*Hei Lao Wu*—because she had dark skin. Her mother, though rehabilitated by this time, had been locked up for five years of the Cultural Revolution for who-knows-what political errors, and without her salary, Xiaoming and her sisters had had to scramble. For food, they'd sold off their mother's high-heeled shoes and fine clothes for a few yuan each.

Xiaoming and I were best friends, soul siblings. We had learned to play the accordion and the guitar together. Music remained the bond between us, even more so now that I was taking voice lessons. We loved to sing duets. We had the same taste and feelings for music, plus an instinctive feel for each other's voices. She would start a phrase of a song and I could chime right in. So many times when I came home from work, always so late, I heard her voice calling up to my window, "Tian Xiao Lu, are you home?" I'd yell out the window for her to come up. We'd share dinner or she'd just sit there and talk. Or sing.

Thanks to her, I was spared punishment for my involvement in the Tiananmen Square Incident. But that only meant that life didn't get even worse for me than it had become for all of us now. All of our hopes for change were gone. We were so depressed and dispirited. Jiang Qing and her gang retained their power. We had no saviors on our horizon, although the cloud over my head did have one silver lining. The audition for the Central Conservatory-Central Philharmonic Society was set to continue.

But how would I get permission from the factory to participate? I was barely showing up at work anymore. I was in agony over what to do.

Then I had an inspiration.

In the past, I had always sought permission from the lowest level in the complicated factory political hierarchy. It was clear that they would refuse me now, since they'd already reduced my salary by half. So I decided to skip protocol and go straight to the top—to the factory Party secretary himself, Mr. Li. Of course, if I failed, that would be the end of me since I couldn't appeal beyond him. I had a good feeling about him, though. He'd been at the factory a long time. We'd had no personal contact, but he seemed like a straightforward, no-nonsense person.

"I feel I can talk to you directly," I said. "I hope you can give me this chance. I'm sorry to bother you"—I was talking very fast—"I really love music. Please say yes."

Mr. Li said, "I know you. You are having trouble in your working group." I died in the silence that followed. "All right," he said finally. "I think you have talent. I will write you this letter of permission. But if you do not get in," he added ominously, "you must promise me personally that you will be a good worker and that you will never try to leave again."

I didn't have to think about it. "I will make this promise to you."

I presented the letter at the Central Conservatory and was told the July date on which to appear for the first round. In this audition, I would compete with five hundred singers from the Beijing area. From these, they would choose twelve finalists, who would compete a few days later in the second and final round. What I didn't know then was that only one singer from the Beijing area would make the cut; if I had known, I would have given up hope too soon.

I worked with my teacher. I rehearsed my two audition songs over and over and over. I was so well prepared.

But I never got to audition. Two days before the date, I woke up with a fever and a sore throat so severe that I could not speak. I had what turned out to be tonsillitis, but the rules for the competition were very clear: if I didn't participate in the first round of the auditions for whatever reason, I could not be in the finals.

So there would never be a way out of the factory for me. Never. No way out. The end of me. That's all I could think during the depression that spread its dark shadow over the rest of my life.

Within a couple of days, when the fever had gone down, although my voice wasn't back, I tracked down one of the main judges, Shen Rei Feng, at her home and pleaded with her to allow me to join the final round of the competition. She was nice enough about it, but she said that there was nothing she could do. I came back again and again, sometimes twice a day.

"Help me!"

Once I just sat in her home as the family ate dinner. "I'm busy," she said, "but you can stay if you want."

I didn't know what else to do. I contacted my mother in Wuhan. She phoned a classmate from her class at the conservatory in 1949, who was now a famous conductor in Beijing. He knew Mrs. Shen, whom I had been entreating. And thus, through him, my mother—who eventually retired from the People's Liberation Army at the well-deserved rank equivalent to full colonel—succeeded in getting me permission to sing in the final round.

I felt as if I'd been rescued from the grave and given one last chance to live. I knew I had no way back from here and that I would never get such an opportunity again. I revved myself up—win or die! I will fight!—until I was sufficiently energized to compete against the twelve extraordinary singers who had made it through the first round. I listened to them all, one by one, as I awaited my turn in the large, crowded hall. Each singer seemed so confident. I began to sweat, and not just because it was a hot summer day. It made me nervous that I was number thirteen, a bad number—this I knew from reading Western literature.

My turn. First I sang a strident revolutionary song, whose strong rhythms and melody released all my tension. By the time I came to my second song, I knew I was one hundred percent into it. This was such a lovely tune—so pretty, I still sing it in recitals. It was "Ode to Beijing," set to an old Tibetan folk melody.

Thousands of horses in the meadow,
but only one is the fastest.
Millions of flowers in the field,
but only one is the most beautiful.
Thousands of silk hadas in our land,
but only one is the whitest and purest.
Thousands of cities in the country,
but only one is the most beloved.
Let's ride the fastest horse,
let's choose the most beautiful flower,
and the whitest, purest hada,

and carry them all to our most beloved city,
Beijing.

July went by, then August. I received no word about the final decision. Back and forth I went to Shen Rei Feng, pleading to know something. She just said, "When the decision is made, you will receive a letter."

September 9. It is Thursday at three in the afternoon and I am at home, since I rarely go to work anymore. The propaganda ensemble doesn't perform now—not since the April 5 incident. There is a knock on my door. I open it to find Auntie, as I call the woman who now lives with the rest of her family in our apartment.

"Chairman Mao has passed away." Auntie goes from sobbing to wailing before she retreats down the hall.

I turn on the radio. It's true. He's dead.

I neither cry nor feel relief. What will happen now? Probably, it will get worse.

For once, I was wrong. On October 5, Jiang Qing and the Gang of Four were arrested. All of Beijing, it seemed, spilled out in the streets in spontaneous celebration. Alcohol sold out everywhere. Rumor had it that the Beijing military drank themselves into a joyful stupor that night. I know I did. The night sky lit up with fireworks and firecrackers.

The Cultural Revolution was over.

Then came the bad news. With Jiang Qing's arrest the Central Conservatory balked at training any more students for the Central Philharmonic. That had been her program, not theirs. Again, I began to make regular appearances at Mrs. Shen's house. She told me that the culture ministry was trying to decide what to do about the program. And she still couldn't tell me whether I would get in.

A month later I was home—as usual these days—when the long-awaited letter from the Central Philharmonic Society arrived. The envelope was so thin. My hands shook as I opened it. The letter consisted of three sentences. "We are very happy to inform you that you are accepted. . . . " Now came the miracle: I was the *only* singer from Beijing. Tears flowed. I didn't try to stop them.

The culture ministry had worked it out with the Central Conservatory that they would train this one last class of thirty musicians for the Central Philharmonic Society.

Of course, there was one more hitch.

I went to the Central Philharmonic to fill out some paperwork and was told they were about to send a letter to the Beijing Boiler Factory to tell them I had been accepted as a singer. But I had never mentioned to Mr. Li that I was going to audition as a singer. I let him assume I was trying for a place as a professional accordionist. No one at the factory knew I had been taking voice lessons, and even if they did, they'd think I was using this as just another way to get out of working. Now that I'd been accepted, they could accuse me of lying to them and could block my admission to the program.

The people at the Central Philharmonic understood my problem and wanted to help. They concocted an elaborate ruse. They would notify the factory that the Central Philharmonic Society wanted to offer an open audition for all factory workers in order to find new instrumental talent. Mr. Li would not be suspicious because he had granted me permission to try out for the Central Conservatory for Jiang Qing's special program. Now she was out of the picture, and the Central Philharmonic, which had tremendous national prestige, was a different organization. I would audition with my accordion, and then . . .

When the audition was announced, everyone was excited and flabbergasted. What an honor! The Central Philharmonic wanted to find new talent at the Beijing Boiler Factory! The factory workers practiced on their instruments for hours. I showed up at work every day now and, of course, practiced my accordion.

When the day came, one of the office clerks from the Central Philharmonic admissions office, dressed in a fancy-looking uniform (a costume from one of its opera groups), drove up to the factory gate on his motorbike, which made him seem even more impressive. All the factory leaders were present as, one by one, the workers demonstrated their talents. They were so prepared. I felt bad for them.

When my turn came, I introduced myself and played my accordion. After I finished, the clerk said to me, "You have an interesting speaking voice. Do you sing?"

"Yes, sometimes," I answered modestly.

"Please sing for me."

I feigned surprise. "Okay." I sang the same two songs from my real audition.

A week later, a formal letter of admittance came to the factory, admitting Tian Hao Jiang to their young artist program for training as a singer.

"Impossible!" I exclaimed when a factory leader called me in. "Me? A singer?"

9

A Card Game

MY PARENTS' SITUATION had greatly improved by the end of the Cultural Revolution. My father had become the director of the Wuhan military song-and-dance ensemble, and he and my mother were back to working a full and satisfying schedule, although they remained hundreds of miles from Beijing. I visited them once a year for a week or two each time, in the summer at first. But Wuhan is known as one of the ovens of China in the summer, just as hot as hell. So at some point I started to go in the winter, during the Spring Festival, the two-week national celebration of the lunar new year when the Chinese traditionally venture back to their families.

My parents' apartment was in Wuchang, on the south bank of the Yangtze River, in a place called Nanwangshan (Hill Overlooking the South). The beautiful brick buildings that housed the ensemble had originally been built for experts from the Soviet Union in the 1950s. They had high ceilings, broad corridors, and tall columns. The compound faced East Lake and was landscaped like a park; the magnolias were breathtaking when they were in bloom. Inside, my parents had a number of cape jasmine plants, which were very popular in south China. The profusion of flowers gave off a beguiling fragrance, and I contributed the scent of pinecones that I gathered when I visited. I loved to walk alone in the evergreen forest behind the buildings. Sometimes I found mushrooms under the pine needles. I had become adept at identifying which ones were edible, and oh, they tasted so good.

But Wuhan in winter, though beautiful and green, was damp and could be awfully cold. The Yangtze River was the official dividing line between north and south China. The houses on the north side of the river had indoor heating systems, while those on south had none, as if the weather differed between the two sides of the same city on any given day. But there we were on the south side, hovering around the small coal stoves that were brought inside for warmth in the winter months. Even the clothes issued to the military were different, depending on which side of the river you were stationed. If my parents had been stationed on the north side, they'd have had heavy overcoats and boots; instead, their army-issue consisted of light clothes and shoes.

The winter of 1978, when I visited during Spring Festival, seemed particularly cold. I felt no warmth from the little stove in the room. I wrapped myself in a thick sweater and kept on my thick cotton-filled boots, fur hat, and long army overcoat all day long, reading or writing next to the stove. The damp cold at night bored into my bones; it took forever to warm up enough to fall asleep. Night or day, I just couldn't get warm. Or maybe—as it began to dawn on me and my parents, especially after I had the hiccups for three days—I was ill. I went to the infirmary and got an injection of something that finally put an end to the hiccups, but I still did not feel well. I was so tired. When I began to run a low but persistent fever, I went to the main Wuhan military hospital. Blood work showed that my liver enzymes were up. I had hepatitis. Again.

Liver disease was so common in China, where it remains a major public health problem, even though now there are vaccines for type A and type B viral hepatitis. I'd had type A the first time, which one gets only once, thanks to resulting antibodies in the blood. So many people I knew had had some form of hepatitis, sometimes from mass outbreaks caused by contaminated food or water, and everyone knew somebody or had someone in the family with cirrhosis or liver cancer, which certain kinds of hepatitis can lead to. Liver infections often occur because of poor hygiene. I am a nearly obsessive hand washer now. I carry my own water if need be—certainly, when I'm in China—to wash my hands and any food

I buy from street vendors. I never eat anything that's fallen on the floor or the ground or even onto a restaurant table. Back then, we had no sinks for hand washing, and people did not necessarily wash before or after food preparation, before eating, after feeding animals, or after working in the garden. Indoor bathrooms were extremely scarce and still are in the old sections of the big cities and the countryside. I hadn't worried about having hepatitis when I was a boy, but now, at twenty-three, having a sick liver was a big concern. For sure, I was worried about having chronic hepatitis. My more immediate concern, though, was *bingtui*. *Bing* means "disease." *Bingtui* meant back to the Beijing Boiler Factory.

I'd moved into the Central Philharmonic Society dormitory and begun my training almost a full year before I got sick, but the factory still loomed menacingly behind me. During the training period, my monthly salary was paid by the Beijing Boiler Factory, which also kept possession of my *dangan*, that personal secret dossier that follows every Chinese person from employer to employer. If I slipped up in any of three ways, only two of which were in my control, back I'd go. First was my performance in the program. I was not about to flunk out and be dragged back in shame to my steel-cutting machine. For the first time in my life I became a model student.

Second was *zuofeng*, moral integrity. Given my history, this was the drawer full of demons that would be hard to keep closed. In my last years at the factory I'd been rebellious, loose, and wild—something of a hippie, I guess you'd call it. I drank, smoked, played guitar, told lies at work, stole and hoarded books, and loved women. All of these counted as bad *zuofeng*, even in the somewhat looser environment that followed the demise of the Cultural Revolution. My past was a mess, and I had to distance myself from it now. So I stopped smoking, steered clear of girls, and did not invite my rough-and-tough old friends to visit me in the dormitory. No dirty words, no wine bottles or even a guitar in my room. It meant everything to me to be there, and I worked hard on having the right attitude. I was an angel. In the dormitory, girls lived on one side, boys on the other, and that first year I tried so hard to be good and stay on my own side.

The possibility that I could be booted out because I was too ill to continue my studies—*bingtui*—had never crossed my mind.

In the Wuhan hospital I received an infusion that normalized my body temperature, and I began to take the medication they gave me. My parents wanted me to stay with them until I was better, but I wouldn't hear of it. At the end of the Spring Festival, I returned to Beijing to continue my musical training, no matter what. If I could not have a singing career . . . In my mind the huge gear wheels in the factory turned round and round, over and over, faster and faster, until I had a pounding headache and was in despair. I told myself I would hold out, that nobody would know I was sick, and that somehow I would be able to sing.

After the journey back, I was so yellow with jaundice—the whites of my eyes looked like egg yolks—that there was no hiding my illness. I collapsed on my bed and couldn't get up. Hepatitis can be very contagious, and my two roommates were very frightened. Nobody at the Central Philharmonic would get close to me. The director told me I had to go to the hospital. I did not want to go to the one with which the Central Philharmonic had a contract, since it did not specialize in infectious diseases and did not offer the superior standard of care of a military hospital, so I asked to be taken to the 262 Military Hospital. It was across the street from the military compound I'd lived in until the year before, in what was left of my family's apartment. More important, my parents were good friends with the hospital's political director, Mrs. Hu, whose husband had been a member of the Zhongzheng. After the director called Mrs. Hu and she said to come immediately, I left the dormitory with a bag containing my toothbrush, a towel, and a couple of textbooks, including one on Italian opera. I turned back as I left the gate, uncertain whether I would ever return.

The chief doctor, a short woman wearing a gauze mask and trailed by doctors and nurses in their masks, got right down to business: how did I know Mrs. Hu? I had not yet changed from my street clothes when she came to see me. I saw her eyeing my brown woolen military pants, which signified that I was from a family of high-ranking military officials. I'm sure she was assessing whether I deserved the highest-quality treatment. Satisfied, apparently, with my father's military rank, she turned her attention to my disease. I found out later that she was a little put out when she learned that my father was only an orchestra conductor. When the doctor left, I looked around to face an odd tableau, my four roommates staring at me in unconcealed awe. They were all low-ranking soldiers from the countryside, wearing blue-striped hospital gowns and military caps, even in bed. Once I changed into my own gown, I looked just like them, although I was hatless, and they began to treat me as similarly human. I lay back, comforted by that wonderful smell of disinfectant that infused the gown, the room, the corridors, and all the people.

The other guys had been there for weeks or months. Worst off was Xiao Huang, a warm-hearted fellow from Sichuan province who was only twenty years old. He had already been there six months, and his illness had progressed to cirrhosis. "Do you know, I'm the sickest guy in the room?" he said, smiling. For him, the hospital was a better place to be than the army. His battalion worked on constructing the railway to Tibet, up and down and through steep mountains, in the hottest summer and during icy winters. He told me about taking his pickaxe to the frozen ground day after day and managing to make only a small white indentation for all his efforts. Five hundred people in his battalion came down with hepatitis, half of them in his own unit.

"Our commander decided that we should have more protein in our food, but there were not enough meat rations for us in the mountains," he told me one day. "So we were given soybean soup, which was supposed to have protein. So you see, isn't it better here, where I have meat with every meal, than back there drinking soybean soup?"

Out of pride, perhaps, Xiao Huang refused to see his mother, who had come to Beijing from the countryside in Sichuan after finding out he was ill. He told the nurse to tell the guard at the gate to say that he had recovered and returned to his unit. But his mother came asking for him every day, anyway. When I asked why he had hardened his heart, he answered, "What shall I say if I see her? I can't tell her when I'll be back to my unit or when I'll be back home. She expected me to be promoted or to return home to get married and have a child. But if you have cirrhosis, your wife will leave you. So what can I tell my mother?"

Xiao Huang liked to play poker, a popular patient activity, and occasionally we used his deck of cards, which were in good shape from lack of use since few people wanted to handle them. But even using someone else's cards, a lot of people were reluctant to play with him because he was so sick. Once a guy from Hunan joined the game when we were using Xiao Huang's deck. He dipped his finger in his mouth before spreading out his five cards to look at them. Then, all of a sudden, he looked at Xiao Huang, threw down the cards, and rushed into the bathroom. We heard the sounds of vomiting. Then everybody was looking at Xiao Huang, realizing that the guy from Hunan had put his finger in his mouth after touching the cards covered with Xiao Huang's germs. Most of the others soon dispersed. Xiao Huang stayed for a long time, then finally packed up the cards and slowly put them back in their box.

I played cards a lot to distract myself from my gloomy mood. My condition did not improve at all during that whole first month. One day I went out into the hospital yard, where many of us walked for a while each day. I wanted to try to see whether I could sing. It was relatively early, and few others were out yet. I walked to the farthest corner and tried to sing my favorite Italian song, "Nina," from my songbook. My voice was strange—weak and dry, with no glamor. I tried again and again and again. Since I was facing the wall, I did not realize that many patients had gathered behind me or that people inside heard my strange noises. I had not talked much about what I did for a living because they had no notion of Western classical music, and I did not want to make them even more uncomfortable about the class differences between us than they already seemed to be. From then on, they called me *Changxide*—Peking Opera Singer.

Many people visited and tried to cheer me up—friends from the factory, from my old building, and from the Central Philharmonic, including students and teachers. In fact, so many people showed up that I became known as the "famous *Changxide.*" They brought fruit in glass jars, chocolate, and pastries, which overflowed from my nightstand, and which I shared with my fellow patients as soon as my visitors left. These were luxuries to the other patients. The treats made them happy, and seeing them happy made me happy, too, for those moments. We were told that having a good mood was healing for liver patients, because depression and sadness were symptoms of our illnesses.

Although there was no obvious improvement in my health for six weeks, my friends and teachers from the Central Philharmonic tried to persuade me that I would be able to sing when I recovered, but I did not believe them. One day my old friend Hong, from the Cultural Revolution period, telephoned after she'd heard I was in the hospital. I hadn't seen her for at least two years, but within moments I blurted out my despair. "This is my second time with hepatitis. This is the end of my life. I cannot sing anymore. I have no other way to escape the factory. I'm sure they will send me back now. Maybe this is my fate."

She was quiet on the other end for some seconds. Then she asked whether I could come out of the hospital the next day to meet her. I said I wasn't allowed out. She said, "If you want to get out, you will find a way. Come to your old apartment after dinner."

So, as the sky grew dark the next evening, I sneaked outside. The wall was about seven feet high, but there were loose bricks lying around, and I piled them up until I could climb on them and then flip myself over. I'd done this kind of thing when I was a boy.

My brother had married and moved back in with his wife, but none of the people who lived in the apartment now were there when I arrived in my hospital gown. When Hong showed up, she said I didn't look all that bad, but I let loose again with my miserable lament, so she suggested that we talk about something else. She chatted about her boyfriend for a while, then stopped and said I should come and sit next to her on the bed. I'd been sitting as far away from her as I could in the small room, to avoid contaminating her with germs. She insisted. I moved closer. She looked straight into my eyes and told me, "You cannot be like this anymore. I just cannot tolerate seeing you like this."

"What can I do?"

"You have to be strong!"

I continued to complain about how horrible it was to live like this, day after day, when she interrupted me. "Do you want to kiss me?"

This was a very shocking request. We were definitely not boyfriend and girlfriend. Her face and eyes looked so determined to help me, but I had hepatitis, and people avoided intimate contact with hepatitis patients for good reason. The incident of the playing cards and the guy running to the bathroom to throw up after handling Xiao Huang's cards came to mind. Yet my friend's eyes, when I looked back up, told me that she would do anything for me, to give me any support I needed. She just wanted me to be strong and positive. I was needy. "Are you sure?" I asked. She reached out. We held each other for a long time, kissing, not saying a word.

This was the only time that Hong and I kissed. I will never forget that precious moment. When I sauntered through the hospital front gate in my gown—the guard's eyes bugging out as he grabbed the phone to report me—I felt different, more positive. I was ready to fight my illness and get on with my life.

I was released from the hospital about three weeks later. I had not completely recovered, but my voice had renewed strength and polish. As I played the piano and sang a tune, my joy was incomparable.

I saw Hong again twenty years later when I visited Beijing. With a glass of wine in her hand and a cigarette between her fingers, she was waiting for me at the bar in the lobby of my hotel. Quite casually, she told me she had been having problems with her liver for a long time and recently had a liver biopsy. I asked her how she was feeling now. "Okay," she said, without much spirit. She'd always been an optimistic person, enjoying every day and living her life with great enthusiasm. Then she said she had hepatitis B and that it was chronic and she would have to live with it the rest of her life.

Eyeing her wine glass and cigarette, I told her she must be careful with her health. Then I wondered aloud, "Why do you have hepatitis B?"

"Because you had it," she said, puffing on her cigarette.

Except that I had not had that chronic kind of illness, fortunately for me. I did not know before her healing kiss years earlier that I had contracted a noninfectious, nonviral hepatitis, possibly from some poison or bad medicine. (You can also get it from drinking, but I was still in my model-student phase in those days.)

"Oh, well, who cares?" she said.

The day I was discharged from the hospital, Xiao Huang stretched out his hand to me with a gift. It was his deck of cards, which he loved so much. "I know you like playing cards, too," he said. I hesitated, wondering whether it was too dangerous to take something from a hospital for infectious diseases, but I could see how happy he was to give them to me. I thanked him. "Who knows?" I told him. "Someday we may still play cards together."

About two months later, I ran into a nurse from the 262 Military Hospital. I asked her how Xiao Huang was doing. "Xiao Huang? He died," she said matter-of-factly. My heart fell.

I stood there thinking about Xiao Huang for a few minutes after the nurse climbed back on her bicycle and pedaled away. Maybe he gave me his prized deck of cards because he knew he wouldn't last much longer. He would never know, fortunately, that the day I left the hospital, as I waited to transfer to a second bus to return to the Central Philharmonic, I threw the cards in a trash bin. I had to. The germs.

Poor Xiao Huang. He told me he had never touched a girl in his life.

With the threat of *bingtui* behind me, the specter of the factory faded. I settled back into my training and gradually into my old skin. I started to let my hair grow and returned to my hippielike,

Western-influenced clothes. Western classical music was gradually returning to our concert stages. The Philadelphia Orchestra had actually broken through the official ban in 1973, a year after the meeting of Nixon and Mao. Now I was studying classical harmony and counterpoint and learning the songs of Mozart and Schumann. In 1979, Seiji Ozawa, the music director of the Boston Symphony, brought the orchestra to the Beijing Workers' Stadium and performed *An American in Paris* and even "The Star-Spangled Banner." The audience responded with ecstatic rhythmic applause. And now with Chairman Mao gone and Jiang Qing behind bars, popular music from Taiwan and Hong Kong was trickling back in. The tight reins on our lives that I had grown up with were beginning to loosen. Which is not to say that there weren't political movements and struggle. One faction would insist that we still had to carry out Chairman Mao's teachings, while another loudly proclaimed that truth could only be proved by practice and result.

My wild and passionate heart was pounding to its own tune. I cared deeply about all the emerging arts. Literature, poetry, and the visual arts, too, were shedding their old skin. During the Cultural Revolution, all poetry and painting had to feature Chairman Mao and the revolutionary working class. Now we were heading, still cautiously, into a modern, even abstract era. In 1979, I went to an art exhibit unlike anything I'd ever seen, by a group of artists who had become contemporary but definitely unofficial stars. The government viewed the exhibit as a gathering of radicals. Without official approval, the works could not be shown inside the China Art Gallery so the paintings and the sculptures were displayed in front of the fence outside it, and they attracted a big crowd. Many had come primarily to see the wooden sculpture that everyone knew was Mao, which looked like an ancient emperor, with a red star on its head and the typical Mao suit collar. It was called *Idol*.

You have to understand that despite everything that had happened to us, Mao Zedong remained a kind of god in China, though a tarnished one, even after his death. To account for the hardships that had come our way under Mao's leadership, Deng Xiaoping, who became our next leader, and who had suffered tremendously during the Cultural Revolution, declared the official formula for the national ambivalence: Mao's influence would be seen ever after as 70 percent good and 30 percent bad.

Bei Dao, an important voice of our generation, who was one of the poets of the so-called Misty or Obscurist style—*Meng Long*—rose from the underground to confront the old restrictions. Even today, I can recite his poem "The Answer" by heart in Mandarin. I am grateful to have come to know this inspiring hero years later in the United States.

Debasement is the passport of the base,
Nobility is the epitaph of the noble.
Look at the gold-plated sky
Filled with the drifting rippled reflections of the dead.

The Ice Age is over,
Why then are there ice peaks everywhere?
The Cape of Good Hope has already been discovered,
Why then do a thousand sails compete on a Dead Sea?

I'll tell you, world,
I do not believe!
If a thousand challengers already lie under your feet,
Count me number one thousand and one.

I do not believe that the sky is blue;
I do not believe in the echoes of thunder;
I do not believe that dreams are false;
I do not believe that death brings no recompense.

If the ocean is fated to burst its banks,
Let every bitter wave flow into my heart.
If the dry land is fated to rise,
Let humanity choose a new peak for its survival.

The new departure and the sparkling Dipper
Are patching together a sky with nothing to hide.
It is a five thousand years' pictogram,
It is the gaze in the eyes of people yet to come.

And this poem, "Trust in the Future," by Shi Zhi lodges forever in my mind. I probably recited it a hundred times in the 1970s, although it did not emerge from the underground until the 1980s.

When spiders' webs mercilessly sealed up my stove,
When the ashes from my last cigarette sighed with the sorrow
   of poverty,
I stubbornly sowed the ashes of lost hope,
With beautiful snowflakes I wrote: Trust the future.

When purple grapes became deep autumn's dew,
When my bouquet was held in someone else's arms,
I stubbornly still took the wet withered vine
On desolate earth to write: Trust the future.

I want to point with my finger to the waves rushing towards
   the horizon,
With the palm of my hand to raise up the ocean of the sun,
Flickering light of dawn, that beautiful warm writing brush,
With childlike strokes I write: Trust the future.

The eyes of the people who trust in the future
Make me firmly believe in the future myself—
Their eyelashes bat off the dust of history,
Their pupils pierce the years of writings.

No matter what people think about our rotting flesh,
That sadness of a lost way, the pain of defeat,
I don't care if they're moved to tears in deep sympathy
Or whether they sneer and laugh with contempt.

Words like these had such an influence on us. When our confidence flagged, they brought us strength and hope.

When I returned from the 262 Military Hospital to the Central Philharmonic Society, I was ready to trust that my future would be in the arts, not in boilers. Now I found little reward in appearing to be a model student. I was a young man in a new China, and I was ready to open my mouth.

10

Son of a Gun

"POP MUSIC IS not good for the country!" my father yelled.

"What's wrong with pop music? That is the future of Chinese music. None of *you* can stop it!" I shouted back.

It was the worst fight I ever had with my father. Certainly, we'd had our disputes, but I had always kept my resentment, and my hurt, simmering hot and deep inside me. In the autumn of 1982, however, I could not or would not contain it any longer. I had found my voice, in more ways than one. Our argument exploded like a cannon shot.

My father slammed his hand on his desk, rattling family pictures and certificates of merit (Outstanding Communist Party Member, Outstanding Conductor). His voice rose high and piercing. "This music is bourgeois and rotten! We won't let these unhealthy things ruin our socialism!" His eyes narrowed as he stared at me, as if I was the cause of the "ruinous" changes to our country. "Look at yourself," he said with disgust. "You do not look like someone from our kind of family. Look at your hair, your clothes! I don't think you are a decent person."

"Look at *you*, so conservative, so reluctant to change," I countered. "Our country will never make progress with people like you!"

In his People's Liberation Army uniform, with the collar buttoned, my father continued to sit stiffly at his desk, while I stood alongside, shaking with rage, in my bell-bottom pants, long hair, black-rimmed glasses, and burgundy leather shoes.

The trigger for this eruption was a newspaper editorial titled "What Is Revolutionary Music? What Is Bourgeois Music?" My father completely agreed with the writer's view that unbearable things—as typified by the decadent music of the times—were happening to our society.

Editorials in the government-controlled newspapers voiced official positions, and my father had always studied Party directives thoroughly, to achieve a correct stance for himself. I wonder whether he ever asked himself why he should do as he was instructed, whether the policy of the moment was right to carry out. Unfailingly, he worked conscientiously to carry out the Party's policies, no matter how the Party treated him, and to adhere to the Party's course. After he died, I found a small note under his glass desktop on which he had written: "Do my best as an elder. If I can still be useful to the Party, that is my good fortune."

The editorial that day voiced the viewpoint that military musicians should not be singing the new light and soft kind of music that smelled too sweet to old noses. What had prompted it was a song called "A Night in Naval Port," sung by none other than my old pal Su Xiaoming. It had become a huge sensation after she'd sung it in a large rally at the Beijing Workers' Stadium. Since 1976, she'd been a member of the navy song-and-dance ensemble, in the chorus but vying for a solo spot. This was her debut. The song, composed just for her, seemed to us so light, so sweet, so mellow, so lyrical, so like a wave:

> The night in the naval port is quiet.
> The tide rocks the fleet so slightly.
> The young naval sailors show such sweet smiles in their sleep
> As the waves become their pillows.

Hardly a pop song by today's standards, but compared with all the strident military music that had come before ("The fleet breaks the waves to cruise onward as Chairman Mao waves his hand to point the way"), this stood out as soft and emotional. It contained not one word about revolution.

My best friend, Su Xiaoming, and I grew up in the same building complex. We learned to play the accordion and the guitar together. We auditioned for military song-and-dance ensembles as a team; she got into a navy unit, though I didn't. She went on to become one of the most famous pop singers in China. I took this photo of her back in 1971 in the summer palace in Beijing.

The thousands of people in the audience went wild when Su Xiaoming finished. She became an instant celebrity, sought after for appearances on radio and TV. To this day in China, anyone over age thirty knows her name. But the old revolutionary Party faithfuls reacted with fear and concern, and the editorial writer expressed exactly my father's opinion that it was a bad influence that would undermine our revolutionary future. Needless to say, the old music had been my parents' raison d'être. Needless to say as well, I had to defend Su Xiaoming and my generation of artists. I had to defend myself.

The day my parents' twelve-year exile finally ended, in 1981, had provided a rare tender moment between my father and me. As I rode to my parents' temporary lodgings on my bicycle, I spotted them walking toward me. I braked and jumped off.

"Dad! Mom!"

My father put his hand over mine on the handlebar and uttered with unusual excitement, "We're finally back!" He looked straight at me and his eyes sparkled with happiness. And this gladdened my heart.

They had always wanted to come back, but my father was never one to push the authorities. Not so my mother, whose trips back to Beijing to request reassignment had finally paid off. They returned to the Zhongzheng, still the premier military song-and-dance ensemble, in far better positions than they had been before. My father was named vice president and artistic director, and he resumed the post of principal conductor. My mother, underpaid and undervalued throughout the Cultural Revolution, was promoted three levels higher when she returned to the Zhongzheng. These were significant honors for both of them. Their history was no longer in question, and they felt fully respected at long last. But my father especially felt that he had lost a significant number of his most productive years. Still, their welcome back was such a warm one, so long past due.

The leaders wanted to do whatever they could to please my parents. My mother and father asked for their piano back. They were offered a brand-new one. No, my mother insisted, they wanted the very piano that they had had before they left. Its value to them was largely sentimental and was closely associated with their early career in Beijing, when their future seemed so bright. It was the piano that my sister, who by that time was studying at the Central Conservatory, had practiced on as a child. For me, of course, it had been my nemesis-turned-muse in those brief and lonely first months when I was a fourteen-year-old alone in Beijing. It proved to be difficult to locate, though. In the decade since it had been spirited away from my little room, it had been transferred from place to place. At last, my mother called and uttered excitedly, "Xiao Lu, your piano is back!"

My mind was filled with its image—the carved patterns on the shiny black wood—as I raced over after work at the Central

Philharmonic Society. So I was at a loss for words when I laid eyes on the damaged and dull, partially toothless instrument. I felt that the piano was looking at me, equally speechless, trying to tell me what it had been through during the Cultural Revolution. Neither of us could utter a sound, until I opened the lid and pressed my favorite note, the A above middle C, the pitch that all orchestra instruments are tuned to so that they can play in concert. The piano gave out a weather-beaten noise, like the voice of an old man who has lost the brightness of his youth. But after major refurbishing, it became the official property of my parents and still remains in my mother's Beijing apartment.

When my parents had left Beijing during the depths of the Cultural Revolution, "American imperialists" were on a par with "class enemies" in the large, threatening slogans that appeared all over the city. Now there was a virtual obsession among many in my generation—but not my parents'—with all things American. Books by American writers were translated into Chinese for the first time or reprinted at long last. I read *Catch-22* by Joseph Heller, even *Love Story*, by Erich Segal (which, I will confess, I had with me when I first came to the United States), and *On the Road*, by Jack Kerouac, among many others. At the movies, *The Sound of Music* was so popular that it showed repeatedly throughout the day, like Jiang Qing's model operas.

At my first solo concert appearance, the year before my parents moved back, two of the three songs I sang were American; one was an art song, the other, "Oh! What a Beautiful Morning'," from the Broadway musical *Oklahoma!*. Another piece was by Bach. Notably, none was Chinese. The occasion was the gala concert marking the completion of the master class taught by American singer Elizabeth Bishop. She was the first Western voice teacher to be invited by the Central Philharmonic Society since the beginning of the Cultural Revolution, so it was an especially celebrated and well-attended event, held at the National Theater. Elizabeth Bishop had selected me and two other soloists as the best in her class. Conducting the Central Philharmonic Orchestra was another American, David

Gilbert, the first foreign conductor they'd invited in all those years. This was very heady stuff, and I was scared to death. I'd never performed in front of such a large audience, and my mind kept searching for a way out. Shortly before the concert, in the winter, I slipped on some ice as I was boarding a bus and broke my wrist. My arm, in a plaster cast, had to be held in a sling around my neck.

"You only broke your wrist, not your voice or your neck," Elizabeth Bishop told me not unkindly.

"Oh, but it will be inconvenient for me, and it will not look good on the stage!"

I guess it became clear to her that I was suffering from stage fright. "Let me tell you a story," she said. "There is a famous Israeli American violinist named Itzhak Perlman who is paralyzed and has to be on crutches or in a wheelchair. But he has never given up. He comes on stage on crutches, then slides into a chair to perform, and he always plays his best. So do you think you can sing in this concert with your broken wrist?"

I couldn't refuse her.

Twenty-two years later, in the summer of 2002, Itzhak Perlman was teaching master classes at the Shanghai Conservatory of Music when I held a recital in that city. He came to hear me sing. I was so honored.

I'd started to learn American folk songs on my own, from Voice of America broadcasts, to which we'd begun to listen more openly, even though they were still officially forbidden. I didn't have a tape recorder, so each time I heard a song I liked, I tried to commit it to memory. The melodies weren't so difficult to memorize, but the English lyrics were a challenge since I didn't know the language. Eventually I'd repeat the nonsense sounds I'd memorized to somebody who knew English, who would try to make out some words. That's how I learned "Jambalaya." One day I accompanied myself on my guitar and proudly sang this song for two American teachers I had come to know. Afterward, the young women were surprised to learn that I had been singing in English.

"Jambalaya" was a *bad* song. It had sparked an attack even before Su Xiaoming sang "A Night in Naval Port." Cheng Fangyuan, a friend from our conservatory days together, had begun to perform this song frequently in Beijing. The *People's Daily* ran a whole page of articles criticizing the song and the singer, without mentioning her name. The gist, as usual, was that the general mood of our society was deteriorating. Not only was music from Hong Kong and Taiwan tempting them, now even the songs from capitalist countries were corrupting the souls of our younger generation. After all, one of the writers pointed out, anyone who understood English would know that the song contained vulgar words. What she was referring to was the "disgusting" line that ended each stanza, repeated three times at the end of the song: "Son of a gun, we'll have fun on the bayou."

The writer of this commentary was herself a singer—a coloratura soprano, in fact, who had trained in Paris in the 1930s—named Zhou Xiaoyan, who became a famous voice professor at the Shanghai Conservatory of Music. Singers now call her Madame Zhou and virtually kowtow in her esteemed presence. Six years after her *People's Daily* article, however, I was quite prepared to dislike her when I met her in the United States. I was one of a group that greeted her at the Denver airport when she arrived with her students for a concert. As I helped her with her luggage, I risked telling her, ever so politely, that I had been one of the first people to sing "Jambalaya" in China. "I liked that song. You criticized it," I said. The small, graceful, intelligent woman had a good laugh. "It is unavoidable to have disputes about the arts," she responded cheerfully.

Today Madame Zhou is one of the greatest supporters of the give-and-take between Chinese and Western forms of music and its ability to make better art and a better world.

Cheng Fangyuan was not damaged in the long run by the criticism directed against her. Although trained to play the *erhu*, the traditional Chinese two-stringed instrument, this free spirit taught herself to sing, to play the guitar, and to speak English. She went on to introduce much American music to China, including the sweet and inoffensive song "Do-Re-Mi" from *The Sound of Music*. In 1993, she was named China's most popular singer.

I, however, in an impulsive act of artistic rebellion, put myself at extreme risk when I performed "Jambalaya" in front of six thousand people in the northern city of Harbin.

Professionally, I had been a Central Philharmonic Society chorus member since graduation early in 1980. This organization held enormous prestige and traveled throughout the country performing Chinese and Western symphonic and chorale works, including Handel's *Messiah* and Mozart's *Requiem*. I wanted to become a company soloist, but the Harbin solo performance was strictly unofficial. The Central Philharmonic was about to leave on a tour to south China. Six of us men from the chorus pleaded to be left behind to try a new singing style and to write compositions that required a lot of time and practice, or so we told them. The leaders finally gave us permission to remain in Beijing.

The day after they left, we jumped on a train for our own tour of towns and cities in northeast China. Since the late 1970s, private concert organizers had begun to pay troupes such as ours to perform unofficially. Until then, only the state ensembles could appear in any venue, and no one could perform without the permission of the company leaders.

We called ourselves Liu Shen Wan, which was the name of a famous throat medicine—which, incidentally, never worked for me—and we performed with a small local band from Harbin and a couple of largely unknown women singers from Beijing. We were ecstatic to have no higher-ups in charge of us and to be paid directly in amounts that were several times our monthly salary. We performed Chinese folk and pop songs and some American film music, like the themes from *The Godfather* and *Love Story*, in Jixi and a number of other smaller cities. Harbin was big, though, and the stadium was huge. Long over my stage fright, I was so inspired by these six thousand cheering people. Suddenly, I announced that I was going to sing "Jambalaya." I had never performed this song in public, and I had barely rehearsed it with the band. We had no sheet music to play from, so the run-through was a joke. But there I was onstage singing, and I started to move and sway, to shake my body—like disco dancing. (I'd call it Elvis-like today, only I'd never heard of

Our sextet, Liu Shen Wan, from the Central Philharmonic Society performed without permission in an outdoor stadium in Harbin in 1982, where I (second from right) scandalized the local cultural department by singing "Jambalaya" and wiggling my hips. Notice how we embraced Western clothing and longer hair. The West was "in," to the dismay of the older, traditional generation.

him then.) This was *never* done in China; we always sang standing stiffly, perhaps using a few gestures. The audience went crazy, screaming as I sang, wiggled, and swayed to the irresistible rhythm. It was momentous for me. It was the first time in professional performance that I had chosen my own material and performed with complete artistic freedom, vocally and physically. I was jubilant. Then the trouble came.

Somebody reported to the Culture Ministry, which immediately phoned the head of the Central Philharmonic, that performers affiliated with that esteemed institution had come to Harbin to sing unhealthy American songs in a foreign language and that the singer had demonstrated dirty movements. His butt was moving! He used ugly gestures! This was not healthy for the audience! This man is a bad influence!

The six of us had agreed beforehand that we would rather die than reveal to anyone where we had gone, what we had sung, and that we had accepted money for it. Nobody knew our names, only the name of our group and our affiliation with the Central Philharmonic. Since we had never performed as a group before, it took some time for them to find out who we were, which, of course, they did. I had committed the most grievous of our collective crimes. Fortunately, in the end, I suffered no immediate consequences because they respected my father's position. Maestro Li Delun, a famous conductor and one of the leaders of the Central Philharmonic, in the late 1940s had taught my mother to play the violin and encouraged my father to learn conducting. He was a powerful man in the musical life of the country, with an imposing presence; he was unusually tall and heavy for a Chinese. The other leader, Mr. Yan, thought I was a gifted singer and was reluctant to have me lose my future over this incident. So they did not report back to the authorities about their discovery, and I was not kicked out of the Central Philharmonic Society. But I was on notice, and it was a taste of things to come.

My parents never found out about this incident. Had my father known, he would have ordered me out of his house earlier than in fact he did. Not many months after the Harbin incident, after our brutal fight over "A Night in Naval Port," my father pointed toward the door and yelled, "Get out!" After that, we were no longer on speaking terms.

I wrote to my girlfriend about all these controversies, at first playing down my own escapades since she did not usually approve of the risks I took and could have a very sharp, sometimes biting tongue. I had met Xiao Xia, a soprano, when I began my Central Philharmonic training; she had been chosen as part of the same program, representing Shanghai. We barely communicated with each other during those three years, although she lived on the same floor of the dormitory. It was obvious that she disapproved of me, especially after I returned from my months in the hospital and stopped trying to appear to be such an industrious student. A very bright and self-directed person, she always worked hard and did well on her exams. Studious—that was my continued impression of her, as she held her pencils and clung to her books. She was the first student there to study English, and she practiced every day. Clearly from an educated family, she always looked neat and well groomed and comported herself with polished manners.

I was not her type. After the first year I never studied hard and preferred to hang out with my friends and ride around on my motorbike, which was quite a luxury at that time since there were no private cars. With my long hair, my bell-bottoms, and my penchant for poker, I struck her as just another spoiled brat from a military-official family.

We struck up our first real conversation on the way to a performance in Shanxi province. We were seated next to each other on the train and finally began to chat. In Shanxi, we explored the local sights together. Each of us was surprised that we enjoyed being together. She was a special lady; I began to see and feel this deeply. We kept our growing relationship a secret upon our return, for a couple of reasons. She had a reputation as a very restrained and dignified person; she loathed the idea that people would talk about her spending time with somebody she was long known to dislike. Second, she was arranging to study abroad. China was beginning to allow some people to leave the country to study, even in the United States, and Xia had managed to get a full scholarship to the master's program at Lamont School of Music at the University of Denver. It was much more difficult to get permission for independently arranged programs than for those that the government directly supported and paid for. Xia still had much bureaucratic red tape to cut through, so we did not wish to add any complications. When either of us wanted to meet, we left the other a secret sign on the door to the roof, where everyone hung their wet laundry to dry. We were together only at parks, movies, or restaurants that were far from the Central Philharmonic.

Xia left for Denver in 1981, and our correspondence, in which we could open our hearts more comfortably, brought us closer. She wanted me to join her in Denver and urged me to send an audition tape to the dean of the vocal music department at Lamont. I was deeply in love with Xia, in a mature way I had not experienced before. I was twenty-seven years old. I wanted to settle down. Most of all, I didn't want to lose her, and far away from me, anything could happen. So I sent the tape from my master-class concert. It was my heart, not politics, that first pressured me to think of leaving China. Yet it was fortunate that I began the agonizingly slow process when I did, because my troubles began mounting so fast that I would need an escape hatch soon.

I did not tell any of my friends or colleagues that I had sent the audition tape. I certainly did not tell my parents.

I had not spoken to my father or gone to my parents' home for three months since our fight. Then one day my mother phoned and implored me to come see him. Her beseeching tone was unusual. "What's wrong?" I asked.

"Your father may have liver cancer." She sounded terrible.

I didn't know what to say when I stepped into his room at the 301 Military Hospital (where I had been born) a short while later. Should I ask about his health? Should I tell him about myself? "Dad!" was all that came out of my mouth. He seemed pretty calm.

"Has your mother told you about it?" he asked.

She had told me that he had gone to the dentist for bleeding gums, which resulted in a full physical exam. That day the hospital had called and said that one of the tests was highly abnormal, and they needed him to come back for further testing for liver cancer, although they never mentioned that possibility to my father, and neither did my mother. Now the doctors wanted him to be transferred for more tests to the Second Military University Hospital in Shanghai, which was famous for its liver and gallbladder department.

"Can you go with me?" he asked.

"Of course," I answered.

I took a leave from the Central Philharmonic and stayed for three months in the hotel attached to the hospital. The doctors found a tumor and the tests confirmed cancer. Professor Wu Menghao, the chief surgeon, a kind man, was very well known and had a long waiting list, so my father had to remain there for a month before the tumor could be removed. I could sense that he was anxious, but typically he did not share his feelings. He tried to look optimistic and told jokes and stories to his roommate. This was the first time I'd seen such amiability, which also made him popular with the doctors and the nurses, but I also understood that he was using it to cover up his worries. A month later, when he was wheeled out of the operating room, both my brother and I were there to hear Professor Wu say that the operation had gone very smoothly. (My mother had to remain in Beijing to work.) "Hopefully, he will recover soon," the surgeon told us. I remained with my father in Shanghai for another month. Especially in military hospitals, the conditions for patients were clean and luxurious, better than the way most people lived. So there was no urgency to leave, and patients convalesced for long periods.

The day my father told me the good news that a key blood test indicated almost normal values, he grabbed my hands. How I remember those wonderful times—the only two—that he reached for me and I felt his warmth.

Not long after I took my father back to Beijing, in the summer of 1982, I received a letter of acceptance to the master's program in vocal arts at the University of Denver Lamont School of Music— with a full scholarship! I was happy, of course, but I knew that even with the letter and the scholarship, I had many hurdles to jump before I would be permitted to leave.

My immediate goal at that time was to become a solo singer with the Central Philharmonic. I auditioned for another big-deal master class, this one given by Italian opera star Gino Bechi, a baritone. He was the first foreigner to be invited by the minister of culture himself since the Cultural Revolution. The focus of the class was Italian opera. I did not know any complete arias with which to audition, so I sang a Schubert song, "Der Erlkönig," instead, in front of a hundred people. When I finished, Maestro Bechi threw his arm around my shoulder and told me, "If you want to be an opera singer, I would love to help you. You have a beautiful voice. But if you only want to sing in concerts, I can't help you."

"Yes! Yes!" I agreed. "I would love to be an opera singer." Not that I knew much about opera at that time. I knew some names—*La Traviata*, *Madama Butterfly*, *Carmen*—but I had never heard or seen one myself. All I wanted was to get into his class and become a Central Philharmonic soloist.

Maestro Bechi turned to the pile of music on the piano and selected a score from it. "Here is the score for a bass aria that is one of the most difficult in opera. It is King Philip's aria from *Don Carlo* by Verdi. Four days from today, you will sing it for me."

Four days to learn one of the most difficult arias in all of opera, when I had never sung a complete opera aria and had never even heard of *Don Carlo*. "Sure!" I replied.

Fortunately for me, he added, "I know you won't be able to sing it well. I am giving you this most difficult aria because I want to show you the best I know about opera in the shortest time. You won't understand everything I tell you in the two months I will stay here, but hopefully in the future you will remember what I have told you and will take away many benefits from this training class."

I barely slept during those four days, I was so busy practicing. I had never heard the music, and I couldn't get any tapes or recordings. It was so hard! My eyes were bloodshot and my throat dry when I appeared at Maestro Bechi's class four days later. I did not, as he had anticipated, sing it well. After a few classes in which we worked on it, probably just to stoke my confidence or my singer's ego, he told me, "I believe someday you will sing this role."

I did, twenty years later, in Genoa, in Maestro Bechi's country, in Verdi's country, in Italy, the birthplace of opera! I remember how I felt in one solemn scene, in which heretics condemned by the Spanish Inquisition are burned to death. I walked down the stage in my regal clothing and crown, with hundreds of chorus members and extras on stage as nobles, soldiers, monks, and common people, all of them, and the two thousand people in the audience, with their eyes on me. I was King Philip, and I was Chinese.

Afterward, two Chinese voice students who had been in the audience came to see me backstage. They were in tears, touched by my performance, they said, and by the fact that a Chinese singer could carry off such a role on an Italian stage.

After the master class with Gino Bechi, I was on track to become a company soloist. I had already begun the passport application process. Nobody could tell me how long it would take. That all depended on each person's "situation," connections, family, character, and politics. For the passport, I would also need permission from several departments in the Central Philharmonic Society hierarchy and from the Culture Ministry, of which it was a part. And finally I would need a visa from the U.S. embassy; this was the easy part in those days, unlike now, when so many more people are applying.

I was about to start the Central Philharmonic permission process when I found out that solo singers who were trained by the state could not leave the country unless the government sent them. Xia had been in the chorus when she got permission to study abroad. So now I had to say I didn't want to be a soloist after all! But what if I didn't get permission to leave? Then I would have no further opportunity. Every singer within the organization dreamed of becoming a soloist. I remember the summer day in 1983 that I returned to the chorus department, with everyone turning to watch me take my seat in the bass section at the back of the room. What was I doing? Even I didn't know for sure.

Then things started to get really complicated.

A new political movement sprang up: the Anti–Spiritual Pollution Campaign, a reaction to Western art and culture and to the changes that had been proceeding too fast for the old-liners. Most of my friends and I now wore Western-style clothing—sport jackets instead of Mao jackets. Some people—nobody in my crowd—started wearing big sunglasses with their made-in-Italy labels noticeably attached. Young people were dating openly and having sex outside of marriage. Official newspapers began to attack foreign movies, music, and literature and works by Chinese that had been "polluted" by Western influences. They even criticized social dancing. Young people who were adopting the more relaxed Western lifestyle came under particular harassment. It felt like a throwback to the Cultural Revolution. An incident that happened to a friend of mine, a professional photographer, was typical. All he did was snap a picture of a beautiful naked woman from a page in a classy foreign magazine. He put this print into one of his books and forgot it was there. One of his friends borrowed the book, came upon the print, and enlarged it into a poster. Somehow, the authorities got wind of this, tracked the original photo back to my friend, searched his home, and confiscated his cameras, his lenses, and all of his printing equipment. Then they sent him to a labor camp for a year. When he returned, he could no longer be employed as a photographer.

X-rated movies, which were absolutely forbidden, had become an underground phenomenon, probably because during the Cultural Revolution we could not even see people kissing on screen and we were very curious. We would get word where one was going to be shown, usually after midnight. When the crackdown came, anybody connected with showing these movies got in terrible trouble. One man, in charge of the projection room at a military hospital, committed suicide after an investigation of an X-rated show he had arranged.

Then trouble came my way. I had acquired six blank videotapes and asked a friend to copy Hong Kong martial arts movies on them. He never made the copies for me, though, and weeks later came to me in a panic, admitting that he'd used them to copy X-rated movies. When pressured to confess where he had got them from, he told them my name! I was so scared. The police came to the Central Philharmonic security office and interrogated me like a criminal. I insisted that I knew nothing. They drove up again in their green jeep the next day, but they could prove nothing.

Now everything my friends or I did caused problems. Security officers followed me when I bicycled to a Japanese pop music concert with two American girls I'd met who were teaching English at Beijing Normal University—the same ones for whom I'd sung "Jambalaya" in what I thought was English. When I went to their dormitory with them afterward, I was reported to my employer. Then the police came after me to try to get information on friends of mine who had had a party in which the lights had been turned off and they all had kissed and touched one another in the dark. Who knows, maybe somebody had made love? Every few days I had visits from police and security officers from different units, often to demand that I inform on other people. To scare me, they'd say, "We know that you know everything. You'd better be careful." I was under terrible pressure. If I denied everything, they would think I wasn't being honest, and that would increase the odds that I would not be allowed to leave—the only path I could see for myself now.

To complicate things further, the Central Philharmonic security officers were required to report to the police any misdeeds. I had become notorious at my work for having done wrong things and having "complicated social relations," although I was innocent of most of the "crimes" of which I was accused. I worried that the security officers would report to the police that I was also under investigation at my workplace. By this time, the Central Philharmonic had given me permission to study abroad, but the security office could have it rescinded. I thought maybe that was why it was going on two years since I'd applied for my passport and I'd heard not a word about it. Then a rumor spread that each work unit would have to turn in a certain quota of spiritual polluters to the police. At the Central Philharmonic, that would definitely include me. Now I was determined to do anything I had to in order to get out. There is a saying in Chinese, *zou houmen*—go by the back door, use back channels to get people to fix things for you. I had no family or close friends who could help out, and asking my parents was out of the question.

My parents knew by now that I was trying to go abroad, but because of the current political situation and their own allegiances, my father's in particular, they did not show support for me. I wanted to go to the United States, an imperialist country and the biggest enemy of socialism! My father, who had taken a leave from his work after his operation, never spoke a word to me about my plans. Even my mother and I avoided the topic. We didn't talk about the trouble I was in, either. I knew that friends of theirs were having similar problems in their families; the son of a couple close to them had been arrested and sent to jail for a year.

Finally, I located a low-ranking security official who said he would talk to his supervisors about my passport, but I essentially had to bribe him. He wanted a tape recorder with four speakers, a very luxurious item at that time. I traveled all the way to Shenzhen in south China, where you could buy merchandise smuggled from Hong Kong. The money he gave me didn't cover half the price. I paid the rest, which amounted to three months' salary, although I wasn't even sure he could help me. Who knows whether he did?

My financial woes compounded my problems. How would I pay for an airplane ticket? I made 46 yuan a month ($5 in today's currency); the ticket would cost two years of work! I did not ask my parents for money, and they did not offer. My brother had little money. My sister, now married and a mother and working as a piano teacher and an accompanist in Hong Kong, could not help me.

And then, because I was not being sent by the government, I had to come up with a personal sponsor in the United States, which both governments required, except that the Chinese insisted that the sponsor be a relative. I had no relatives in America.

From Denver, Xiao Xia tried to help me in every way she could, urging the Lamont School to write to the Chinese authorities to help free my passport. Her letters were my greatest emotional support in those anxious days. And it was she who came up with the idea of how to find a sponsor: ask Dr. Martha Liao. I had been introduced to this scientist in Shanghai just before I brought my father back home. Then a visiting scholar in genetics at Fudan University, Dr. Liao was now back at the University of Colorado medical school. Raised in Hong Kong, she had been educated in the United States and now lived with her Chinese husband, a surgeon, in Denver; both were naturalized U.S. citizens. An accomplished pianist, she was very helpful to Chinese music and science students who had come to Denver, Xia included. At Xia's behest and mine, Dr. Liao agreed that she would claim to be the daughter of my mother's brother, the one who disappeared during the anti-Japanese war.

To raise the cash for the ticket, I resorted to smuggling.

A friend arranged for me to go south to Guangzhou to buy one thousand LCD watches, which we would resell on the black market in the north for three to four times the price we had paid and would share the profits. At that time, merchandise in China could be purchased only through state-run stores. Personal trade was illegal and would result in a jail sentence. My friend supplied the money, and I took the risk. He gave me 5,000 yuan, and I put this fortune in cash in a bag that I hung around my neck. I had never seen so much money in my life. At the Beijing Railway Station he introduced me to a train attendant, who in turn presented me to a uniformed policeman working on the train who was in on the deal. The cop arranged a seat for me next to his guard room. I glanced up and noticed a framed award on the wall; this was a Red Flag Train, which signified a model train crew—the best in the country. Finally, in my fear, I was able to smile: I was going smuggling with a corrupt cop and a model train crew.

The cop changed into plain clothes after we arrived in Guangzhou more than twenty hours later. I followed him through the city's narrow, crowded streets to the house of a very short man—people in the south were usually shorter than many of us from the north. The man ushered us upstairs and told us to wait there while he went to get the merchandise. Not long afterward, we heard loud knocking at the door below. The train cop pulled a pistol out from under his jacket and placed it on the table. A gun! The police were yelling to open up, but we didn't answer, and they went away. I thought I might drown in the sweat running down my neck and back. When the short man didn't return, the train cop told me where I should go to find watches by myself but to wait until after dark. He said to meet him back at the train by ten that night. It was only four o'clock, and I had nothing to do besides wander around with all that money. I decided to take a chance and look up a doctor friend who worked in a military hospital there to see whether he could help. He was not surprised to hear what my business was, since it was business as usual for Guangzhou.

My doctor friend took me to a street where he knew there were smugglers selling their Hong Kong goods. It was scary. "Smokes!" "Sunglasses!" "Lighters!" unseen men called out from the shadows in these narrow, winding streets. Finally, I got up the nerve and approached a man who flashed an array of watches on the insides of his coat. He said he had eighty of them. I needed a thousand. He said he would take us to a place where we could get them. We got into a taxi for what turned out to be an hourlong drive to the suburbs. Except for the chatty driver, no one spoke the whole way there. We finally arrived in a small village, where the man told the driver to stop and wait outside a partially constructed house with a low roof and as yet no doors or windows. Men who were at least five inches shorter than me and my friend began to stream in, with bags and boxes of watches, which they dumped out onto a table. I could see right away that many of the watches were no good.

"Don't try to fool me with this garbage!"

My loud voice startled them, but only briefly, and suddenly they were threatening us. "Take it or leave it! We have seen enough like you!"

I reached into the bag of cash, at the bottom of which I had put a small, triangular dagger, which I had made for myself at the factory in 1974. I had never meant to use it as a weapon. My movement caught the smugglers' attention. With my free hand I struck the table and shouted, in my deep, trained voice, "Stop! Let me tell you where I come from. I'm from the Guangzhou military region. If you dare to touch us, we'll take this village by force and grind it into the dust."

As I was shouting, my friend backed up against the wall and grabbed a long bench, which he held up menacingly. The room fell silent.

"Now show me the watches one by one, and remove the bad ones. Don't try to fool me."

How I managed to pull this off, I can't tell you. I suppose it was my first great solo role, and it proved that I was destined for grand opera. The smugglers certainly outnumbered us and could have robbed or even killed us. The taxi driver could have left us stranded or driven us straight to the police station. He, too, was silent on the trip back to the station, where I arrived without a ticket and only fifteen minutes before the train departed. I met the train cop, who

As if they really are happy I am leaving China, my parents smile along with me the day of my departure, December 16, 1983, just a few days after I finally got the passport that I had been seeking for two years. I was shocked to find my father wearing my Western-style jacket, which I had left at home in a closet. I had never before seen him in Western clothes.

was back in uniform and pacing nervously at the crew entrance. We had to walk past two other cops, to whom he introduced me as "a friend from Beijing." Searches of passengers returning from Guangzhou were routine, and there I was hauling two heavy bags. But they nodded and let me through. My cop conspirator put me into his guardroom, locked the door, and told me just to stay there. I obliged.

I'd come up with only eight hundred watches, but my share of the take was a good start. Almost immediately, I got a letter from the Beijing Public Security Bureau—in other words, the police— that I could come get my passport. I borrowed money from everybody I could to make up the balance for my ticket. I handed in the forms and the documents through a small window to an officer at the U.S. embassy. Two minutes later I had my visa.

"Good luck in America," he said.

Son of a gun.

Circling

I REMEMBER THE LIGHTS down below, so many, so bright. The pilot could not lower the landing gear. We circled and circled around New York City. I had never been on an airplane before. I had never been outside of China. I was at the far edge of my youth, looking down on my next life. So many tall buildings, so many lights, like stars, only far beneath the heavens. I remember thinking, If the plane never lands, that is fine with me, just to see this beauty, just to have come this far.

Of course, I could not dream too much because I did not know what was waiting for me.

PART II

Big Old Yankee

11

John Peking

LUCIANO PAVAROTTI LUMBERED past me to his dressing room, dismissing me with a wave of his hand. "Yes, yes, bravo, bravo."

It was December 17, 1993, the fifth performance of the new production of *I Lombardi*. The Metropolitan Opera was staging this relatively obscure Verdi opera for the very first time to mark Pavarotti's twenty-fifth anniversary at the greatest opera house in the world. I was singing a small supporting role in this opera. Needless to say, an unknown singer does not ordinarily approach a star of Pavarotti's stature. Besides, when I'm nervous and shy, I tend to keep to myself. For these reasons, I had stayed clear of him during the weeks of rehearsals. But when I realized the anniversary that this performance marked for me, I felt compelled to tell him. After the first intermission, I waited for him to leave the stage, then followed him, jabbering in my quasi-English, through the concrete backstage hallways to his dressing room.

"Maestro," I blubbered, "ten years ago I came from China. I had only thirty-five dollars left in my pocket. My first night in this country I spent eight dollars for standing room here at the Met. I had never seen a real Western opera. And you, such a great singer, sang that night.

"Maestro, today I realized that exactly ten years have passed *to the day*. And here I am *on* the Metropolitan Opera stage *with* you! Maestro, this is why I had to tell you. This is such an honor! I am so lucky!"

"Yes, yes, bravo, bravo," he muttered, without turning to face me. The dressing room door shut tight behind him.

Maybe he hadn't understood me. My English was terrible. If I hadn't had to prepare for my own imminent appearance onstage, it might have occurred to me that I was behaving like a fool.

In the ritual of grand opera, when the cast comes out together to take their bows between acts and at the final curtain, the major singers are always at center stage, and the minor ones range outward to either side. I was a solo singer and therefore entitled to take my bow with the rest of them, albeit in last place. Pavarotti was the one the audience had come to hear, of course, and the bravos that greeted him after each of his arias and at curtain calls went on and on and on. I hadn't appeared in the first act. At the end of the second act, in which he and I were both onstage, I dutifully waited my turn at the end of the line as, one by one, the cast members filed out to take their bows. When Pavarotti's time came, though, he signaled the others to proceed onto the stage ahead of him, confusing everyone. Finally, there was no one left behind the curtain except him and me. He grabbed my hand and led me out onstage. With his free hand, the great man gestured to the audience to direct their thunderous bravos to me. I wept.

He repeated this grand gesture in all of the remaining six performances of the opera, including the one that was televised.

From then on, until the end of his life, Luciano Pavarotti always greeted me as "the Chinaman," with his big sweet smile.

What I had blurted to him about my arrival in the United States was the two-minute, stage-to-dressing-room version of my exceptional first day. My parents, my brother and his family, and four friends from the Central Philharmonic had accompanied me on the bus to the Beijing airport in the very early hours of morning the morning of December 16. None of them had known that I was leaving until two days earlier, when I had my ticket in hand. They seemed to understand that my political situation was too precarious for me to risk word getting out. It shouldn't have surprised me that my father asked no questions, but my ambivalent feelings toward him were swept aside when he said he would come to see me off.

Luciano Pavarotti embraces Martha and me on December 17, 1993, after we appeared together in Verdi's I Lombardi, *staged to celebrate his twenty-fifth season at the Met. This was the tenth anniversary of my first day in the United States, my first visit to the Met, and the first time I ever saw Pavarotti perform. This is the day I told Pavarotti that story after the first act of the opera.*

He and my mother were not wearing their normal PLA garb. They were dressed in street clothes, but my father didn't have on his usual Chinese "civvies." Instead, he wore the sporty blue Western jacket that my sister had brought me from Hong Kong, and which I had left in the closet at my parents' home. I had never seen him in such an outfit, and I was touched. I do think that on some level he was happy for me; he had to have known that my situation in China had become untenable. Carrying just two big bags—which included ten brass cloisonné vases that Xia had told me to bring because in the United States they could fetch ten times the price I paid—I threw my guitar over my shoulder and headed into the customs area. I did not look back. Tears streamed down my face. I did not know whether I would see my friends or family again. Travel abroad was so inconvenient and politically fraught that going to the United States was like going to another world.

It was another world.

I had fifty U.S. dollars with me when I arrived at John F. Kennedy Airport, but I handed fifteen dollars over to customs upon arrival, for reasons I can only guess. The agent asked questions and in my polite Chinese way I kept nodding agreeably, although I didn't understand a word. (I didn't think that "Long live Chairman Mao," the only complete English sentence I could remember, would get me very far.) Probably, I had agreed that I had goods to declare.

My departure from China had been as much a necessary getaway as it was the positive pursuit of a new life path. Sure, I wanted to be a singer, but what did that mean? I was going to the Lamont School of Music because it had accepted me and provided a scholarship and because Xia was there—and because I needed to get out. Maybe I would be a pop singer. Who knew whether I had a future in the United States or whether I'd be going back to China in the short or long run?

The direction of my life came into ecstatic focus that first night at the Metropolitan Opera. The opera was *Ernani*, a Verdi opera I had never heard of. I just wanted to see a real Western opera and to be at the real Met, the most famous opera house in the world even to us in Beijing. Pavarotti's fame had spread to China, as had that of the great baritone Sherrill Milnes, who also sang that night, and the renowned conductor James Levine, who led the most beautiful orchestra I had ever heard. The stark, gray, pillared formality of the Soviet-inspired halls in China, with their dimly lit lobbies, were all

I had known of concert halls. Here, everything was astonishingly gold and plush, crystal-bright and sparkling—like pictures from art books about the Renaissance I had stolen during the Cultural Revolution. Eight dollars was a large chunk of my remaining cash, but I gladly paid it to stand at the back of the orchestra level. During the first intermission, an elderly couple, carrying their coats, approached me and waved a ticket at me. Fearing a repeat of the expensive customs transaction earlier that day, in a panic I gestured them away. So they grabbed my hand, put the ticket in it, and left. Through the body language of nearby standees, I began to understand that these nice people were leaving and giving me one of their seats for the remainder of the opera. I showed the ticket to the usher, who took me down closer and closer to the stage in this huge, glamorous opera house.

Picture this: A twenty-nine-year-old Chinese man in his drab clothes, on his first day in the United States, sits in the center of the fifth row from the stage, surrounded by men in fine suits and women in jewels and furs, watching his first opera performance, which stars Luciano Pavarotti, one of the most famous opera singers in the world. Before the end of the second act, I knew I had to become an opera singer. That's what I was trying to tell Pavarotti exactly ten years later backstage at the Met, when on that anniversary I felt such a clear sense of *yuan*, my fate.

If you can give in to it, opera can lift you to such moments of divine clarity. That operatic bubble of mine burst pretty quickly, though, when I began my studies at the University of Denver.

Xia had written to me so much about Denver that it seemed less foreign than New York. The buildings were fewer and much lower to the ground, and Xia had not cautioned me to be vigilant and watch my possessions, as she had warned about New York. Yet I was unprepared for the dazzling whiteness that greeted me. A huge snowstorm the day before had covered the city in snow. It snows in Beijing but rarely enough to conceal the city's gray dust. The blazing sun illuminated the Rocky Mountains in the distance. It was like a fairy tale, and I was like a kid who insisted on marching into piles of snow instead of walking on the cleared walkways.

I was no kid. I was nearly thirty, the age to have a family, the age to have an established career, and maybe not the age to begin a rigorous education for the first time in life. I had not worried too much about what it would be like to study for a master's degree. My three years of training for the Central Philharmonic had come so easily, especially after I felt secure there. After I became a member of the company, my life between performances ran from pleasure to play: Chinese chess (*xiangqi*), military chess, novels and poetry, a lot of smoking (cigarettes, cigars, pipes, whatever I could get my hands on—great for the voice, no?), and hard drinking, plus fast driving on my motorbike.

If Xia had any fear that I would return to the idle ways she had once resented, she needn't have worried. I had no time. For the first seven months, I studied voice and opera performance and went to language school five hours a day. I also worked in the student union five days a week. Xia had tried to warn me that life would not be easy here, despite all the Chinese fantasies about the good life in the West. Scraping and washing plates while singing "Red River Valley" in Chinese was the most fun I'd have in a typical day.

I cannot tell you whether I loved or hated my voice professor, Dr. Ronald Worstell, because he pushed me so hard to study and sing and learn English. At our first meeting, I attempted to sing the so-difficult King Philip aria from *Don Carlo* that I'd learned with Gino Bechi in Beijing. He leaned back in his chair and asked me, through Xia, what I wanted to do with my future, and I told my little joke: "I want to be an opera star."

His response: "Learn English first." For the first couple of months, we communicated by gesture and with five English words: up (higher), down (lower), no, yes, and forward (the direction I should project my voice).

Everybody was incredibly nice to me, even strangers on the street. They tried to help me understand what was being taught in my classes by using the simplest English words, often just gestures, and Xia, who was now in her third year at Lamont and very busy herself, tried to help me with the papers and homework I had to complete once my English was good enough for me to take music history and vocal pedagogy classes. But there were so many times I just couldn't bear it all and came close to collapse. In one semester in Beijing I had learned three songs. Here, in the first semester alone, I had to learn arias, lieder, and art songs, forty-four pieces in all—in English, French, German, Latin, and Italian—commit them to memory, and perform what I'd learned in front of other students each week.

The papers and the tests were my mission impossible. It was better to be tortured by the Red Guards or chased by my father waving his leather slipper. Xia, whose English was proficient, lent me her notes from classes she had already taken, but I could barely understand them. When I had to write my first paper, on a topic in vocal pedagogy (physiology and acoustics of the singing voice), I went to the library with a dictionary and found some books that seemed to discuss the subject. I proceeded to copy from them, word for word. So my first paper consisted of a dozen para-graphs pieced together from eight books, which I hoped could be taken as coherent. I submitted it to Professor Worstell and be-came increasingly anxious when he did not hand it back for longer than a week. When he finally did, there wasn't a mark on it except for one sentence on the cover: "I don't think you wrote this paper."

Today I'm thankful for everything that made me so desperate then. It forced me to my own edge, to confront the vast precipice over which only my own artistry would carry me. I could turn back and fall or search deep inside myself and fly. Thrown into the most serious study of music, forced to challenge myself in ways I never had, at last I began to discover the depth of my own singular, origi-nal passion for music and its expression, and I took wing. So far, I had gotten by on my natural instrument. Now, whenever I sang with true understanding of a work, I became overjoyed, especially when I saw the smiles on people's faces. I could not get my point across using spoken words. But in the language of music, I was be-ginning to make my heart known.

There was also the language of the dinner table. "Fork," Mrs. Schug would say to me as she placed the implement beside my plate.

"Fork," I attempted to repeat. "Knife" and "spoon" naturally followed, as did learning how to use them.

Xia, who lived with an American family, had arranged for me to live in the home of Walt and Rondeau Schug, a wonderful retired couple, for my first two months in Denver. Besides basic vocabulary, they taught me the fundamentals of the American lifestyle, such as showering. In China at that time, homes had no bathing facilities, so we went to public bathhouses maybe twice a week in the winter. When the Schugs figured out that I wasn't bathing or even changing my clothes every day, by using gestures and simple words and pointing out the plumbing, they made their point that a daily shower and a change of clothes were the American way. Walt apparently misread my confused facial expression during a "discussion" about clothing. Believing that I didn't have enough of them, he handed me his own shirts. "For you," he said earnestly.

In those two months I also learned that I should not make noise when eating and to close my mouth when chewing. But how can a man eat with his mouth closed? I found this difficult to master. Table manners were not the same in China, where I always enjoyed sucking noodles into my mouth straight from the bowl. My friend Su Xiaoming had once asked whether I wanted to go on a date with a friend of hers, who had been attracted to me because I'd made a bigger noise than anybody else while I ate noodles. I was so *shuai*, so totally cool.

These lovely people tried so hard to make my transition to the United States comfortable. Every day they made me a peanut butter sandwich to take to school, and I mean every day, with the same carrots and celery sticks alongside it. I had never tasted food like this before. The first time they served me this meal, they asked me whether I liked it.

"Very good," I said, to the limits of my English. "Very, very good," I said in response the next day. They seemed so happy that I enjoyed this meal. I had sixty peanut butter sandwiches in sixty days. By the tenth, I wasn't so happy with it. My Chinese manners prohibited me from requesting a change of menu. Xia came to my rescue, and we began to share our sandwiches; her host family had more imagination with luncheon spreads.

The Schug home was small—only two small bedrooms—and I did not want to disturb them with my singing, so I practiced when I was vacuuming, which I often did for them. They heard me anyway, I soon found out, because they asked me to entertain for their friends. I sang and played my guitar, which was so much easier than trying to carry on a conversation. Then Walt asked me to entertain for his group of retired chemistry teachers. That was my professional U.S. debut. They paid me twenty-five for three songs, one of which was "Red River Valley" in Chinese. This always went over big in cowboy country.

After that, Walt and his friends started to call me "John Peking," after Colorado's own John Denver, whose songs I also began to perform for them. I had been a big fan of John Denver's since Deng Xiaoping's historic visit to the United States in 1979, when John Denver was one of the performers in a gala concert televised live to China from Kennedy Center. (After a visit to a Texas rodeo on that trip, Deng liked to wear cowboy hats).

The day I moved out of the Schug's house to move in with Xia, the Schugs announced that they had a gift for me. With a big grin, Walt pulled out from behind his back a huge industrial-size can of, of course . . .

"Thank you, thank you, I love it!" I exclaimed.

I did not open the can and have never had another taste of peanut butter in my life.

Xia had been in the States longer than me, and she bugged me every time I slurped my food. She had learned her American manners by imitating Dr. Liao. When I had lunch with Xia and Dr. Liao—Martha—shortly after my arrival, Xia instructed me to sit with my back straight, then take the napkin that was on the table and spread it on my lap. I objected. I couldn't move my legs at all with the napkin on them.

"You have to do it," Xia insisted.

The lunch was very stressful for me. "I'm exhausted from this," I complained. "My legs are stiff and cramped."

Martha, who had been born in England, raised in Hong Kong, and educated in the United States at Bryn Mawr College and the University of Pennsylvania, broke out in peals of laughter.

I didn't understand food prices in Denver at all. In China, milk and chicken were luxuries. We ate chicken on special holidays or if we needed extra nutrition because of illness or pregnancy. Milk was always reserved for babies and old people. In Denver, chicken and milk were the cheapest foods Xia and I could buy! And there was so much soft white bread; in China it was coarse, dark, and chewy. Beef and lamb, which were cheap back home, were costly in Denver, which made no sense at all. And the price of tomatoes, not to mention their strange shape! In Beijing, I'd paid the equivalent of ten cents for a bucket. The first time I went to a supermarket with Xia—and we didn't have supermarkets in China at that time—I noticed that all the tomatoes were the same size, as if they had been made from the same mold. I gathered up eight or nine of them, shocking Xia. "Hey, can't you see how expensive they are?" she asked.

I couldn't read English and didn't understand price tags, but I put five tomatoes back when I finally figured out that buying them all—at about a dollar a pound then—worked out to one week's salary in China.

It bothered me that there was so much waste of food in the United States. I worked the morning shift at the student union cafeteria. After breakfast service, we emptied heaping platters of French toast, scrambled eggs, and sausages straight into the garbage bins. The first time I saw this, I gestured to the food and to my mouth: all this food was edible. Not only could I not take any of it home—no leftover food was allowed beyond the door—but we couldn't give it away to needy people. How horrible! In China, we were taught to finish all the food in front of us and never to waste a single grain of rice. "I'm a grain of rice and don't despise me. The farmers raised me with their hard work. Don't throw me out," we sang in kindergarten. Chairman Mao said, "Corruption and waste are the worst crimes."

I ate everything on my plate in Denver, including the white bread. I gained thirty pounds.

I liked my job, which required no brainwork and enabled me to support myself. Since I couldn't talk to anybody, I sang all the time. I sang, too, as Xia and I cleaned people's houses on weekends. We rewarded ourselves with Kentucky Fried Chicken. It seemed so very foreign to us students from Beijing, where now it's almost as Chinese as McDonald's. Xia's regular job was at a Chinese restaurant.

Although I was around people all the time—my host family, my teachers, my fellow students and workers—I experienced a privacy I had never imagined, coming from a country as crowded as China. Back then, we all had to share kitchens and bathrooms, and we dwelled in such small individual living spaces amid so many others that there was always somebody poking into our personal business. What were you doing here? Who were you visiting? Who was that who came for dinner? What decorations do you have on your wall? People just opened doors and came into our rooms. If you locked your door, you must be doing something indecent. And they always asked strangers, "How much do you make?" and "How old are you?" During the Cultural Revolution, Mao promoted to vice-premier level some former model workers and peasants, who became a national joke for their propensity to ask international visitors how old they were, how much money they made, and even, "Do you have a boyfriend?"

Here, remarkably, people didn't get all that involved in one another's lives. So I didn't worry too much about what others thought of me.

I was missing Beijing, though, missing China, and missing my friends and family. Telephones were becoming much more widespread back home. They were no longer reserved only for high officials, so I could call my brother and his wife or my friends, but at $2.99 a minute I could rarely afford to. Even calling my parents was complicated because I had to go through their military switchboard and had to call on a prearranged schedule. Mostly, we wrote letters, and seeing my family's handwritten communications brought me much happiness. It was so much better than receiving e-mails today. Through handwriting, you can feel the person, experience his or her personality. And in China, where calligraphy and poetry are closely associated, beautiful handwriting touches you. We also recorded messages on tape and mailed them to one another. (I even recorded love songs for Chinese students to send back to their wives and husbands and heartthrobs.) I still have the tape that my father sent to me, the only recording of his voice that I possess. I sent him a VHS tape once, my second year in Denver. I borrowed the video camera from Martha Liao and shot my school, the cafeteria where I worked, and, of course, my car. I knew my father's health was fading, but neither of us referred to this. Needless to say, neither he nor I discussed politics. Yet now that I was in the United States, I found myself defending Mao and even the Cultural Revolution.

In China, we learned that the United States had been our number-one enemy, which impressed me as a child, when the world was more easily understood in black and white. I had learned in school about the War to Resist U.S. Aggression and Aid Korea, which ended a couple of years before I was born. I remember when I was nine, standing in a huge gathering on Tiananmen Square, surrounded by red flags, and watching a parade that celebrated the assassination of John F. Kennedy. This was the fate of our enemy, and we cheered. People carried big banners that said, "Kennedy was killed by the people," and "Down with U.S. imperialism." Now, almost twenty years later, in Denver, I winced at this memory. But I was very proud to be Chinese. It was so confusing. In America, I discovered a passion for my country I had never felt before. Everyone I met in the United States welcomed me as a Chinese. No one mistook me for an American, even though when I was a small child in Beijing I'd fight with anyone who called me *Da Lao Mei*, meaning "Big Old Yankee." They thought I looked like the cartoons of Uncle Sam that circulated for years after the war against

Americans in Korea. What an insult. Uncle Sam had a long face, and so did I.

I was surprised at how little Americans knew about China. Sure, everybody knew about kung fu, Bruce Lee, and fried rice. But they did not know, for example, that the Japanese had invaded China during World War II and had committed terrible atrocities, leaving more than thirty million people dead or wounded. They had heard about Mao and the Cultural Revolution and about the Red Guards, but they did not know that in the beginning, the Red Guards were young people with high ideals. In fact, Americans knew very little about the history of that era. My English was not good enough to explain this to them, although I felt the need to. How strange it was that despite my family's experiences during those years, I could not tolerate people criticizing the Cultural Revolution or Mao. I guess this is natural—we can ridicule or attack ourselves from within, but we defend ourselves from attacks from outside. If it weren't for the Anti–Spiritual Pollution Campaign in China in 1983, I might never have come to the United States, yet here I was arguing with Taiwanese students in Denver who dared to disparage the Communists.

"If the KMT is as good as you say, how come they lost mainland China in 1949?" I asked, nonsensically.

After a political argument that I soon regretted with a Taiwanese medical student, I called him first thing the next morning to apologize. I jokingly identified myself as "the Communist Party member Tian."

Silence.

"Hello? Hello?"

"I'm busy right now," came the eventual response. Click.

The medical student told the other Taiwanese students that I had admitted to being a Party member. Now none of them would speak to me. After that, I became much more careful with my jokes.

Yet I found out from other Chinese people in Denver that there was a lot I didn't know about the Cultural Revolution. I remember talking to a scholar about the famine in the 1950s and early 1960s, at the end of Mao's "Great Leap Forward" program. I made some comment that it wasn't such a big deal. "I wasn't ever hungry," I said.

I remember how he stared at me before he angrily shot back, "You are from Beijing. I'm the son of a farmer. While you were drinking milk, ninety percent of the people in my village died."

Ninety percent! And this information I got from a very good Communist, who would return to serve his country after he finished his studies.

Gradually, I grew more comfortable with being in the United States and more certain about my Chinese identity vis-à-vis modern Chinese history. I didn't have a long view of Chinese history then; as far as I was taught, history began in the twentieth century when the peasants overthrew the landowners. At least, I wasn't forced to study U.S. propaganda as part of my music education in the United States. Even at the Central Philharmonic, we all had to study Party history, documents, and newspaper editorials; the works of Lenin; and Marx's *Das Kapital*, which I still don't understand. Little by little, I began to appreciate that a person's politics—and religious beliefs—cannot come from forced learning but are acquired naturally through life.

As I approached my thirtieth birthday in this new country where I was trying to find my place, I yearned for spiritual sustenance. What was my faith? In my childhood, I was told to worship Mao. I did what I was told, but if I ever believed in Mao as a god, that had faded into memory. Xia and I lived together in a garage apartment belonging to a very religious woman, Betty Lamonica, who often held Bible studies at her house. Sometimes we went to church with her. The congregation was so nice, but the ritual reminded me too much of life during the Mao years. We'd stood up, read Mao's works, bowed to his portrait, sung songs about him or composed from his words, and criticized our wrongdoings. In America, we stood in front of the savior on the cross, recited passages from the Bible, sang hymns, and criticized our wrongdoings.

It was through the grandeur of music, including the great religious music of the West, that I discovered my true faith. Music—its beauty, power, depth, joy, spirit, and passion—became my religion. It inspired me. It comforted me. It transformed me. It allowed me to give of myself to others. It was ethereal. It was human. It was history. It was the future. It was my daily bread. It was my spiritual sustenance. It was the key to my understanding all of the people and cultures of the world.

From the music of Handel and Bach, I learned about Western religion and felt its spirit. From German lieder, French art songs, and contemporary American music, I experienced the high beauty of Western history and culture. From American folk songs, country and western, and especially jazz music I learned the common loves and longings of my new culture. The music of some great American jazz musicians, like Quincy Jones, was so free, simple, unpretentious, and warm. Jones's music seemed to speak to my yearnings from the 1970s, for love, freedom, peace, a rhythm for my soul.

I gave voice to my new faith, but I could not express it in my body. I could wiggle my hips a bit like Elvis but could not yet emote as a singing actor, which is what Western opera performance is all about. In Chinese opera, emotion is implied through ritualized movements. Women show sorrow by dabbing their eyes with their long sleeves; they always seem shy. Men show their bravery by standing in stiff postures with their chests up. I was a man of my culture, trained in a tradition of restraint that was hard to overcome. Learning the emotional language of Western performance proved to be one of two most troublesome challenges for me. It limits many an Asian career in opera even now, splendid voices notwithstanding.

The other challenge was learning to count the beat of the music. In China, the pianist or the conductor always follows the soloist's rhythms. Here, you're a part of one big performing team.

I made my opera debut at Lamont in a production of the American opera *Susannah*, about a young woman in Tennessee who is falsely accused of immoral behavior after church elders see her swimming in the nude. I had only one phrase to sing, a total of seven words—and my big voice boomed to the back of the room—but the hard part for me was the acting. I could not put the music in my body. It was agony, as was the square-dancing scene.

Yet one Denver day I had a kind of epiphany: what do I have to fear in opening myself up to this art form in front of everyone, even in my body, when I have gone through so much in my life already? Actors draw from their life experiences, and of these, I daresay, I had far more than most of my student colleagues. What shame could I experience that was worse than, say, destroying my parents' treasured record collection and living with that memory?

It would take several more years for me to really open up to acting and Western expression. But from that day on, early in my Denver years, I realized that music is inside, outside, and all around me, body and soul. It makes me one with everyone. I sang "This Land Is Your Land" in a Denver synagogue and felt as if I was experiencing Jewish history, Chinese history, all history. I learned "Silent Night" for a Christmas party that Martha invited us to. Here, I met a man named Lou Walsh, a handsome Irishman who became a close friend. He taught me "Danny Boy," such a beautiful song; each time I sing it, I can see the green mountains, the trees, and the coastline of Ireland. This moves Chinese audiences when I perform it in recitals back there now, although many do not understand a word.

I even sang "Danny Boy" from the float of a mayoral candidate in the Denver St. Patrick's Day Parade. Look at me, world: just another singing Irishman from Beijing.

12

Facing the Music

It was a Chinese American honeymoon. The American part was Yellowstone National Park. The Chinese part was that six of us slept and ate in one room. Xia and I, Martha Liao, and three musicians—plus a violin and a cello and three days' worth of food prepared by Martha—squeezed into our honeymoon suite at the Old Faithful Inn for three nights. It was Martha's idea. When she found out that we had no honeymoon plans for after the wedding—the wedding she helped us put together—she volunteered her big Jeep, we invited three of our music-student friends, and off we drove. Martha's husband, a thoracic surgeon who was frequently on call, could not take the time off. Even if he could have, this kind of poor-student vacation was not his style.

Martha and her husband were high-achieving, highly educated, beautiful Hong Kong Chinese in their mid-thirties. Hong Kong had been a British colony when they grew up, and the two were very Western, her husband in particular. By 1984, the year Xia and I got married, both of them were arts supporters and very active in Denver society. Martha seemed to identify more with Chinese culture than her husband did at that time, but on the surface she had little in common with us students. We had no money and no social position and possibly no future.

Although Martha had masqueraded as my *biao jie*—cousin—to help me leave China, in fact she acted as family and producer-promoter for music students from China and Taiwan. She arranged an impromptu performance for us even on our honeymoon. Martha sweet-talked the initially reluctant hotel restaurant manager into letting the five of us perform between the regular band's sets.

"Ladies and gentlemen, attention please! We have some talented musicians from China who are going to perform for you!" Drinkers and diners looked up in surprise and people peeked in from the lobby, as Martha claimed the microphone and the five of us jumped up to sing and play the piano, the violin, and the cello. As she interjected comments about who we were and what we were performing, I think she was even happier than we were. We put a tip glass on the piano with a few dollars in it. Afterward, we ran back to our room and counted out the bills, one by one, as we threw them all over the bed and jumped on it like children, whooping and hollering. Twenty-one dollars! What a success! Maybe we could afford to eat one meal out now. What a honeymoon!

Who needed privacy? Xia and I had enough of that back in our garage apartment in Denver.

Martha had a great influence on Xia, who was more refined than I was to begin with. The two of them had similarly lovely figures, so Xia was delighted to receive gifts of Martha's elegant clothes. Martha liked to cut hair and took the scissors to mine when I first arrived in Denver. "Your hair is too long!" she had pronounced disapprovingly. So I let her do it because it saved me money and made me presentable in the United States. Xia was always well put together; not so most of the other Chinese students in our circle, whom Martha groomed in many ways and often took to task for their messy hair and infrequent showering.

Martha and her husband had a magnificent house in the foothills about a half-hour west of Denver. In China, we had always felt sorry for the poor people who had to live in the hills and the mountains, for they had no transportation and no communication. But here in the United States, it was poor people like us who didn't have transportation to get to rich people's homes in the mountains. Until Xia and I bought our treasured, secondhand, two-door Chevy sedan for $750, Martha often drove down to pick us up.

Martha threw two kinds of parties, for which she always did her own cooking. At the elegant parties where she entertained her husband's doctor friends and his relatives and their own social circle, we students helped with the cooking, the serving, the cleaning up, and finishing off the leftovers. Sometimes we performed at fund-raisers she threw at her home for arts organizations, including the brand-new Opera Colorado. At these events, the driveway would be lined with BMWs, Mercedeses, and Jaguars, all new and shiny. But at the casual get-togethers just for us, you'd see a lineup of shabby wrecks, although some of these poor old things gave up the ghost before making it to the top of the hill. We'd laugh and sing and play and make dumplings together as Martha chopped, grated, minced, sliced, boiled, stirred, fried, and served us in her effortlessly graceful, flying kung-fu cooking style. It could be a little awkward when her husband came home from the hospital since he spoke only the Cantonese dialect at the time, which we did not, and our English wasn't fit for extended conversation. Martha's Mandarin wasn't so great, but she kept improving.

I could barely communicate with most Americans, but I watched and learned the rules. For example, I learned by observation the proper way to greet and bid farewell to a woman one has met before: kiss her on the cheek and hug her slightly. This was very interesting but fraught with anxiety for us Chinese, who are culturally more reserved; men and women do not touch when meeting, unless they know each other extremely well. As I tried out this new custom, I discovered that hugging too tight or kissing too long or hard is likely to be misinterpreted. Operatic greetings, which I observed in performances, were more easily acquired and less dangerous to practice. If I were to give a class in this important skill, I would tell my students: you must not raise the hand too high and you should not bend down too low and appear to bow; you have to look in the woman's eyes and touch the back of her hand with your lips ever so lightly, not smashing your whole face on it as if you're about to take a bite. My Chinese friends and classmates, even those who were somewhat used to Western ways, thought that kissing the hand was very unnatural, but I liked it. I still do, although some people think it's an affectation. But it feels right to me—I'm an opera singer, after all.

I observed lips and faces especially carefully in my attempts to understand what people were saying, and this proved to be unexpectedly broadening. I noticed that Americans smiled very naturally and freely. Among the Chinese, the smile is always related to the relationship and the degree of acquaintance. Traditionally, we need time to understand you, so upon first meeting we'll smile politely, while we wait and see. Among the older generations, the facial expressions, even in families, were always related to status and authority: the higher the person's rank, the more imperceptible his or her smile. And old-style Chinese women were brought up never to show their teeth when smiling, which could impart a tight quality in Western eyes. Babies everywhere, of course, have the most genuine smiles; how I love this open, spontaneous expression of feeling, before culture reins it in. Compared to what I had grown up with, I thought that Americans had naturally peaceful expressions and looked very sincere. I began to realize that when you smile, even if the other person does not seem happy, everybody becomes more at ease. Martha always smiled, and she laughed like a bell. She even smiled the day she taught me how to drive, although Xia was horror-stricken. Xia did not trust my wild-man ways.

Before I came to the United States, I had been in a car only two or three times in my whole life, when a driver picked my father up and on the rare occasion that he invited me along. Here, I would have been happy enough just to sleep in it. Then Martha said she'd teach me to drive, so one day she picked me up for a quick lesson during her lunch hour. Here's how the lesson went: "This is the gas. This is the shift. This is the brake." Then she said, "I am very tired." She kicked off her shoes, leaned back, and went to sleep. I started the car, it bucked, the gears screeched, and the car died. I started the process over and over again and finally got the car moving. Martha napped throughout, and we both survived.

Her ski lesson was not so different. Xia and I were brand-new to this sport. We borrowed equipment from Martha. She gave us a two-minute explanation of skiing basics, took us up the mountain, then pointed us toward the blue—intermediate—trail, and down we tumbled. I took off the skis and walked the rest of the way.

I would not know Martha's full story for some years, since she was more inclined to listen and to encourage us to share our stories than to claim the spotlight herself or to "bother" us with her concerns. If I have a headache, you'll know the first minute. If Martha has one, I began to learn, you'll hear about it only when it's over. Slowly, the basics of her background emerged. Though her family was from Hubei province in China, Martha had been born in Leeds, England, where the Nationalist Chinese government had sent her father to study engineering. Her birth was a big local event, since the newspaper reported that she was the first Chinese baby born in that city. People apparently flocked to the hospital to see the infant with the straight black hair. Once her father received his PhD, just before Liberation, Martha's mother had the intuition to steer the family to British Hong Kong, rather than back to Beijing where they had been living. Their extended family remained in China, however, and suffered greatly there because they had been landowners. Although Martha's parents never returned to mainland China, they passed on to their four children their great love for the country and its people.

During her student years in the United States, Martha was swept up in all the popular youth movements of that time. She knew some of our Chinese revolutionary songs, although she did not touch a toe on mainland Chinese soil until 1979. She went there initially out of intense curiosity and then as a visiting scientist, always on her own, since her husband was too busy. She searched for missing relatives at her mother's behest and made the grim discovery that her mother's sister had drowned herself during the Cultural Revolution. The sister had fled to the countryside with her grandson and with her husband's concubine. The jealous concubine had been about to report the boy's grandmother to the authorities. Martha arranged for the impoverished boy—a young man by the time she met him—to be educated in the United States.

It was on one of her trips to China that I first made Martha's acquaintance, thanks to Xia, who had been swept up into Martha's circle of students after she'd arrived in Denver. When Xia found out that both Martha and I would be in Shanghai at the same time in 1982 (I was there for my father's surgery), she arranged for us to meet. I looked around the room for an old lady with thick glasses and gray hair pulled back in a bun. What else would a woman scientist look like? Instead, my host pointed out a very beautiful, thirty-something, energetic Chinese woman with short hair wearing jeans, a polo shirt, and tennis shoes—and cutting a little girl's hair while laughing and dancing around the girl to catch the best angle. She was totally different from any of the other Chinese people in the room. Her laughter created a beautiful movement in her eyes and mouth. She was the first American Chinese I had ever set eyes on. I was deeply impressed by this American scholar, married to a rich American surgeon. Her helping hand reached my way a year later, when she assisted in my departure to the West. And from Denver,

This photo was taken right after my graduation recital from the Lamont School of Music at the University of Denver in June 1987. Martha, my accompanist, had studied piano since childhood. The program was full of art songs by Brahms and Poulenc, difficult for both of us. At one point Martha offered to pay a "real" accompanist to take her place. But the recital was a success and I graduated with flying colors.

she even helped Chinese culture take root in the American West, which would have a totally unexpected influence in a future I could not have anticipated in those days.

At school, the horrid vocal pedagogy classes were at last behind me, and I could concentrate on my singing. I was the top vocal performance student in the school. Professor Worstell consistently encouraged me. So did the founders of the new Opera Colorado, Nathaniel Merrill and Louise Sherman, who had been at the Metropolitan Opera for years before that; he was a very important stage director, she a vocal coach. (They had collaborated on the first opera ever performed at the White House, *The Magic Flute*, for President and Mrs. John F. Kennedy.) I auditioned for the Opera Colorado chorus in 1984, and although I had difficulty understanding what they were telling me afterward, I finally comprehended that they were suggesting I work with Louise privately. I did not have the money for that, so I never pursued it.

I encountered Nat and Louise again several months later at one of the fancy events at Martha's house to which students were invited. They did not appear to be happy with me. "Where have you been?" Louise asked. "I was expecting you to come for the lessons."

"I would love to come for the lessons," I murmured, "but I have no money to pay."

Nat said, his eyes bulging in annoyance, "I told you already, your lessons will be free."

Free? I had not understood. *Free!* Louise coached me for five years and never charged me. After I had won a vocal competition awarding me two thousand dollars specifically for lessons, I was so excited that finally I could pay her. So she billed the organization for the two-thousand-dollar prize, and every subsequent lesson, she handed me sixty dollars in cash. She paid me for coming to my lessons!

Nat and Louise became my stand-in musical professional parents in the United States. Their encouragement was so very important to me, emotionally. Eventually, they gave me some small roles with Opera Colorado at just a few hundred dollars apiece—my first professional stage experience. These supporting roles were big steps for me, but I wasn't looking ahead to a career then. I was indulging in my student life, which I had missed out on at an age when that would have been appropriate. Although I was no longer young, I loved being a student and living in such a rich present tense, discovering my voice and discovering me.

But the present did not remain carefree.

My father's illness returned suddenly and aggressively in late 1985. I flew to Beijing for ten days. It was a sad and strange trip. I had left my old life so abruptly, yet I did not dare tell anyone I had returned for fear of my past troubles catching up with me. My father was so weak and had lost so much weight since I had seen him last. He was obviously suffering. Though he had a very nice hospital room, suited to his high rank, I asked him whether he would like to go back home. He brightened at this suggestion so we took him home, although he could hardly walk. We did not talk much about his illness. I told him about my studies and life in the United States. He was interested. We said our final good-byes in our way: I talked about coming to see him again. I said, "See you next time."

One sunny morning several months later, in 1986, I was still in bed when Xia came upstairs to tell me that my mother was on the phone. By the look on her face, I knew that my father had died. He was only sixty-two. Xia had never met my father or anyone in my family. I had met her mother only once, the week Xia left for the United States.

I thought so much about my father in the days that followed, about all the young players he had recruited and helped and about his colleagues who loved him. He gave so much to them. With us, he was always so worried and serious, so careful, so cautious. Had he loved me? In his unspoken, undemonstrative way, I believe he had. Some years later, my brother told me that Dad had urged our mother not to tell me that he was close to death. "Tell Xiao Lu, don't come back. He may not be able to leave again if he comes back." I was very moved to hear of his concern for me in his last days because he never had agreed with my decision to leave China, nor had he acknowledged that I was having problems there that put pressure on me to leave. I felt that in his dying days, he had finally acknowledged the realities of my life and had given me his approval.

How short life was. How short happiness.

Xia and I were having problems.

Xia had graduated from the Lamont School of Music in 1985 and immediately faced reality in her very practical way. She had been a top student, but for all her hard work and accomplishment, she did not believe she had what it takes to become a professional singer. So she packed her musical ambitions away and began a course in computer science. She wanted me to prepare for a career outside of music. I was not sure I could make a living in music, either, but I would not consider changing course or playing it safe. I was content to do odd jobs, clean houses and movie theaters, sing at weddings, clerk in the DU library, make dumplings at a Chinese restaurant, and dog sit (for a dog named Tosca), if that's what I needed to do. We were both in our early thirties, and the differences in our outlook began to divide us. She sought a direction, while I reveled in the present and was willing to follow fortune as it came my way.

We could not talk about what lay ahead for us. Like every couple that does not know how to resolve the real problems, we fought over the littlest things. Here is a typical scenario: Xia has been working very hard many evenings after school as a waitress and is usually exhausted when she gets home. This particular night I am home a little earlier than usual and decide to surprise her with a special meal, including a whole fish, when she comes home. I am so pleased with myself as I direct her to the table. But before she even sits down, her eyes fall on the frying oil and soy sauce splattered all over the stovetop.

"How could you make such a mess!" she cries.

So I become hurt and angry. I have worked so hard to cook this meal, and now it is totally ruined, and I feel misunderstood. Xia can't get over the mess I am making of our kitchen and of our lives.

It got to the point where I became so jumpy anticipating that she might lose her temper that I would lose mine first. Both of us grew very nervous about our relationship. Yet despite everything, Xia supported me in my studies and worked more hours than I did to earn money so that I could do well. She always wanted the best for me, and I for her, although we could not provide this for each other.

Because the tension between us grew so bad, Xia and I decided it would be better to live apart for a while and let things calm down. After she got her degree in computer science, she decided to get a temporary job in New York and live with her sister, with whom she was close. Immediately, just as we had hoped, we missed each other very much and telephoned each other all the time. It was like the period after she had left Beijing and I was trying so hard to be able to join her. We could be kind and loving and gentle with each other from afar. When she returned for a couple of days at a time, we were overjoyed and fell into each other's arms. But in no time we were fighting again. That was our pattern for the year: separated and missing each other, together and at war. Our fighting began to erupt in front of others, which was terrible for everybody. But I just could not control myself and became more and more irritated with myself and with her. Of course, she was right most of the time. She was rational with our financial planning and very careful with our spending. I spent money more freely. Ever since the Cultural Revolution, I think, I just couldn't tolerate any outside restraint over my life.

In those months following my father's death and during my de facto separation from my wife, my inner life dipped very low. Yet I had two major projects to prepare for, on the heels of each other, which took me outside of my miserable self. The first was my graduation recital in June 1987. This was my first-ever recital anywhere, and for months I prepared a very difficult set of pieces, including Brahms and Poulenc song cycles, opera arias, and American art songs (such as those by Charles Ives, Samuel Barber, and Aaron Copland). The song cycles were the hardest—for me and for Martha. Along with everything else she was doing, Martha was studying piano with a teacher at our school. She was talked into accompanying me for this important event, which was far more challenging than anything she had ever done. Practicing pushed her close to tears. At one point, she pleaded with Professor Worstell to hire an accompanist at her expense. He reassured her that she would perform flawlessly, which she did. My performance went extremely well by all accounts.

Perhaps the highest of the high points of that day was the arrival of my mother in the concert hall, although the recital almost had to go on without her. She was flying in that very day from China with a troupe from the Zhongzheng, of which she was the creative team leader. They were scheduled to appear in the Celebrate China week events, sponsored by the Denver Downtown Partnership. Martha's newly formed organization, Asian Performing Arts of Colorado, was in charge of performing arts. The events were scheduled for the following week, and my mother and her group were among the first who were due to arrive. Their plane was late. We delayed the beginning of the concert and delayed it another five minutes, then another. Finally, we had to begin, and as *yuan*—fate—would have it, I saw my mother and a dozen of her performers walk through the door as I stepped onstage. To have her there, both as my mother and as a professional musician representing China, meant so much to me. Of course, I thought about my father a lot that day. He had heard me sing only once before, at the concert following my master class with Elizabeth Bishop in Beijing. His only reaction was surprise that my voice could carry all the way to the back of the hall. I wanted to believe that he would have found more to say today, that he would have been among the many people congratulating me for the success of this recital, and that he would have liked what he heard.

Xia, who had returned from New York for these events, was very happy that day and finally got to meet my mother. The two of them left to go back to our garage apartment to have some time together. Before Martha finally departed, we hugged each other meaningfully; we had worked so hard together for this event, and it turned out so successfully. I didn't know then that Xia had driven back to the concert hall to retrieve something she had forgotten. She saw that hug and didn't like it at all. That came out much later.

In downtown Denver during Celebrate China week, office workers and shoppers came outside to watch Chinese performers singing traditional opera, playing ping-pong, tumbling, or playing the two-stringed *erhu* on temporary stages. Martha appeared in Chinese garments to introduce these arts or artists during the lunch hour, then, like Supersciencewoman, changed back into her work clothes and returned to her lab. As for me, I served as the liaison between the organizers and the performers, plus I played the accordion and sang Chinese songs in front of the ladies' lingerie department at the Joslin store (a festival sponsor), which my friends will never let me forget.

Chinese festivals in New York City or San Francisco are very popular tourist events. But Denver does not have a large Asian population, and it was even smaller in the mid-eighties. It was a risk that our "inscrutable" culture might come across as strange and comical, but in fact the festival was a popular success. The final gala concert—singing, dancing, traditional instruments, Peking opera, modern Chinese compositions, and Western opera sung by Chinese singers—in the twenty-three-hundred-seat Paramount Theater was completely sold out.

I thought when I came to the United States that I was here only to acquire Western culture and education in order to make a career. I did not think that Chinese culture and learning could enrich the West and my own singing career. Now, a quarter-century later, I am a citizen of the United States, I work all over the world and my wife and I bring Western operas and teachers to China, we help Chinese students and musicians in the United States to get scholarships and find sponsors, and we developed and produced our first Chinese-written opera, which premiered the summer of 2007—in Colorado. Not long after this book is published, I will have originated the roles of genuine Chinese characters and a Chinese-speaking Jesuit in China in world premieres of four modern operas in four consecutive years: *The First Emperor*, at the Met (2006); *Poet Li Bai*, at Central City Opera (2007); *The Bonesetter's Daughter*, at the San Francisco Opera (2008); and *Matteo Ricci* in Hong Kong (2009).

China has changed, the world has changed, music and opera have changed, and I have transformed in ways I would never have

During Celebrate China week in Denver in 1987, Martha's newly formed organization, Asian Performing Arts of Colorado, produced all the performances. Here she's explaining Peking Opera to the downtown business crowd during lunch. I sang Chinese songs in front of the ladies' lingerie department at the Joslin store.

dreamed. I grow dizzy projecting so far forward from my Denver days in the mid-eighties because what developed for me makes no sense from the point of view of who I was at that moment. I had absolutely no plan for myself or my future. None.

The excitement of Celebrate China was over, my mother had gone home, and I was no longer a student. Now it was just Xia and me and our fights and my depression. Xia knew what she wanted to do; she had been accepted into a graduate business program in Arizona. I still felt that I might be able to make it someday in opera, but Xia was adamant that I should face the music, as the American expression aptly goes. I had to agree with her that the majority of graduates from conservatories and graduate music programs never go on to make a living in music. So, okay, I had done well in school and I completely enjoyed any opportunity I had to perform, but maybe my voice wasn't all that special. (Recently, when I watched my graduation recital videotape, I cringed at the language, the diction, the technique, and the high notes.) I was almost thirty-three years old, by which time a professional singer should already have an agent and experience in some major roles, if only at regional opera houses. Nat Merrill and Louise Sherman were still giving me a lot of attention, and I'd made my Opera Colorado house debut in a small role in Puccini's *Manon Lescaut*. So maybe the most memorable part of my performance was that I'd forgotten my contact lenses, and when I was supposed to push the leading man onto a boat, like a blind man I walked right past him.

Time and time again Xia reminded me that I didn't have enough singing contracts and that I still cleaned houses and mowed lawns. She pleaded with me to learn something useful. "How about accounting?" she suggested. "You'll find a job as soon as you finish the program." Accounting? The only numbers I was interested in were the kind I could sing.

My mother always said that my father's liver cancer came from his unhappiness during the years of the Cultural Revolution when he'd held his feelings in. Now I was worried myself, because of my family history of liver disease, and because in traditional Chinese medicine, anxiety and anger cause damage to the liver. I began to feel pain in my abdomen, and my appetite was not good. The more I dwelled on my father's death and my conflicts with Xia, the worse I felt, physically and mentally.

Finally, one day I said to Xia, "I think we should divorce."

She left for Arizona, and I got a job playing the piano and singing in the piano bar at Wang's Mandarin House Restaurant. I worked three nights a week and earned seventy dollars a night. "Yesterday," "Moon River," "Yellow Submarine," "Smoke Gets in Your Eyes," "Only You," Broadway musical tunes—I crooned them all. My spirits began to lift. My appetite returned. Business at the restaurant flourished. Maybe I did have a future in music—or a future in the restaurant business.

13

Love Conquers All

I SANG AT Wang's Mandarin House for three years. Night after night at closing time, I watched Peter Wang and his partner counting out piles of fifties, twenties, tens, and fives. The restaurant, up in the foothills, catered to the people in Martha's neighborhood and did pretty well. Peter and his partner both owned nice houses and drove good cars.

So one day I had this brilliant idea: maybe Martha would be interested in opening a restaurant with me. I would sing and play the piano. With Martha's knowledge of fine Chinese cooking and with all the people she knew who would flock to our place, it would be the best and most popular restaurant in town. Think of all the money we'd make!

Martha laughed. "So you see me standing at a stove in my apron, with you ushering people in!" But she didn't say no. She knew that at long last I was becoming concerned about my prospects, which right now amounted to little more than eight hundred dollars a month.

During the same week back in 1987 that I had asked Xia for a divorce, Martha's husband told her that he wanted to end their marriage, too. Martha's brigades of student admirers were all stunned. From our perspective, Martha and her husband had a perfect life and a perfect marriage. What could go wrong with such a beautiful couple, working at important careers, supporting the arts, living in luxury? Martha had never spoken to us about her problems. To me, she was my sponsor, my "cousin," my big sister, my adviser. My life was a mess. How could hers be, too?

We became closer friends once we were both living singly, I was no longer in school, and she was alone in that big beautiful house with just her two dogs, Chili and Pepper, and her talking and singing parrot, Luke. I confided my troubles to her, and she, little by little, began to open up to me. "You should be a psychiatrist, if not a singer," she said to me, and I was very gratified that at last I could return the attention. I hadn't realized how lonely she had been in her marriage. Her surgeon husband was thoroughly absorbed in his time-consuming career, was on call every other night, and was involved in his solitary hobbies, including horseback riding.

Now I began to understand why Martha always had all of us around. "I'm a people person!" she told me.

She met her first husband when was she was just a teenager and then was sent to Bryn Mawr to be educated to be a proper Chinese wife. But Bryn Mawr was no finishing school, Martha told me. Though it was a women's college, the students were encouraged to pursue independent careers. Those were the early days of the women's movement, which influenced Martha strongly, and she persevered in her own science career, even staying behind at the University of Pennsylvania to complete her PhD in physical chemistry after her husband had accepted a position in Denver. Perhaps Martha had grown up to be a woman far different from what he and his Hong Kong family had wanted for him. Yet, independent as they both were, nevertheless, Martha's devotion to her marriage had always seemed evident. That's why we were all stunned.

Tongues wagged about Martha and me getting divorced at the same time, but there was nothing to it, except, as time went on, in the silence of my heart, where a thousand blossoms began to bloom.

The job at Wang's Mandarin House Restaurant took some pressure off me, but now I began to feel self-conscious about my poverty around Martha. It was one thing to be a poor student, but being a poor grown-man-with-no-career-and-few-prospects had little romance to it, not with a friend like Martha. Better to be a starving artist. Who didn't sympathize with the four young men in Puccini's beautiful *La Bohème*, who lived in their freezing Parisian garret and sang so gloriously of love and art? Martha always encouraged me in that art-for-art's-sake direction, though, so I tried to believe in myself as well. My boss Peter Wang was generous with time off, and I began to push myself to pursue whatever opportunities I could. These included voice competitions, which can often unlock doors for unknown artists. I won a couple of them. The big one was the regional Bel Canto International Voice Competition, held in San Antonio, Texas, in the fall of 1987. The prize was an all- expense-paid, two-month trip to Italy to study with the great Italian tenor Carlo Bergonzi.

Nat Merrill and Martha came to the December 1987 concert in Chicago for the Bel Canto regional winners, which immediately preceded our departure. As Nat said good-bye afterward, he pressed something into my hand. It was a wad of bills. I protested, but he made sure I put it in my pocket. "I know you don't have much money and that you'll need money in Europe. Take this, and study hard. Use this precious opportunity to work very seriously with this master. When you return, let us meet at Opera Colorado." I had a good role coming up there in Puccini's comic opera, *Gianni Schicchi*. "I think this journey is going to be your turning point," Nat said to me with great feeling, like a father.

I had never been to Europe, and to travel to the birthplace of opera seemed to me even more of an otherworldly journey than my departure from Beijing six years earlier. It was also one from whose spiritual and artistic heights, like going to heaven, I might never again descend. In fact, I almost did not get back, but for very worldly reasons, for which Nat's gift, combined with the contents of my savings account (six hundred dollars), proved essential. He was right, too, that this trip would be my turning point, but the turning point of what I don't think he would have predicted.

Busseto, where we studied, was the home of the great tenor, teacher, and Verdi interpreter Carlo Bergonzi, who was sixty-three years old and still performing (as he did well into his seventies). He was—and still is—a great mentor to singers of the Italian tradition of opera. (In 2005, when he was eighty-one, we brought him to Beijing for a very successful and inspiring master class for Chinese students.) Busseto, and this is no coincidence, was also the home of the great Giuseppe Verdi, who has written the most beautiful body of operatic music of any composer in history. *Aida*, *Rigoletto*, *La Traviata*, *Otello*—even people who think they have no interest in operatic have heard of these and probably can hum along with some of the arias, whose melodies have become so familiar throughout the world.

Great operas have been written in so many languages—Chinese included, I'm happy to say—but it is the Italian language that first gave flight to opera, and no wonder. How lovely the syllables, the vowels that lift the ends of every word. It may seem surprising that in the seventeenth century, opera was invented to express the emotion of a drama, not especially as a form of beautiful music, in and of itself. But the great Italian opera composers of the eighteenth and nineteenth centuries brought such beauty to magnificent melodies, creating the splendid arias that expressed the emotions of the drama with soaring beauty and singing technique—bel canto style. This means, literally, "beautiful singing." Shouldn't singing always be beautiful? I hope so! The term describes a vocal style, as an Australian opera Web site glossary defines it, "emphasizing smooth line, lyricism of tone and phrasing, and even the agility necessary for effortless displays of vocal pyrotechnics, as opposed to the more declamatory, dramatic, straightforward style" of more realistic-sounding, dramatic singing, "sometimes referred to as 'can belto' when not too pleasantly executed."

To me, the bel canto technique is basic to Italian singing. Its beauty is the seamless flow of the notes—the *legato*—flowing from my voice to your heart. And, of course, the place to learn this Italian style, to feel it, to perfect it, is in Italy. The language itself is so musical, connecting from vowel to vowel, "O Sole Mio". . . To stand on this land, to breathe the air, to soak in this culture, the Italian character. Oh, this is opera.

We lived and studied in Bergonzi's hotel, named I Due Foscari after one of Verdi's early operas. Bergonzi is one of the last masters of Italian singing traditional. He is known as a great interpreter of Verdi, and Verdi was the focus of our work. I took three classes with him every week. He was such a serious teacher that he'd demonstrate both the right way and the wrong way for you, not just telling you to try again. That he would use his precious voice this way with six or seven students a day—what dedication! I also focused on style, language, and roles with a famous coach, well into his eighties, who had worked with all the greatest singers at La Scala—Callas, Sutherland, Corelli, and Bergonzi himself.

And, of course, I also took classes in Italian, everything from grammar to conversation. I was the only Chinese singer—the first ever in that program—and my Italian was worse than every other student's. Chinese is so different from Western Romance languages in every imaginable way, from the grammar to the syntax to the very placement of the words in your throat and mouth.

To learn about Verdi, all I had to do was walk and breathe in Busseto. A bronze statue of the revered composer stood like a god in the town's piazza. We rehearsed in Verdi's own study. The piano next to our rehearsal piano was said to be the one Verdi himself had used for composing. It took little effort to imagine that the great man's eyes were watching me, his ears listening attentively. (Would he be surprised that I was Chinese? Or just curious, like the Busseto townspeople? They asked many questions about where I came from, how I got there. One man, who spoke no English, gestured that I should follow him to a nearby shop selling stamps, where he proudly showed me an Italian stamp picturing Zhou Enlai and Richard Nixon toasting each other, commemorating the opening of China to the West. I bought a sheet of them.)

I think everybody in this town felt Verdi's presence, and most claimed some Verdi expertise. Even the old doorkeeper of the small Verdi Theater, where we had our voice classes, was an Italian opera expert and a self-proclaimed teacher. He knew all of the operas that I learned while I was there and could himself sing every word of each character in the whole work. After every master class, this old man, who spoke no English, demonstrated to me what he perceived I had not understood.

But throughout these inspiring weeks, as I so joyfully absorbed Italian culture, history, art, vocal technique, pasta, and wine—definitely a lot of that—a dark theme was developing. It was a Chinese issue. I was traveling on a Chinese passport. Before I left Denver, Opera Colorado, in order for me to sing there upon my return, had issued me a work permit. With this, I was assured that I would readily obtain a reentry visa from any U.S. consulate in Italy. The first week in Italy I took a day off from my studies and traveled by train to Milan, about an hour away, to get the visa business out of the way.

The poker-faced consular agent pushed my passport back to me. "You will have to go back to China to obtain your reentry visa to the United States," she droned.

I had her repeat what she had said. I was stunned. No! I could not go back to China! I knew that once there, I had no guarantee of getting a visa to return to the United States. All my progress in my new life—gone! Maestro Bergonzi, thinking I'd simply had a communication problem, sent an administrator from the program back with me to Milan to try to straighten out the situation. But he only made things worse; he grew irritated and gave the consul a piece of his mind. "The case is closed!" she snapped back. "He has to go back to Beijing to apply for the visa."

I phoned Martha immediately, and after near-daily, increasingly anxious telephone calls and weeks of dead ends, she finally determined through an expensive lawyer that I would be able to get my return visa from a U.S. consulate in France. I was so relieved when I went back to Milan, this time to the French consulate there, for a visa to travel to France. After waiting in line for hours, I learned that I had to go to a different window, the one that dealt with people from Communist countries. No one else had been in that line all day. Yes, they told me, they could issue me this travel visa, but it would take three months. Impossible! The Bergonzi program had ended. I could not stay in Italy much longer on my current visa, and I could not return to the United States. My young Italian teacher from the program, with whom I had become friendly, had volunteered her parents' home while I tried to work this out. Now it seemed the only way out was to go back to China.

I was so depressed when I telephoned Martha again. I was out of options. How could my new life end like this?

Then Martha came up with an idea that proves the rule that has served me ever since: love of opera conquers everything. She knew a very refined French woman in Denver who worked for the French consulate there who was passionate about opera. She would call and explain my plight. And indeed, the woman was so moved that although she wasn't at all sure she could help, she passed my appeal on to a colleague who was going to a meeting with an opera-loving French foreign affairs minister in Los Angeles the following week— and who ultimately agreed that since I was an opera singer, Chinese or not, certainly I should be allowed to travel to France immediately. The message was relayed to the French consul in Milan.

Thank God. I needed an escape now for another reason. I had misread my Italian teacher's feelings toward me, and things at her parents' house were growing very awkward. Maria was a tiny, warm-hearted girl, a little more than half my age, who lived with her family on a farm outside Busseto. Of course, I slept in the guest room, but it became obvious that her parents were not comfortable with me there. I could hardly communicate with them and did not know whether their discomfort had to do with me being Chinese or a much older man, or both. Probably they understood what was in their daughter's heart, which I did not suspect, perhaps because I was so preoccupied with my problems. I thought she was a sweet young woman who understood my plight. Without complaint, she drove me back and forth to Milan in her tiny Fiat, the smallest car I had ever been in, which I was forced to enter body part by body part. We talked freely, and I often mentioned my friend Martha.

"Martha, Martha, Martha, everything is Martha! I don't want to hear about her!" the *signorina* exploded one day as we sat in a café. She stubbed out her cigarette, then rose abruptly and walked away from me.

I was astonished at her outburst and increasingly troubled by it, because she was right. Everything *was* Martha. Martha, Martha, Martha, Martha. I had to face it: I was in love with Martha. But who was I kidding? There were so many differences between us in every way. Martha was respected, high in society, an accomplished scientist with a prominent academic position, and older than me. I had nothing. I was fighting for survival. Wasn't I always fighting for survival? I sat for hours mulling all of this over, as my love for Martha grew uncontrollably inside me and I felt alternately hopeless and hopeful.

A few days later, Maria agreed to drive me back to the French consulate in Milan. I sat self-consciously stuffed into her car. This time the French consular agent at the Communists-only window waved to me with a big smile and handed the visa to me with one proviso: I would have to sing for my visa. So right there, with crowds lined up at the other windows, this Chinese basso sang a Verdi aria into the thick glass that separated me from yet another Italian opera fan. Everybody in the room applauded.

I stayed in Milan the night before I left for France. To my surprise, Maria was at the train station, chain smoking, when I got there the next morning. I started to make some silly chitchat about how smoking was bad for her, but before I could finish, she grabbed me, kissed me passionately, and wept so hard. Just then came the announcement that my train was about to depart. I gave her a big hug and thanked her sincerely. I said, "Maybe someday I will see you again, here or in America." But she just shook her head sadly, knowing it would never happen.

On the train my thoughts were all about Martha, whom I would be seeing in a couple of days. What could I do to make *us* happen?

A day later I was in Lyon at the U.S. consulate. They were waiting for me to apply for the visa, which they provided to me on the spot. I took a long look at the American flag and for the first time felt something stir in my heart for my adopted country. Except for my idiocy in leaving my bags on an unattended cart in the Paris train station, from which my bag with the visa and my passport was stolen but was returned by a plainclothes cop before I even knew it was gone, and my missing the plane back to the United States because a friend in Paris who was driving me to the airport passed the exit—because we were listening too intently to *The Marriage of Figaro* on the radio—I returned without further incident.

I officially reentered the United States in Chicago. "Welcome home," said the immigration officer. Home? Before now, I had always thought of Beijing as home. But now, yes, I was coming home.

Martha met me at the Denver airport, and I took her in my arms right away. "I'm so thankful to you," I said.

She brushed off my gratitude, as she always did when anyone thanked her. "I'm just so glad you came back." I had not seen such a beautiful smile on her face since before her divorce. How I love that smile.

That night she took me to a Michael Jackson concert in the stadium. What a bizarre welcome-home experience. I'd never seen anything like this—the beams of light, fireworks, the dancing, the extraordinary energy of this gifted man. The audience went wild for him. Is this what it would take to become a successful performer? We'd been sitting under a bank of speakers and I'd grown almost deaf, so my head was spinning and I could barely hear Martha's voice as we drove up the hill to her house afterward. I had given up my garage apartment before I left, now almost three months earlier, and had stored my few possessions at Martha's house, where I was going to stay while looking for a new place.

It was past midnight when we arrived back. I felt unsure of what to say or do, although my gratitude and my passion were building. Martha was quite at ease, making me some food, chatting with me, telling me my room was ready any time I wanted to go to sleep. I was agitated. Was she in love with me? I was not at all sure. She said good night and went to her room. When I passed by, I saw her reading a book. In her nightgown, with no makeup, she was a beauty in the soft lamplight. She looked happy. Happiness itself is so beautiful. I turned and came back.

"Can I kiss you goodnight?"

"Of course," she said, with that smile, putting aside her book.

Martha never discouraged me from the restaurant idea. She would look at me and smile when I brought it up or perhaps make jokes about my wanting to put an apron on her. But I was under such pressure to make something of myself now that we were together, and she knew that. I had so little income. Martha's family was so worried for her after her divorce—her parents; her scientist brother and sister, both with PhDs, in Hong Kong; and her New York sister with an important UN job. They were very open-minded people and weren't against me or Martha's love for me. It's just that I had no prospects, and hers were much reduced. Her old friends from Hong Kong thought she was being cheated—a penniless singer from Beijing? Martha, have you lost your mind?

One day, when I mentioned opening a restaurant yet again, Martha simply said, "Okay, if that's what you think you want to do, start looking for a good location." I drove around Denver in a frenzy.

Of course, I knew nothing about the restaurant business, and, as Martha rightly pointed out, "All you know is how to sing." I had come back from Italy to Martha, but now Verdi would have to

By 1989 Martha, an established geneticist, and I, a jobless singer, were madly in love in the American Wild West. I vowed to work my butt off for two years in order to make it in the world of opera so that I could ask her to marry me. I fulfilled my vow, and we got married in March 1991.

make me man enough to deserve her. All day long I practiced opera, and at night I returned to the piano at Wang's. Verdi caught up with me even there. I was singing "Moon River" on the night a restaurant writer from the *Denver Post* came to report on the place. He asked who I was, and Peter said that I was an opera singer, which the writer doubted since I was singing so softly. So Peter came up and told me to sing some opera. I whispered to him that I had no voice for this tonight. I had been singing for three hours already, my voice was tired, I needed to warm up operatically—people don't understand this when they ask opera singers to belt out an aria—and anyway, I needed an accompanist for that kind of singing.

"No, no, you must sing! The reporter is very interested in this," Peter insisted. So I phoned Martha to hurry over to play for me and then ran into the bathroom to warm up, which turned out to be so loud and unmusical to the patrons' ears that everybody in the place apparently stopped eating, the reporter jumped to the door of the bathroom, and he got himself a good story. Then Martha rushed in and played while I sang an aria from Verdi's *Macbeth*, after which the reporter interviewed me. The story that appeared a few days later was almost entirely about me, with just a few sentences about the restaurant and the food, but then customers started to come up to hear me sing opera, although I had to manage to accompany myself much of the time. Martha was awfully busy.

Martha is a scientist, very logical and decisive. One day she decided she had to sell the big house, which was too expensive to maintain, and move down into the city, where she rented an old house half the size in the Cherry Creek North neighborhood of shops and galleries and cafés. Chili and Pepper had so much less space to romp, but as the Chinese expression goes, dogs do not care how poor their owners are (and cats do not care how rich). Money was a lot tighter than it was before Martha's divorce, especially after she decided to build a new house in this neighborhood. Happy as we were, I felt increasingly irresponsible. I could be the errand boy, the occasional carpenter, the ski and tennis partner, but I could not contribute a penny to this beautiful, if more restrained, life. We were both so much in love, and Martha expressed so much faith in me, but faith could only go so far without results. I gave up the restaurant idea, realizing that I could not make Martha happy that way. The time had come: I would have to have a career in opera within two years or I would give it up. I designed a step-by-step plan to work at Wang's restaurant and earn enough money to travel back and forth to New York City and study with the best teachers and coaches, take auditions, enter competitions, and make contacts whenever I could. I set myself a deadline: December 31, 1990. By that time I would be thirty-six years old. I had to make myself an opera singer by that date so that I could ask Martha to be my wife.

If not, there would be no marriage.

I made at least twenty trips to New York in those two years—back to the capital of culture where, listening to Pavarotti, I had determined to be an opera singer my first night in the United States. Each time I stayed until my money ran out, from a week to a month on one occasion. Sometimes I cut it a little too close, like the time I took an eighty-dollar lesson knowing that I had only seventy-five dollars in my checking account. I went immediately to the airport and flew back to Denver, got my seventy dollars at the restaurant that night, and deposited it in my account the next morning. The check bounced anyway. But this is the tight world of music teachers and students: my coach said she'd give me that lesson for free.

During each visit, I stayed with my old friend Wei Fugen, a famous pianist from China, who had just come to the United States and was supporting himself by giving piano lessons, playing as an accompanist for voice teachers in their studios, and doing odd jobs (and who, although neither of us could have imagined it then, accompanied me later in recitals in the United States, Singapore, Hong Kong, and China for more than fifteen years, and who is now on the faculty of the Shanghai Conservatory of Music). He rented a cheap apartment in Queens, where we both lived very frugally, and where he often insisted on giving me the best bed, although sometimes I slept on the floor. He shared the apartment with another fellow, a writer. Wei usually cooked. One day he'd stew a chicken in water, and we'd eat the meat. The second day, he'd add vegetables to the broth, and we would have soup with vegetables. The third day, he'd add noodles. We were so happy. It really was like the fellows in the attic in *La Bohème*—who may have inspired me and helped soon enough to decide my fate.

In New York, when I went to art exhibits or bought standing-room tickets at operas, gobbling down a sandwich I had made at home, I couldn't help thinking back to those days after the end of the Cultural Revolution when the young people had little wealth and little pressure, just a huge appetite for culture and knowledge.

Except that I did have pressure. The deadline. Love was my driving force and gave me the energy to go forward.

One of the few English expressions I had learned while still in Beijing was "catch-22"—or "number 22 rule," as translated literally from the Chinese. You certainly did not have to be American to get stuck in those impossible paradoxes, and the Joseph Heller novel became one of my favorites when it was translated into Chinese after the Cultural Revolution. At a garage sale in Denver in 1990, when I spotted a worn old *Catch-22* paperback, I bought it immediately. I did not manage to get through the book in English, but it was enough to have it with me as I waded into the thicket of my own catch-22 of the moment: in order to become an opera singer, I needed an agent to set up auditions and negotiate contracts; in order to get an agent, I needed more experience as an opera singer. After getting to know many gifted singers and seeing how they struggled to get a hearing, I suspected that my hope of finding an agent was extravagant.

Nat Merrill came to my rescue in the spring of 1990, a few months before Martha and I moved into the new house. "Tian, I think you are ready to find an agent in New York," he said, "and I am going to help you." Within the week, he told me that he had contacted eight agents who were willing to listen to me the very next week. I could not believe my good fortune. With the general director of Opera Colorado on my side, how could I fail? For months, Louise and I had been working on five arias for me to sing in competitions and auditions. She coached me on which ones to sing first, which styles and characters to demonstrate, and how to handle agents. Now my time had come.

I left for New York immediately. The first morning I began to phone the numbers that Nat had given me.

"Yes, Mr. Tian," the first agent replied. "Nat called me. How could I say no to Nat? But I can't take any new singers right now. Good-bye."

Second agent: "I'm so busy now, but I hope to see you the next time when I have an audition schedule."

People in New York speak so much faster than Denver people do that before I understood enough to say, "Okay, thank you," they'd already hung up.

Numbers three through five were versions of numbers one and two. The sixth call got me a hearing. "Okay. I've booked a place for some singers tomorrow at four o'clock. You can come," the agent said. I arrived to find a man in a sports jacket with a silk scarf wrapped around his neck. I sang my big opening audition number, "O Tu Palermo," from the Verdi opera *I Vespri Siciliani*, in which Dr. Procida sings of his love for his country and his attempts to get help for the Sicilians to overthrow the occupying French. This is a very difficult aria, which demonstrates my big Verdi voice to the fullest. The agent's hands remained in his pockets, and he looked steadily at the floor. He paced a few steps forward, then turned around and spoke to the ground. "I think you have a good voice. You should go to Europe and become a house singer [on yearly contract] there. That's my advice. I will tell Mr. Merrill. Good-bye." He never looked at me.

Although the seventh agent also agreed to hear me, I was quickly shown the door there, too. I did not report back to Nat, who had such high expectations for me, and I dreaded facing Martha. Not that she ever demanded anything of me. Why did I think that I was any different from any other singer with no experience? If only to avoid making those more difficult calls to Denver, I dialed the final number on Nat's list.

"I would love to hear you," the man said so cheerfully that I wondered whether I had the wrong number. He said that he was going to hear another Colorado singer, a soprano, at the recommendation of Mr. Merrill and would hear us both the next day. Two men greeted me, both well dressed, polite, and very attentive to my audition. Probably because I thought this was the end of everything for me anyway, I sang very freely, very relaxed. They asked for more. I sang the next one on Louise's list: "See, the Raging Flames Arise," one of Caleb's arias from Handel's *Joshua*. He sings this aria as he and Joshua fight the battle of Jericho: "See, the raging flames arise," he sings. "Hear, the dismal groans and cries! The fatal day of wrath is come. Proud Jericho hath met her doom."

The technique to sing Handel is very different from what it takes to sing Verdi. Handel's arias can be very fast, and where Verdi singing is very smooth, with Handel it is as if the voice is running up and down dozens of stairs, one at a time. Usually, a bass with a big, heavy voice like mine cannot move the voice that quickly. It is risky to offer this difficult aria in an audition. As I sang, the two men began to smile at each other. Every singer loves a smiling audience. I sang the fast passages confidently and clearly.

I don't know what I said—"Of course, sure, wow, okay, um"—when the taller man, Paul Côté, invited me to their office the next day. He turned out to be a known agent with a small but good roster, especially of young singers. We did not talk contracts since there was nothing to contract for. He told me, "We would like to try, with no guarantees. We think you have great potential." I promised Paul and his partner, Peter Randsman, that I would fly in for auditions, which I did throughout the final months of 1990, as the last weeks before my deadline slipped away. When a local or an international opera company, a conductor, or a visiting general director is looking for singers for a specific opera or a certain type of singer—a Verdian baritone, a Wagnerian bass—or wants to beef up his company, he calls around to the agents, who might show up with a number of their singers. Thus, the hallways at auditions can be teeming with agents and singers. The first impression is everything; within seconds, your fate may be decided as you walk to center stage and introduce yourself, assume a dramatic stance, announce your aria, then open your mouth to sing for maybe three or four minutes total. It's not just your voice; your gestures, your facial expressions, your style, and your body language all speak loudly. Do you sound like the character who you are singing? Do you *look* the part? I was worried about being—about looking—Chinese. We were not known commodities in opera. Other than the Bonze, Butterfly's uncle in *Madama Butterfly*, who sings for one minute and twenty-four seconds, there is really only one Asian bass character in all of Italian opera—blind old King Timur, in Puccini's *Turandot*. Without makeup and costumes, how could I look Italian, even if my voice was trained in Verdi?

All too often, singers are not educated in how to take auditions, where their futures are decided sometimes before they open their mouths. We could not be in the room when another singer was auditioning, so I usually tried to peek in the door to see how other vocalists were handling it. I practiced walking onto the stage with vigor and confidence, but not too fast and not too casually. I practiced pronouncing the titles of the arias accurately, so that people would know I had a command of the languages, and I spoke directly to and established eye contact with at least one of my listeners. Of course, in the beginning, my English was not even fluent, let alone my Italian or French. So I practiced, practiced, practiced, practiced, and I rehearsed with accompanists, whom singers have to bring to auditions. My time was short, my deadline was near.

Most singers figure that if you get called back 25 percent of the time, you are successful. I got five offers for future productions out of seven or eight auditions. Opera companies are always looking for big and beautiful bass voices, which are harder to find than lighter voices, to cast in the most difficult Verdi and Wagner roles. It helps to look big and imposing, and fortunately I am big for an Asian. Some of the offers were for big parts with regional opera companies, such as the Delaware Opera, which offered me the role of the cold and cunning assassin Sparafucile in Verdi's *Rigoletto*. Sarasota Opera invited me to sing the noble and dark Fiesco in Verdi's *Simon Boccanegra*. Both are famous bass roles. I was very excited, even though I was not sure whether I was ready for such a challenge. The pay was not great, but offers they were. And what good starting gigs these were for young singers, who need to work up from small regional opera companies, often for years, before hoping to successfully audition at a major house. I was an inexperienced singer, but, at thirty-six, hardly a young one. At my age, did these admittedly good starting offers amount to success within my deadline? Did they really make me an opera singer? Or would I be starting out too late to achieve success in time to share it with Martha?

My agent, Paul, of course, was very pleased and became more confident of my abilities. So one day he called me in Denver and told me that he had set up auditions for the New York City Opera and the Metropolitan Opera, both in the following week. You can't get any bigger in New York than these two Lincoln Center companies or, in the case of the Met, in the entire world. The *world*.

It was a disastrous week.

On Wednesday, I went to the City Opera. A silver-haired gentleman sat far away in the otherwise empty hall. He walked down a few rows as I was singing. After one aria, he said, "Thank you," and that was it. The next morning Paul called to tell me that the City Opera didn't think my voice was big enough to fill the hall.

"Cancel the Met audition," I told him at once.

"Hao Jiang . . . "

"If they don't think my voice can fill this hall, well, the Met auditorium is huge! I will never make it. It will be humiliating."

"Everybody knows the acoustics at the City Opera are terrible," Paul said, but I did not think acoustics had anything to do with it. They just did not want me.

"You should never say no to the Met," Paul warned me. "You never know until you try."

The Met audition was scheduled for Friday, but on Thursday my accompanist canceled. Paul gave me a bunch of names, and I finally found one who could play for me on short notice. Although I was supposed to be at the Met at eleven, he said he couldn't meet me at his apartment until ten-thirty; he assured me that since he lived only five minutes from Lincoln Center, we would have time for a quick run-through. At fifteen minutes to eleven, he showed up in a sweat that rivaled my own. He started to play the first few bars of "O Tu Palermo" and kept missing the notes. I was horrified. I sang maybe two lines before we had to run to the Met. My name was called just as we came in to List Hall, a rehearsal hall where the stage is at the bottom and perhaps fifteen rows of seats rise sharply from it. I didn't even have time for a drink of water. My heart was racing. I could not breathe. I stood by the piano, announced what I was going to sing, and nodded to the pianist to start. The two well-dressed, very attractive women who were to listen to me sat in one of the high rows, and as I began to sing, I raised my head so that I could sing directly to them. Too late, I realized that my head was angled too high for me to sing this aria properly; I could not connect my voice to the breath support and risked losing control (just as in athletics you have to set the muscles properly for each move). Meanwhile, the pianist was making so many mistakes that he played more and more quietly until I could hardly hear a thing. With my head raised too high and no piano support, I was totally at a loss. The ladies smiled professionally and asked me what else I wanted to sing. I went on to the Handel piece, pulling my head back down, so that this time I was at eye level with the empty seats. I was in despair. The pianist was killing me and destroying my audition. I yearned for Martha. I sang with all that was left in me. When I finished, the women smiled politely and said, "Thank you." That's all. "Thank you."

I still had to pay the pianist. "I know I made some mistakes," he conceded. He took the money anyway.

I went back to Wei Fugen's apartment in Queens and called Martha. I was despondent. She tried to comfort me with the usual things one says after a bad audition: "It's only an audition. You'll have others." Then she changed the subject. Something about curtains for the new house. I tossed and turned all night, feeling enraged, then pitiful, then overcome with loss. Of all the auditions to have blown. I knew I should have canceled it. Why did my agent pressure me into this? I had failed to come through for Martha.

At last I slept, and I was still sleeping at ten-thirty the next morning when the phone rang.

"They like your singing," Paul said.

"What?"

"They want to arrange an audition on the stage with Maestro Jimmy Levine," he said. They want the artistic director of the Met to listen to me? This is crazy.

"But I had a terrible audition," I protested.

"Hao Jiang," Paul said patiently, "this is *good* news."

I returned to New York a week before the audition was scheduled. I rehearsed three times with my pianist, a man who came highly recommended. The audition was scheduled for noon. I pleaded with him not to be late. "Don't worry," he said, reassuring me that he had been through this with singers at this opera many times before. He would meet me at ten minutes to twelve at the backstage entrance.

I went to bed early, slept long and surprisingly well, and had time for a leisurely breakfast on the morning of the audition. I dressed in a suit and a tie, which I usually try avoid because sometimes it makes me feel as if I can't breathe. But I believed that I needed to look well-dressed and serious to sing from the stage of the Met. My composure lasted until I dropped my contact lens in the bathroom. Wei and I crawled around on the floor until time was growing short. It was a hard lens, and I did not have a replacement. (I now wear disposable lenses and have boxes of them around, so my onstage contact lens issues are at last behind me.) Well, at least I did not lose my voice, I said to myself to calm the sudden tide of anxiety. Instead, I lost my pianist. He never showed up. Five minutes to twelve, four minutes to twelve, three minutes to twelve, two minutes, one . . . "Mr. Tian, we can't wait any longer," insisted the stage manager, who ushered the singers in to their auditions. I had been going back and forth to the stage door. "You must come in now."

A soprano was completing her audition as I stumbled backstage. I was blind in one eye, I was worried to death, and my head was pounding. How could I audition without a piano? The soprano and her pianist passed me on their way out, just as the stage manager announced, "Mr. Tian, it is your turn." I lunged for the pianist and grabbed him by the collar. His eyes were round with terror as I blabbered, "You must play for me. I need your help! I have no pianist."

"Okay, let's go," he gamely replied after a moment. I handed him my music, with which he said he was familiar. He turned around and followed me onto the stage, straightening his collar.

My voice had become hoarse with anxiety, but this mercifully vanished as I announced that I would start with "O Tu Palermo." There were five or six people sitting perhaps ten rows back in the dark auditorium, and in my semiblindness I could not make out who was who. I looked out into this splendid hall, all gold and red, with seats for four thousand people. This stage was so big, the light was so strong. The piano began, beautifully. I had passed through this crisis. I was on the stage of the Metropolitan Opera. I opened my mouth and just sang. That's all I remember. I just sang.

A man's voice asked me what else I had prepared. I was so nervous, I forgot to offer the Handel aria, so they selected the aria from *La Bohème* in which Colline, the starving young philosopher, sings farewell to his beloved overcoat in the freezing garret. He will pawn it to buy something to help the seamstress Mimi as she lies dying of consumption. One of the shortest in opera, this emotional aria is actually quite difficult, although it should come across as easy.

After I finished, I heard that same voice saying, "Thank you very much." And that was all.

I thanked the pianist repeatedly. I told him I would pay him any amount he wanted. He asked for the standard thirty dollars. Paul showed up backstage. "Hao Jiang, you were absolutely wonderful. Congratulations. That was a great audition."

"I don't think so," I said.

I was working on my income taxes on March 18, the day my contract arrived. Although I knew I had gotten the job—and had met my deadline—my hands were shaking as I opened the thick white envelope from Paul's office. The contract specified that I would be a house singer at the Metropolitan Opera for the 1991–1992 season, beginning in the fall and including the Met's tour to Europe the following summer. It listed my roles—two that I would actually sing and the handful that I would cover. I had made six thousand dollars in the previous year. Now I would be making nearly ten times that.

I called Martha at work and suggested that she take the rest of the day off.

She was a little annoyed. "I can't. I'm very busy."

"Can't you take a few minutes?" I urged.

"Why?"

"I think we should get married today. Please come home."

She was there in ten minutes. We rushed to City Hall with our friend Lou Walsh (the man who taught me "Danny Boy" and became my Irish "father") and his wife, Ann, as our witnesses. It was a beautiful day, sparkling with sunshine, and I was the happiest man on earth.

14

Hao Giovanni

Luke, now my legal step-parrot, was only slightly more the novice opera singer than I was as we drove east to our new perches in New York City. In his cage by the window of our apartment on the eighth floor of the Battery Park City complex in lower Manhattan, he chattered in Chinese and English and sang in Italian, bel canto style. We had a view of the Statue of Liberty, whose symbolism was not lost on me as I reflected on the strange journey of the roaring river of my life, from Mao to the Met. I loved sitting in the dark at my desk and watching the lights twinkling around the statue and the harbor. I remember thinking, I do not want this to pass too quickly.

On the other side of our apartment building rose the massive twin towers of the World Trade Center. It was September 1991.

Luke's perch has risen steadily in the years since. Now he can sing for his preferred supper of Martha's homemade Chinese dumplings, while gazing down at the Metropolitan Opera House across the street to the west or over Central Park to the east. His ability to mimic my singing or the earnest rehearsing of the many young singers who stay with him while Martha and I travel throughout the world is legendary. My own progress was not so seamless, especially at the beginning, when I was literally lost in the warren of floors, hallways, dressing rooms, and rehearsal halls that make up the enormous backstage world of the Metropolitan Opera. I knew neither where I was nor who was who. One day in a rehearsal I was standing next to a well-dressed man in a suit and a tie who looked very serious.

"You must be an important person," I said.

"Why?" he responded, stone-faced.

"Because you are so nicely dressed," I answered.

"I'm Joe Volpe." The well-dressed man was the powerful general manager of the Metropolitan Opera, and I didn't even know that. No wonder he was not friendly to me. The place was crawling with people—hundreds of artists, crew, and staff members. Conductors, directors, costume designers and tailors, set designers, dancers, carpenters, wardrobe clerks, technicians, stage crew, accompanists, and language coaches. Chorus and orchestra members numbered in the hundreds. And there were at least two hundred soloists from all over the world who came to perform there, so many of them big stars.

Then there was me. The Metropolitan Opera, with the highest budget of any opera house anywhere, is not a place where singers at my age ordinarily start out. Most have established careers by the time they achieve these great heights. Indeed, most of the singers I encountered knew their way around the opera house and the opera world. I, of course, was brand-new to both. I didn't even know what to wear to work. Because in Italy singers usually dress rather formally, even for rehearsals, I thought that I should dress for business and even carry a briefcase to add to my operatic image. After a month, I told someone I met in the cafeteria that I was a new singer there. "I thought you were an insurance salesman," he said, surprised. So I changed my look: casual pants and shirts or sweaters, like the rest of my colleagues.

As a house singer, my job that year was to sing two supporting roles and cover (understudy) three or four others. No role was really small for me then, even if I had only five lines to sing. I took coaching in singing and certainly in diction from the extraordinary artistic staff at the Met; they helped me in the characterization, the pronunciation, and the style of a particular opera and its background. And I took—and paid for—lessons with my own voice teacher, Arthur Levy (and later Ruth Falcon). But I was at a disadvantage from the start.

For one thing, I had no training in acting, which has become increasingly important as the theatrical and even cinematic aspects of the opera grow more central to the productions. This is especially important today, as live high-definition productions are being beamed into movie theaters worldwide. This successful innovation was introduced by the Met's general manager Peter Gelb when he took over for Joe Volpe in the 2006–2007 season. The close-ups that are a part of the new productions are far more revealing than anything the opera house audience will see, even with opera glasses. When I began at the Met in 1991, audiences were already demanding more than great singing out of this old art form. They've been getting it, from the directors and the designers who increasingly come from the worlds of theater, movies, and multimedia. (There's a trend in opera to go for a cinematic look; the demands on the singer's physical appearance are now becoming as great as those on his or her vocal bravura.)

So I learned by watching, and at the Met I had the biggest stars in the world to learn from. During rehearsals, while I stood on the side of the stage or sat in the audience, I observed how these great performers expressed the drama in the operas in their eyes, their eyebrows, their hands, and their facial expressions as they sang and moved. I noticed their phrasing, how just one note, one consonant (perhaps a single sharp T) could convey so much. I saw how they opened themselves to passionate expression, which is always an education for Asian singers raised in cultures of restraint. I learned from the questions that even the greatest singers asked the director about their characters and how they should move on the set. And, eventually, the great Met basses themselves—such as Paul Plishka—showed me acting techniques that were essential to the roles they had performed time and again.

Not only did most of the singers have much more stage experience than I did, they usually knew several languages—Italian, for sure. I was most fluent in Mandarin, not a staple language in opera, and this was my biggest problem when I started out.

Diction for singers is quite different from speaking a word correctly in a particular language. Even if you manage to say a word, you still have to learn to sing it, with appropriate color: light and bright or dark and resonant and ringing. All of these have different placements in the throat and require trained muscular support from the breath. The language changes how the sounds are produced and delivered so that they are understood while you sing. And all of this has to be done without amplification. Pop singers need only whisper into their microphones. At the Met and most other great houses, there are no mikes. You make yourself heard clearly on your own. Even for people who grow up speaking a language, some languages—such as English—are harder to sing than others.

Many people who are new to opera believe that they'd rather hear an opera in English than in a language that's foreign to them. Then they find themselves grateful for the supertitles that virtually all opera houses now use to provide the dialogue in the language or languages of the audience (as at the Met, which provides discreet LED translations in three languages on the backs of the seats). Just think of one of the most popular emotions in opera: love. Now sing that word in English. Your voice rides a little on the *luh*, but then you have to crash land on the *ve*. Ah, but sing it in Italian, *amore*— ah . . . mo . . . ray. You can lift your audience to heaven with those pure vowels.

I must say, even now that I am conversant in English, I find it a difficult language to sing. English, for better or for worse, was the language of the text of Tan Dun's new opera *The First Emperor*. This first-ever collaboration between the Met and a Chinese artistic team had its world premiere in 2006. Some critics believed that the subject matter—the story of Emperor Qin Shi Huang, who unified China in 221 BC and began construction of the Great Wall—would have been better served in Chinese. Not that the Met would likely have commissioned a Chinese-language opera, although Plácido Domingo, who sang the title role, would have learned the language, even at this stage of his exceptional career. Remarkably, in one review of this controversial opera, my English diction was praised. I was dumbfounded to read this, and I'm not sure that I agree. I do know that I worked and worked and worked on my role of General Wang, to whom the emperor has promised his daughter as a bride, but she gives her love and her virginity to the emperor's former best friend, Gao Jian Li. Gao bites off his own tongue at the end, by which time I have been murdered, although I still get to sing some beautiful music as a ghost.

Diction and language were so daunting for me as a Chinese, even after eight years of opera training. The language system, the grammar, and the syntax of the Chinese language are so different from those of Western languages; the consonant and vowel sounds are so different.

I do not think I worried so much about each performance before I arrived at the Met, but I became a worrier on my first day there. Now that I had come this far, I felt, I had so much to lose if I failed. I had gained Martha's love through opera, and I meant to keep it. I did not want to disappoint all the people who had supported me, including everyone in Denver who had put their faith in me, from my first landlady and the dog Tosca's owner to all those at Opera Colorado, plus Martha's colleagues from Asian Performing Arts of Colorado.

I put enormous pressure on myself to master all the skills and the languages of grand opera—because I was a neophyte and because I was Chinese. Especially when my career became global, I saw how great the disadvantages were for Chinese singers in the international opera world. There were so few of us singing at the highest levels in those days, and China itself was only beginning to emerge from being the closed-off society it had been when I grew up. The odds were stacked against us for many reasons—culture, language and diction, acting, familiarity with the background and the history of this music—and not all of them related to skill. Too many people in the business thought that Asian singers could not master this form or that audiences would not wish to see or hear Chinese people in Western roles.

From my first day at the Met, though, the top-notch coaches worked with a zeal to match my own. I worked so hard to justify their decision to hire me. Perhaps I sometimes put too much pressure on myself, to the point of getting headaches and insomnia. (Now I do yoga to relive stress.) I put so much time into practicing every single word, every gesture of my hands, every glance of my eyes, every turn of my feet. I was so nervous.

"Tian, what's the matter with you?" The loud voice of Giancarlo Del Monaco, a famous Italian opera director (and the son of the great tenor Mario Del Monaco), singled me out time and again as we rehearsed the first opera I worked on at the Met, Puccini's *La Fanciulla del West* (*Girl of the Golden West*). For both of us (and for the conductor Leonard Slatkin), this opera marked our debuts at the Met, but he was a famous director and I had the smallest principal role. The opera was a lavish new production of this shoot-em-up California Gold Rush spaghetti Western opera that would test Del Monaco's talents far more noticeably than it would mine. It featured a big-time cast, including Plácido Domingo, who played Dick Johnson, a bandit in disguise, and Sherrill Milnes, who played Jack Rance, the sheriff. I played the Indian boy Billy Jackrabbitt.

Del Monaco had a quick temper and swore often. In one scene I was lying down drunk, a cowboy hat covering my face. The hat wouldn't stay on, though, because of my glasses. "Would you get your damned glasses off your face!" he hollered. I think my glasses flew up and off and out of the opera house. (I do not wear my contact lenses until dress rehearsal.) Perhaps I was too nervous for Del Monaco's tastes or for the horse's. Plácido Domingo's character rides a horse in this opera, and Billy Jackrabbitt gets to lead it.

Plácido Domingo was such a big hero to me. I was too shy to speak one word to him during rehearsals, but I watched him with awe. He was so handsome, in his long cowboy coat and hat, always making jokes—such a great actor. And he was so gifted musically. Once during a rehearsal break he sat down and brilliantly played a Chopin waltz, while still wearing Dick Johnson's leather gloves. Billy Jackrabbit does not sing with Dick Johnson during this opera, but I was very excited to have the opportunity to stand close to him as he sat astride his horse. This worked out fine until the first dress rehearsal when a real horse made its appearance. That horse would not let me near it. As soon as I reached for the reins, it shook its head so hard I could not get hold of them. I did not want to irritate that big horse any further, for fear I would make it so jumpy that it would throw my hero off its back. When, after two more tries, I still could not get the reins, Del Monaco decided to have someone else stand in for me in this part of my role. I was miserable and also perplexed, for I have loved horses since I was a farmhand with my auntie's family in Jincheng during the Cultural Revolution. Also, as I mentioned previously, I was born in the year of the horse in the Chinese zodiac, which gives me a horse nature. Perhaps that was the problem. As the Chinese saying goes, When two horses come together, they will kick each other.

Another day, during rehearsal, as I was walking offstage and Domingo was in front of me, he suddenly turned to me. "You have a beautiful voice," he said, out of the blue. I was so stunned and flattered, I have no recollection of what I said to him in return. Such a big star says such a nice thing to *me*, a Chinese newcomer in a tiny role! Horse or no horse, I became more relaxed onstage after that. At the gala dinner on opening night, I walked to Domingo's table and introduced Martha to him. Domingo then turned to the VIPs at his table. "I want to introduce this Chinese singer to you," he said. "This is his debut tonight. I believe he will have a great career."

So it did not matter in the end that Plácido Domingo's horse did not take to me, for within a couple of years Maestro Domingo himself would become important to the rest of my career.

My debut—October 10, 1991—went very well, despite my bronchitis. As dress rehearsals approached, I started to cough and run a fever. That I might have to miss my own debut was too horrible to think, and I certainly dared not take off from rehearsals since I was so new. When my symptoms began, Martha was in Hong Kong with her sick mother (her father had died of liver cancer the previous spring), and I suppose her absence on top of all the stress of my upcoming first appearance contributed to my illness. I tried to keep from coughing and didn't tell anyone besides Martha how sick I felt. But on opening night, when a man from the Met artistic department came to wish me good luck in my debut, I blurted out, "Charlie, I really do not feel well. I have bronchitis." My dressing-room mate bolted out the door as soon as he heard me say "bronchitis"—akin to "plague" for an opera singer—although he must have noticed my muffled coughing throughout the week.

Charlie looked at me closely before answering. "If you can still have such a beautiful voice with bronchitis," he said finally, "you should definitely keep the bronchitis."

I always felt that my voice was not good enough, my performance might not be strong enough, and my acting would not come across. My heart would beat like crazy, my hands would feel like ice, and I would be in a cold sweat every time I was about to go onstage, even if the role was minuscule. One day after I became more familiar with Sherrill Milnes, another of my heroes, I confessed my nervousness to him and asked him how he managed to be so steady. He looked into my eyes with complete understanding. "Welcome to the business," he told me.

I still worry. I worry after a part is offered to me and the contract does not come right away. I worry that there will be no more offers for me. I worry that my voice will not be in good form because Martha and I have been having so many guests—we are always entertaining—and I have been talking too much. I worry that flying all over the world will sap my strength and steal my voice. I worry that there will be so many flowers onstage during a recital or in my dressing room that my throat will close up because of my allergies.

Of course, all opera singers worry constantly about their voices. A Stockholm University psychologist found that female opera singers test their voices in the morning to determine how they sound, while the men are more concerned about whether their voices are there at all.

And yet for all the fears and worries, my happiness, excitement, and joy in performing have multiplied beyond measure. Maybe when I'm preparing for a role, I still push myself too hard, and then I must remind myself that the purple yoga mat is spread out and waiting for me. I often feel that I am not ready, but my greatest pleasure in life comes when the curtain opens and I am in costume, in my makeup, and wearing my wig. For every opera, every aria, I am in character. I just cannot describe how I enjoy every single second when I am singing that character onstage. After my debut and then my second opera, these rewards began to accrue.

My second Met role was Count Ceprano, who is cuckolded by the lecherous duke in Verdi's *Rigoletto* in the very first scene. Neither the production nor the director nor the conductor was new to this opera, and I felt like an old hand, having already made my debut. The opportunity to cover the roles of other singers allowed me to add new roles to my repertoire.

My confidence began to grow. So did my concern about Martha.

Both of us were working in unfamiliar environments, but I was at the bottom of a ladder climbing upward, and she was standing on her own ladder wondering which direction to go. Martha had taken a one-year leave of absence from her position at the University of Colorado medical school, where she had been an associate professor. She took an interim position doing research at an institute in New Jersey. It wasn't the same as running her own lab with four postdocs and determining the course of her own work. She felt as if she was starting all over again, and because she was a visiting fellow, she had little space in which to work. She wanted to complete the AIDS research grant she had been working on before she left Colorado. Her heart was not in this new work. She usually came home exhausted after the long bus commute to our little family of Luke and Chili (Pepper had died) and to her worrying husband. Yet, as always, she supported me fully in my career and steadied my emotional ups and downs. She decided to cut back on her work in New Jersey and take a part-time job at Albert Einstein Medical School in the Bronx, working as the managing editor for a genetics journal. With her qualifications she could have been editor in chief, but she wanted a position with less responsibility while she decided the direction of her career. So now she was running between New Jersey and the Bronx—by car—which did not add to her well-being.

One of Martha's postdocs, who had helped us pack up the truck to leave Denver, had predicted we would never return there to live because we were taking so many of our possessions with us, including the contents of Martha's precious kitchen. His prediction was correct, but not for that reason. We continue to take many of our belongings, from computers to duck-roasting racks, as we travel from opera house to opera house throughout the world.

As a house singer for the Met, I would not have time for guest roles at other opera houses; in essence, I belonged to the Met. Just in case they decided not to renew my contract, however, I had gone on auditions and had in fact received two offers for the 1992–1993 season, in Nice and Hong Kong. I was quite willing to give these up when the Met offered me the second-year contract, but Paul thought I had potential for an international career and suggested that I consider broadening my choices. I was reluctant to give up such a good, secure position on a gamble. Martha, Paul Côté, and I discussed the options. There was no limit to what roles I might sing as a guest singer at opera houses throughout the world . . . if I got the offers . . . if I performed well. And if I didn't? I feared that my ambitions were growing too large for my

Here I am as Timur, the exiled king of Tartary, at the Met in Puccini's Turandot. *This is the only Western opera that takes place in Beijing, the city of my birth, so I guess it is* yuan *that I have sung this role over two hundred times in at least ten productions in different opera houses worldwide.*

limited experience. Martha, true to form, believed in me more than I did.

The Met offered me a guest-singer contract, to perform one role the second season and to cover a number of others, essentially as a freelance performer. I accepted.

We never returned to the Denver house Martha built and that she loved so much, in which we had lived for only one year. (Martha is so sentimental about the place that she can't bring herself to sell it, so we rent it out year after year.) Basing ourselves in New York made more sense, in the hopes that I would appear often at the Met in upcoming years and to make it easier for me to go on auditions. So we stayed, for my career, and I felt guilty—guiltier still when Martha gave up her genetics career altogether three years later.

Since I had first tried my luck in New York, I'd had a high success rate in auditions, so I wasn't nervous about the process. It was unnerving, though, that I was older than most of the other unknown singers who were trying to move up to the next step of their careers. But the reality was that except for my two upcoming roles abroad and the supporting role and the cover jobs at the Met, I had no other income for the year. Nobody knew who I was, and I had no name—certainly not a memorable Western name.

In Western cultures today, sports fans will fearlessly tackle any name in any tongue. Chinese Houston Rockets basketball player Yao Ming, Japanese New York Yankees slugger Hideki Matsui, Korean Tampa Bay Devil Rays pitcher Jae Seo—nothing to it, and listen to the way the play-by-play announcers rattle them off. But opera fans are not yet so motivated. In the music world, even as more Asians move upon world stages, our names (with the exception of a cellist named Yo-Yo and a pianist named Lang Lang) remain difficult for Westerners to pronounce and to remember, although they'll remember a good performance or a bad one. Sometimes I think my name, at least to artistic administrators, is That-Chinese-Bass-Whom-We-Like-a-Lot. Many Chinese people routinely adopt Western first names, especially for business purposes. Only Luke the parrot and Martha's sister Diana address her anymore by her original name, Yinghwa (actually, even Luke calls for "Martha!" most of the time, unless he wants something really badly).

So what do you think—Hao Giovanni?

Back in 1988 after I won an international opera competition in New York, the head of the foundation came up with a whole list of names for me, most of them French. One of them, I recall, was Jean-Pierre Tienne. Beautiful. I am not French. Look at my face. I won the competition anyway. Sherrill Milnes, whom I first met at Opera Colorado, suggested I call myself Howard. "You know—Hao, short for Howard." But nobody thought I looked like a Howard. So he started calling me Mao Zedong. He still does. And Pavarotti always greeted me with, "Hey, Chinaman!" How about Ho Jo? I did not know then that Ho Jo was memorable to Americans as a nickname for the Howard Johnson restaurant chain. John Peking, as my first host family called me in Denver? Little Beijing? Little Deer? Big Old Yankee? I've been called so many things!

Just call me Tian. That's pronounced tee-EN, as in T. N. "What is your name?" people asked me the last time I arrived to sing at the Arena di Verona.

> "My name is Tian."
> "What is your first name?"
> "Tian."
> "Then what is your last name?"
> "Tian. My name is Tian. Just call me Tian."
> "Ah," they'd say and smile. "Tian!"
> And the next day, "*Buon giorno*, Tian!"
> Music to my ears.

The truth is, though, that whether or not our names are easily pronounced, basses rarely make a name for themselves. There is a saying in opera that the tenor gets the girl and the bass gets the role. Bass roles in opera are many, but almost always as supporting characters and not usually the sexy ones. Basses are old guys and bad guys, almost never the heroes who woo the (increasingly) beauteous sopranos. In almost all of the several dozen operas that are regularly performed, the starring roles are written for tenors and sopranos, followed by baritones and mezzo-sopranos, with the basses lagging at the bottom. Tenors hog the ranks of superstardom. Nobody has ever dared to organize a Three Basses concert. As rare as basses are in major roles, though, they command many more parts—more jobs—than other voices. Of the seventeen roles in Wagner's *Die Meistersinger von Nürnberg*, for example, nine of them are for the bass voice.

So the opportunities to sing are greater for a bass than for a tenor, in smaller or medium-size roles.

Alas, the rate of pay ranges downward from tenor to bass, unless the bass is an international star. Although singers do not generally discuss with one another what they are being paid, at the opera houses in the United States, the fees per performance now can range from fifteen hundred dollars to about thirty thousand dollars for principal roles. All the rates were lower when I began to perform these roles, but even a thousand dollars each time I sang sounded like a lot of money to me. Two years before this, after all, I was earning seventy dollars a night. Although I was alternately fearful of taking on such a financial responsibility and ecstatic at having the opportunity to make my own way, I knew soon enough that it was not likely to be a rich and luxurious life, superstar style. I began to book up quickly in the United States and in Europe, and the ex-penses of the traveling life mounted equally fast. True, I did not have to pay my airfare, even to go abroad, but the cost of housing was mine to bear. Usually I could get a long-term rate, since most con-tracts called for me to be available for at least a month. Nobody but me paid for Martha to come along, if she could take off from work. Imagine if we had children. Some singers who want to main-tain a sense of family life bring along their spouses, the kids, and even the nannies at their own expense. (Our current dog, Niu Niu, though quite the diva, and good old Luke do not require rooms of their own when they travel with us now, but that's another chapter.)

Also, I had to bear the full costs for my voice teachers (upward of one hundred fifty dollars an hour now), and if I wanted to work on a role before I got to the opera house, I had to hire my own coaches (upward of eighty dollars an hour) because they are a necessity for singers at every level throughout their careers. The human voice is a very subtle and sensitive instrument, and unlike a violin or a piano, you can't hear through your own ears the true sound you make so you constantly need expert "tuning." And you need a coach for delivery of the opera in each language and each role that you are hired to sing.

Normally, the agent's fee comes to 10 percent. And if I had to cancel a performance, for whatever reason—bronchitis, flu, the music is not right for my voice, I lost my voice, or I can't take the pressure—I will not get paid, no matter how much I have spent so far.

Then there are the taxes. If I sing in the United States, I pay as a self-employed person. If I sing in another country, especially in Europe, they take the taxes out of my payment, sometimes as much as 50 percent. What the amount turns out to be in dollars depends on those ever-fluctuating exchange rates (pay me in Euros now, please).

But don't cry for me, Argentina (or Italy, for that matter). Though it is also true that bass roles are usually the last to be signed—tenor and soprano roles are most often booked one to five years in advance, the bass maybe only months before the performance—we get our revenge in the end: the bass voice generally matures latest and lasts the longest. So what if I was already thirty-eight years old when I launched the next important stage of my career? I was in my prime. The lower voices are closer to the natural range of the human voice than are the soprano and the tenor, who push their sounds upward to unnaturally beautiful extremes. Going very low, as does the *basso profondo* voice, does not take such a toll. Perhaps that is why tenors and sopranos are paid more, because their voices are like rare metals, which can run dry, as happens when singers work too much at an early age. And if I sing less in most operas than do the starring singers, well, my voice may last that much longer. With care, skill, and health, this bass may well still be singing at a grand old age—as old as some of the characters I portray.

If you grew up in the Cultural Revolution, in the end it's having a voice that counts.

A Night at the Opera

WHAT IS SO refined about opera? It is an art form that gives vent to the messiest human passions—love, hate, revenge, agony, ecstasy, jealousy, and heartbreak. It can be raucous and boisterous and bloody and completely ridiculous, but is rarely lukewarm or vague. It is like life and human history, in which emotions run high and in the end things do not always work out. There are bad guys and good guys and evil can be more intense than good, but love, for better or for worse, is the most intense emotion of all. This is the same in Western opera as it is in traditional Chinese opera, no matter how different their forms of expression. In the modern world, in which opera audiences are growing larger and becoming younger (unlike other classical-music audiences), opera is a people's art form depicting what it feels like to be human, which means it is loving and bloody. And sometimes it even has a happy ending.

Yet in many places throughout history, opera has been the arena of the rich and the royal. In the grandest opera houses even today, it can seem that only aristocrats—in jewels and furs or jeans and sandals—can afford the most expensive seats. Teatro Colón in Buenos Aires, when I debuted there in 1997, had many season-ticket holders who were descendants of the Italian and French nobility who had settled in that city. I was singing the role of Mephistopheles in Gounod's *Faust*, one of the biggest and best bass roles in opera. Once before, in Singapore, I had sung this great French role of the devil to whom Faust sells his soul, but I had never expected to sing it in one of the most renowned opera houses in the world. I

Mephistopheles, in Gounod's Faust, *is one of the best bass roles in all of opera. The Teatro Colón production in Buenos Aires 1997 was truly spectacular. What I like about being a bad guy is that I have the opportunity to act out on the stage the evils I see happening in everyday life all over the world.*

prepared so hard, along with everyone in the cast. And yet, on opening night, right from the first arias I heard few people applauding. We were all so confused, until someone explained to us that the people in this opening-night gala audience, all dressed up in black tie and gowns, were wearing gloves that rendered the applause almost inaudible.

With all of its unlikely, heartbreaking, hilarious, passionate, and sometimes silly stories, I often think that my life is an opera. Perhaps we are all heroes in our own operas, in lives populated with lovers and friends and foes, and we express our hearts and aspirations in the beauty of song, if only in the shower and utterly off-key or just in our imagination. Opera has changing sets and settings and costumes and hairstyles, and so my life always seems to have unfolded in shifting scenes in different dress, different countries, and different languages. Once my full-time career in international opera took off, it was often hard to distinguish what was opera and what was the opera of my life. Operas for the stage can be edited, their music and their stories made more taut and true, and operatic musicians can practice to perfect their expression. The opera of my life changed scenes so rapidly; it had so many characters and storylines and subplots that sometimes made no sense, at least not to me.

There is nothing polite or genteel about the behavior of Italian opera audiences. Opera was born in Italy, and Italians, well-bred and otherwise, claim it as their own—and they demand to be pleased. They used to throw tomatoes, and they can still boo with a gusto that makes a performer cringe. They can also lift you to the heavens with their bravos. Which would it be for me?

In 1993, I made my European debut in Nice, France, where Italians arriving by the busload from the nearby Italian Riviera made up much of the audience. The opera was Verdi's *Ernani*. My role was Don Ruy Gomez de Silva, an old guy whom the beautiful, young Elvira is being forced to wed. In fact, I got the most enthusiastic applause I had ever received, which was such a wonderful relief on two levels. Making a good impression in my European debut was so important at this new stage of my career. But I'd also had such a bad time with the director that he punished me by not allowing me to appear—unlike anyone else in the cast—in stage makeup. I could not rely on the operatic facial dramatization to help me perform my role. I had to really sing.

It had started out so well. The young French director was clearly talented. He had wonderful ideas about how to stage this opera. This is a complicated and far-fetched story about conspirators against the king and the competition of three men for the same woman and an oath that Ernani, the hero, swears that he will kill himself if Gomez de Silva blows his horn, which in the end he does, of course. But the music is thrilling, and the director's ideas for dramatizing it in authentic seventeenth-century style, with period costumes, makeup, and even gestures from that time in Spanish history, were exciting.

I was in a very upbeat mood. It was May, and my hotel room looked out over the azure waters of the Mediterranean and a nude beach. Martha was not able to come until two days before opening night, but I made friends with the cast, one tenor in particular, with whom I walked along that beach every day to the opera house for rehearsals.

But one by one, all four of the performers in the major roles began to have conflicts with the director because of his tactless and often nasty manner of speaking to them. I tried to mediate the disputes, to restore the pleasant and previously productive rehearsal environment. Eventually, three of the principals and the director stopped talking to one another altogether. Then the director turned on me. We were in the third week of rehearsals when he came into my dressing room and told me, "I want you to change your face. You look too Chinese. Shave your mustache and goatee."

His unpleasant tone upset me. "I've been working hard to be completely in character in this role, but this is what I look like," I shot back.

"No," he said again. "You look too Chinese. I don't like the way that looks."

Deeply offended, I stormed off to the general director and demanded that he instruct this man to apologize to me. "When I signed my contract, you knew I was Chinese. I'm so happy I was hired. This is my European debut, and I'm trying my best to make it successful. I don't know what happened with this director."

He graciously apologized to me on behalf of the opera house and agreed that such a comment was out of line. He promised to speak to the director. The result was that the director stopped talking to me, too. So now there was silence between him and all the major performers, and the atmosphere during the last couple of days of rehearsal was grim. What a shame. He was really talented.

Then, right before the dress rehearsal, the director marched into my dressing room. "You must shave your mustache. I don't like the way you look," he declared with sneering hostility.

For a performer to shave facial hair is not an unreasonable request, but his manner was so offensive I could not consider it. He could have talked to me nicely; he could have discussed this with me. I would have thought it over.

"If you don't shave, I'll tell them not to make up your face," he said.

"Then I'll go on just like this," I retorted.

The makeup man was afraid to get near me for all of the performances. I wore my heavy velvet robe and my face disappeared under my nobleman's wig, except, perhaps, for my facial hair. So I guess I tried that much harder to be in character. The reviewers made much of my singing and failed to mention my ghostly face.

My voice is technically a *basso cantante*, which is a more flexible, more melodic voice than the deep, dark *basso profondo*, and it has a lighter, warmer color. King Philip, in Verdi's *Don Carlo*—whose major aria was my introduction to opera singing in my master class with Gino Bechi back in Beijing—is a *basso cantante* role. I am sometimes called a bass-baritone, although, as my current agent describes me, I'm really a bass with high notes. But there is no bass-baritone designation in Italian opera, and throughout my career I have most often sung the Italian repertoire, including almost every major bass role in Verdi's operas. Still, it took until the year 2000 before I was invited to perform on Italian soil, in Genoa, at the Teatro Carlo Felice. The opera was the rarely performed Verdi work *Jerusalem* (a French-language revision of his *I Lombardi*). It is a long opera, my role was hard to sing, and I ended up having to sing two performances only twelve hours apart—a certain death for the operatic voice, like having to pitch two nine-inning baseball games twelve hours apart. But I defied the odds and sang even better the second time. My reviews were great. I was the only Asian in the cast, and though my French diction was good, these performances did not test how well I would be received by Italians in their own zealously guarded language.

That opportunity came three months later, again in Genoa, where I sang the great role of King Philip, with which Gino Bechi had opened up the world of opera to me two decades before. *This* was a test, of the legacy of my first opera teacher—the first Italian opera teacher invited to Beijing after the Cultural Revolution—and all that I had learned since he predicted I would sing this role. Maestro Bechi was from Florence, and I tried to find him when

"I believe that sooner or later you will sing this role," the great Italian baritone Gino Bechi told me after he heard me sing *"Ella giammai m'amò,"* King Philip's aria from Verdi's Don Carlo. *It was the first homework he assigned me. Without ever hearing it, I learned this piece in four sleepless days. Twenty years later, I was the first Chinese singer to perform this dream role for bass here in Genoa, Italy.*

I first arrived in Italy. I discovered, to my sorrow, that he had died in 1993.

It was also a test of how I would be received as a Chinese singer in a classic Verdi role. Not only was this opera my Italian-language debut in Italy, it was also the first time any Chinese bass had ever sung the role of King Philip in Italy. I shared the role with the great Italian bass Ferruccio Furlanetto. Although he sang the initial performances, I did most of the rehearsals, since he arrived later. The reaction of the other performers was so interesting: even chorus members came up to tell me how much they liked my singing. Was this only because I had a good voice or because I was a Chinese singer who had a good voice?

One night just before my first performance, I took the costume I shared with Furlanetto and went onto the stage. All was dark. Nobody but Martha and our good friend mezzosoprano Marianne Cornetti, who were my audience of two, knew I was there. I wore headphones attached to a tape recording I had made during rehearsal.

As the music played, I walked through my role again and again, holding the costume to me. I was determined to get this right.

During the performance the next day, the audience reaction really touched me. The bravos continued nonstop. Even the chorus chimed in. I wish Maestro Bechi could have been there. Afterward, two Chinese students rushed backstage in tears to congratulate me on being so convincing in this great role. I was Chinese, and I was King Philip.

In 2003, when I showed up for rehearsals of Rossini's *The Barber of Seville* in Florence, immediately an Italian singer in the cast effused, "It is great that you are here." Translation: In this increasingly globalized opera world, once again in Italy I was the only Asian in the cast. One night, when I went home with this singer for dinner, he said to me, "Do you know how many Korean singers are studying in Italy? Over two thousand! Do you see any Korean names among the performers?" Koreans outnumber all other Asians among music students studying in the West. Out of curiosity, I later went online and searched through the performance rosters of a dozen opera houses throughout Italy. No Koreans. No Chinese. No Asians at all that season.

That Rossini opera, though, would turn out to be a real test of language skills for me. *The Barber of Seville* is a comic jewel of a crowd pleaser, which everybody knows at least from the famous "Figaro, Figaro, Figaro," sung by the boastful hero. My role was Don Basilio, the old singing teacher of the beautiful young Rosina and an accomplice to her guardian, old Dr. Bartolo, in his plan to marry her. She is in love with young Lindoro, however, who is actually Count Almaviva in disguise. This role, though not large, like all the other roles in this opera requires extraordinary vocal and Italian-language skills, involving not only florid arias but recitative, the vocal chitchat that mimics conversation and is all too easily understood by those who speak the native tongue. In these extended passages, my accent stuck out, as the saying goes, like a sore thumb. Everybody corrected me—the conductor, the other singers, the director, the coaches. It got so that I was almost afraid to open my mouth. Besides rehearsals, I worked on my diction with coaches for three to four hours each day; I recorded these sessions and then practiced additional hours on my own.

By the end of the first rehearsal week, I was a wreck. Martha was there and made me listen to her. Her message: *Que sera sera*. Whatever will be will be. "You are trying your best. If it doesn't work, then we go home. It isn't the end of the world."

Then the general director came to my rehearsal. He sat down not three feet in front of me and stared directly into my face. It was like my final exam. But at that moment I felt strangely unafraid. Martha was right, *Que sera sera*. I was more confident than I had been. Even I could hear that my diction had improved. "Keep up the good work!" he said, grabbing my hand, and then he sauntered confidently out of the room.

The most meaningful endorsement came the day after my first performance. I was walking over one of the beautiful bridges in Florence when a man on a motorbike screeched to a halt beside me. He lifted his helmet and said to me, in Italian, "Were you Don Basilio last night?"

"*Si.*"

"Oh! Can I shake your hand?"

"*Grazie.*"

I was invited back to sing the wonderful role of Sparafucile, the assassin in Verdi's *Rigoletto*, for the next season.

I did not have the chance to prove myself in the native language in Germany. At the opera in Bonn I had sung two operas in Italian to great success before being offered the principal bass role in Beethoven's German-language *Fidelio*, in 1996—and something went terribly wrong.

The opportunities at Bonn had come through none other than the hot-tempered Giancarlo Del Monaco, who had yelled at me so often in my horse-opera debut at the Met in 1991. At the same time that he was a much sought-after director, Maestro Del Monaco became the general manager of Oper der Bundesstadt in Bonn. Although I could not keep a cowboy hat on my face while stage-drunk, he nevertheless signed me afterward to a three-opera contract in Bonn. The first two went well—*Il Guarany* and *Don Giovanni*, both in the 1994–1995 season. Although Giancarlo (as I began to call him now that we were more familiar) did not direct that Mozart opera there, it was in his opera house that I had my Cultural Revolution suicide inspiration: when dying at the hands of Don Giovanni, I assumed the expression of that poor man who had jumped to his death in the Summer Palace.

Giancarlo himself directed me again at the Met in 1995, in Verdi's *Simon Boccanegra*. In my role as Pietro, a popular leader, I rally the crowd to support the former pirate Boccanegra to become the doge of Genoa. I then incite this horde—there must have been two hundred people onstage—to topple the statue of the current doge. Suddenly, I hear, "Stop! Stop! Stop!" It was Giancarlo, shouting again and running up onstage from the audience. "Everybody," he said, "look at Tian's gesture." I was instinctively waving my fist to the sky the way I had as a boy in rallies in Tiananmen Square during the Cultural Revolution: Down with the bourgeoisie! Del Monaco asked me to demonstrate this gesture for them all to copy, which I was thrilled to do—I was happier still to be on the right side of his emotions.

Giancarlo's offer that I sing Rocco in *Fidelio* was a great honor. Beethoven was born in Bonn, and this was the only opera he ever composed. It is a heroic opera in which Leonore, in disguise as the prison guard Fidelio, rescues her husband, Florestan, who is condemned to death for political crimes. Rocco is the jailer, whose daughter is in love with Fidelio (oblivious that he is a she). There is a lot of spoken dialogue in this opera, so I worked intensively with two internationally known German coaches at the Met, where I was singing before I was due in Bonn. Yet when I arrived for the first rehearsal, I could not find my name anywhere on the schedule. I was very confused. Giancarlo asked me to run through the Rocco role with the coach there. After about twenty minutes,

the coach called his boss and told him I was *sehr gut* ("very good").
I knew enough German to understand that. So Giancarlo asked to
hear me himself. He came down with a load of people from the
opera's artistic department. I started to perform the role again,
but after a few minutes I simply stopped. Something was not
right.

"I have worked on this role night and day for months," I said.
"Now I am here to do my job, and I find you have taken my name
off without explanation. I need to know why."

Giancarlo took me aside and said quietly, "You are a good
singer, Tian, but we have replaced you with a German singer. This
is a new production. Please understand."

"I have had this contract for a year!" I answered. "The only
right thing was to let me know before I started to prepare and
before I came all the way here!"

"We were so busy with so many operas. Yes, we should have
told you. Please understand the situation." Then he offered me the
much smaller role of Don Fernando, the king's minister, at the
same rate of pay.

I looked over at Martha, who had joined me earlier than usual
for those days. She had tears in her eyes. It was a terrible moment.
I could understand if they wanted a native German speaker in this
German role in Beethoven's German birthplace—but why had
they offered me the part in the first place? And why did they not tell
me that they had changed their minds? I did not understand the
politics of the decision. I still don't. That's opera. That's the roaring river of my life.

I accepted the role of Don Fernando halfheartedly.

At Giancarlo's suggestion, we took a week's vacation before
beginning rehearsal. Martha and I were both so upset, but a romantic week in Paris put our minds on other matters. The Fernando
role went well, and the opera later did offer me the role of Rocco,
but the scheduling did not work out. I have never sung the role, but
after all these years, I still can recite some of Rocco's dialogue.

Again and again, I have had to prove that a Chinese singer can
emote, can act, can understand the role, can master the language,

can understand the culture, can follow the conductor, and can love and comprehend the music. I had no Chinese singers to model myself after. I had to suffer these experiences alone. I did not grow up in a Western culture, but I studied it and lived it. I have plenty to pass on to the Chinese singers coming up now. I tell them, You have to work five hundred percent harder than Western singers to make your mark. You study, you learn, you make yourself better, you prove that you can do it, again and again. And if you do that always, they will come to see that you *can* do it. It is not easy for any opera singer to succeed. It is even harder for the Chinese singer. So try harder. It comes down to that: try harder.

In 1997, the offer to sing Mephistopheles in *Faust* in Buenos Aires— a role that a bass would sell his soul for—was a gift to me from a conductor whose mind had been closed to me the first time I sang for him. Michelangelo Veltri, an Argentinian of Italian heritage, had never worked with a Chinese singer before we met on the first day of rehearsal for *Aida* at the San Diego Opera in 1995, and he did not have high expectations. It is at the first musical run-through, with piano accompaniment, that the cast and the conductor meet for the first time and get to know one another. Maestro needs to know our voices and our abilities, and we have to know what he wants from us and how he approaches the opera. As I had done when I was younger, out-of-town singers often arrive the day before the work starts, sometimes after very long, exhausting travel, which can take a toll on the voice. Now I usually try to have a day or two to rest before beginning rehearsal, but that is not always possible.

At the Met we always begin first with staging rehearsals, which involve singing but not at full voice. Musical rehearsals do not begin for another two weeks. In San Diego, though, we started the musical run-through immediately. The general manager, much of the artistic staff, and the stage director were all present, and, of course, I was eager to present myself in best form, never having worked with any of them.

My role was Ramfis, the high priest of Egypt, who sings the very first note of this huge, dramatic Verdi opera. As soon as I opened my mouth, I could feel that my throat was not quite right. After only one sentence, Maestro Veltri stopped me to correct my diction and my pitch. He proceeded to stop me at every phrase. He became increasingly impatient. This kind of antagonism does not often manifest at the first rehearsal, and it had never happened to me. The air froze around me, and everyone felt the chill: the maestro did not like me. Again and again, he stopped me, as if I had never sung this role before, as if I had not prepared. It was humiliating. I think he had made up his mind that I would not be good, and my slightly rough throat at the start confirmed it for him. I had to stay calm and unflustered, all the while that I was screaming inside, I have prepared this piece a hundred times, I know the role. I have watched five versions of this opera on videotape. I have worked with a coach. I have talked to people who have directed this opera. So let us just work and let me show you what I have!

The rehearsal lasted three hours. I did not give up. I showed him. Afterward, with grace and dignity, Maestro Veltri came up to me and said, "I like your voice."

We became close friends. During an intermission of the second *Aida* performance, he summoned me to his dressing room to ask me whether I would come to Santiago, Chile, the next year, 1996, to sing in Dvořák's *Requiem*. I had not sung that magnificent music before, and I had never been to South America. I was delighted to accept. The majestic nineteenth-century Teatro Municipal was inspiring, and I enjoyed every single note I sang there. During the final rehearsal in Chile, Maestro Veltri, who had just been named the artistic director of Teatro Colón in Buenos Aires, asked me whether I would be interested in singing there. Of course! This is one of the most famous opera houses in the world—every great singer has sung there—and I think I would have been excited to sing any role.

"What opera would you like to sing?" he asked.

"How about *Faust*?" I suggested.

"Okay," he said idly, walking away.

Nothing further was said about it. Then, out of the blue, six months later a contract appeared—an impressively high fee, plus two business-class tickets, for Martha and me. We squealed like little children. We could hardly wait to get to Buenos Aires and work with Maestro again. Alas, a month before we departed, Maestro Veltri passed away from a brain aneurysm. He was only fifty-seven years old. The day after the opera opened in 1997, Martha and I carried roses to his tomb. We stayed there for a long time. We missed him. We left feeling that this wonderful gentleman and musician was resting peacefully.

The great lesson of my experience with Michelangelo Veltri, from those first awful hours onward, was how extraordinary a musical collaboration becomes when people overcome their cultural preconceptions about one another.

Another, equally important, theme was emerging: how strong and resilient grow the bonds between people who have, on the surface, only one thing in common: the love of opera.

The multicultural and multinational friendships Martha and I were making through our opera work grew like blood vessels to nourish and sustain us wherever we were. Now we have a worldwide family, a cast of characters in our personal and professional saga on whom we have come to rely. We find them everywhere. And, like many of the family members to whom we are related by blood, many of them follow us everywhere.

Most of these friendships I owe to Martha. People are drawn to her. I just sing for my supper. She draws the thread through our stories and makes sense of our lives.

After Martha left her research fellowship in New Jersey, the development of the Internet made it possible for her to do more of her work for the genetics journal while traveling with me, for which I was so relieved and grateful. Until she retired from her genetics career, though, she could spend only a few days at a time with me, usually arriving for the final dress rehearsal or opening night.

The first time I went to Bonn, in May 1994, I was so lonely. The opera was *Il Guarany*, a beautiful but rarely performed work in Italian by the Brazilian composer Carlos Gomes, a student of Verdi. Giancarlo Del Monaco mounted a brand-new production, directed by filmmaker Werner Herzog and starring Plácido Domingo. Of course, I was very excited to sing with Domingo again. I had just finished *The Pearl Fishers*, an opera by Georges Bizet, and had to rush to catch a plane from Seattle to Germany, where I had never been. New productions require more rehearsal time than usual, and I had to be there for two months; Martha could not be with me until performances began.

I arrived in Bonn at dusk, in a gloomy drizzle. I found my way to the private home where a tiny apartment had been rented for me. The place was below ground level and was very damp; the walls were moist. I just could not stay there. The owner, when I phoned him, explained in limited English that he could find me another place, but he had no time to take me there. I went out in the rain with my two heavy suitcases. The streets were dark and empty. I had no umbrella, and by now my clothes were wet. I felt like an outcast in a strange city with no friends and no one to help me find my way.

I knew I needed to change my despondent mood. I opened my mouth and out popped a popular song from the Cultural Revolution: "Chairman Mao's soldiers follow the Party's orders well. They go wherever they are needed and they settle down wherever there is hardship. When the motherland needs me to guard the pass, I will go there with my gun." The tune was energetic, light, and happy. I began to cheer up. I sang song after song for the whole hour it took me to find the apartment. This place was bigger, lighter, and drier.

Martha arrived with our English springer spaniel, Niu Niu, which means "Little Girl," as she was back then. Now an old lady who has grown deaf to my singing, Niu Niu is the only Chinese American dog I know of who learned to swim in the Rhine. She was my sweet, globe-trotting companion—never chewing on furniture or trampling on flower beds—who kept me from being too lonely when Martha had to return to New York.

Whenever Martha was present, though, we threw open our doors to the opera cast and to our growing cast of friends, often including the people we rented from or who opened their homes to

Peking duck is one of Martha's specialties, and everywhere we travel, ducks are hung out to dry. First they have to drain overnight. Then they have to dry again after Martha puts her special sauce on them. Finally they get cooked, standing up on racks that allow the fat to drain away. Martha serves the sliced meat in warm Chinese buns with hoisin sauce. Cleaning and hanging the ducks is my job.

us wherever we were. It seems like nothing for Martha to prepare the ingredients for a seven-course Chinese dinner, then rush off to see the opera, then bring back twelve or fourteen people to a dinner that she cooks on the spot. Peking duck is her specialty, for which she has to hang ducks to dry all night in our hotel rooms or rental units. It is so much a part of our ritual that I don't even notice it anymore, although visitors and housekeeping staff do.

At first, I was afraid to invite Plácido Domingo to our parties in Bonn. I had to convince myself that I was his colleague, not some hapless guy who couldn't handle a horse. He greeted me in Bonn with a laugh. "Tian, although you were the Indian last time, now it is my turn." His character was the leader of the Guarany Indians in Brazil, who has fallen in love with Cecilia, the daughter of Portuguese aristocrat Don Antonio—my role, and an unexpectedly good one at that. Domingo, as I have learned in the eight productions in which we have worked together since, never acts like the temperamental superstar that celebrity tenors have a reputation for. He puts his entire attention into the work and is a great singing and acting collaborator, not someone who is there to have the light shine upon his illustrious self while he belts it out.

I was very struck with Maestro Domingo's sensitivity, which comes through in his singing. Early on, in the lobby of his hotel, we were meeting with the conductor and the cast to talk about the music of *Il Guarany*. At first, I thought Domingo was distracted since his glance kept darting away, and he didn't seem to be listening to the conductor at all. Suddenly, he jumped up and dashed to the door, where there was a toddler who was about to become trapped in the revolving glass panels. He grabbed the boy and returned him to his parents, who apparently were not paying as much attention to their child as Plácido Domingo was.

After opening night, we all went to a restaurant across the street from the opera house. We ate, laughed, and drank. It was three in the morning when Domingo looked at his watch and said, "I have to go back to my room and get some sleep. I have to catch a plane to Monte Carlo in three hours. I have a rehearsal in the morning and a performance at night, which will be televised."

We were very apologetic for keeping him up so late, but he laughed and waved our regrets away with his big cigar. We asked which opera he was performing.

"No opera," he said, "a Three Tenors concert." So after three hours' sleep he would take the stage with Luciano Pavarotti and José Carreras, in the second of what would eventually be nine hugely popular concerts throughout the 1990s.

After Maestro Domingo took over the Washington National Opera in 1997, he brought the whole production and the original cast of *Il Guarany* to D.C. It was his debut as general director.

Martha has never stood on ceremony with Domingo, whom she addresses informally. To this day, he is still my Maestro and Martha's Plácido. In New York, during rehearsals of *The First Emperor* in 2006, he and the rest of the cast joined us for Thanksgiving at our apartment, where East met West. Martha prepared her Peking ducks, and Siu Li GoGwilt of the Met's artistic administration made the turkey. Maestro Domingo made particular friends with our bird Luke when he told a joke—about parrots—and Luke laughed louder than everyone else. Luke is the step-parrot of an opera singer, after all; he knows how to get the spotlight.

A dog, a parrot, and Peking ducks are loyal supporting players in our life's little dramas. Niu Niu was a world traveler, until flying in the cargo area became too stressful for her as she began to age. (Most European countries have no quarantine requirements, but Niu Niu did require a special visa to go to Argentina, provided upon proof of health and vaccinations.) Luke goes with us when we sometimes travel by car to perform in the United States. Once Martha made the five-hour drive to Washington, D.C., for a performance of *The Pearl Fishers*. Into the car she loaded Niu Niu, Luke, and four dead ducks, which she had already dried in New York. More than a dozen of our Denver friends had come to see me perform—some have joined the retinue that travels with us around the world—and, of course, Martha was planning a party afterward. She

Even a diva like Niu Niu has to practice. She looks about as happy as I felt when I was a child being forced to play the beast with eighty-eight teeth. Niu Niu is very sensitive to voice quality. After hearing beautiful singing, she barks her bravos. So-so singing leaves her silent.

came backstage before the opera began and told me everything would be okay because although the ducks required three and a half hours to cook, they were already in the oven, and since the opera lasted only two and a half hours, she could get everything on the table as soon as we came back. She left them cooking in the hotel? That's all I could think about while I was onstage. I kept hearing fire alarms going off and fire trucks shrieking through traffic as our hotel burned down. My performance was fine, the party was fun, and the ducks were cooked to perfection.

"Do you think we keep Tian here because he's a good singer? Ha! It's because of your cooking," Jonathan Friend, the artistic administrator at the Met, told Martha as he stuffed a spring roll in his mouth.

I don't remember when our backstage Chinese New Year party became an annual tradition at the Met. Probably it was around the mid-nineties, when Martha became my full-time boss and full-time wife, my personal manager, my chief professional critic, and my social organizer, before adding opera producer to her list of credentials. She left behind the worlds of science and business, in which she had had a brief fling. One year we started to put up Chinese decorations on the mirrors and serve up a Chinese buffet. Martha cooked all day, and I ran back home to chop vegetables, stuff dumplings, and help to carry all the food over.

"I love your cooking!" Maestro Levine uttered earnestly after one of Martha's feasts, then later sent his assistant to bring him another helping. He was conducting Verdi's *Un Ballo in Maschera* (*A Masked Ball*), in which I was singing, along with Luciano Pavarotti, when the Chinese New Year fell that year. Pavarotti grabbed five spring rolls and took them off to his dressing room, to be sure they would not disappear while he was onstage. He promised he would not eat them until after the performance. Singers are picky about what and when they eat on performance days. Most will not eat anything for several hours before they sing or at least will avoid spicy food. (I eat only pasta with olive oil and salt, five hours before the performance, a regimen I learned from an Italian singer.) So when, another year, Maestro Domingo swallowed a spring roll as he headed off to his dressing room after the first act of Verdi's *La Forza del Destino* (The Force of Destiny), I got worried. Martha puts ginger and scallions and all sorts of spicy things in her spring rolls. My God, I thought, what if he chokes on it during his big aria in the second act? I stood beside the curtain, listening to his singing and praying that Martha's delicacies stayed quietly in his stomach. Domingo was in exceptionally fine form that night. As the audience clapped and shouted, I understood that Martha had put magic in that spring roll.

I have been part of the Met family since 1991. I have sung there every season, well over three hundred times. Most of my scenes in operas have taken place at the Met, and most of the operatic scenes of my life have taken place in and around the Met.

I used to dream about Maestro Jimmy Levine's eyes. This started during rehearsals for *La Forza del Destino*, the same year that Domingo downed the spring roll before going onstage. I sang the first note in this opera, and I kept missing the beat in rehearsal. I was fine after I finished this first phrase, but I just couldn't get the beat. This occurred during the period in my early career when I was so sensitive and nervous about doing something wrong. I started to take over-the-counter sleeping pills, and although they would not necessarily put me to sleep, at least not for long, they made me drowsy the next day, which in turn made me nervous about my voice and my performance. To cue a singer, Maestro Levine will look up from the orchestra, as he did for me when conducting *La Forza*. He was and is such a great conductor. He is always nice to singers and never has fits of temper. I wanted to deliver my best for him. He never lost patience each time I blew the cue, but in my sleeping-pill-befogged dreams, all I saw were his eyes, his eyes, his eyes.

When I did finally get the beat, Maestro Levine looked up from the orchestra and smiled.

I was so shy with the Met's big stars in the beginning. But as my experience with Pavarotti in 1993 showed me, there can be great care and collegiality among the singers associated with this opera house. I learned tricks of the bass trade from the likes of Samuel Ramey and Paul Plishka. Ramey shared a trade secret after we rehearsed a brief duet we had in the 1993 *I Lombardi*. My character has the first few phrases of the duet, and Ramey suggested, since I was going first, that I step into the place on the stage where the acoustics were best, and my voice would carry throughout the whole house—the sweet spot that he could have kept for himself.

Paul Plishka taught me how to fall on the floor without killing myself the first time I sang in *Turandot*. I took over the role of old Timur from him. There is no opportunity to rehearse onstage with the rest of the cast when you step in for another singer, as I often do. I have to watch the performance very carefully beforehand and hope that I can mimic the steps and the moves. Having to go on blind was very scary for me the first time—doubly so since Timur is blind. *Turandot* is Puccini's "Chinese" opera, in which man-hating Princess Turandot has all of her suitors executed if they fail to answer her three riddles, which, of course, they do. Calaf, the hero, foolish prince, is determined to woo and win her, which in the end he does, but not before Turandot causes him—and me—a lot of trouble. Timur, from Tartary, is Calaf's father, a king in disguise, who during the third act is captured by Turandot's guards and dragged onto the stage, where they throw him harshly to the ground. How should I execute this fall without killing myself? During one intermission, I went to Paul's dressing room and asked for his advice. Immediately, he led me onstage to show me, even though stage hands were busy changing the sets for the next scene.

"Be sure to tell the two guards just to make the gesture of pushing," he said, "and you fall by yourself so that you don't get hurt. But you have to make it look like they really pushed you." He tried to explain the move, but I couldn't picture it. So he acted it out for me, with me being the guard. He threw himself forward as if flying and fell with a loud thud, which he actually accomplished by surreptitiously slapping his hands on the floor. It looked like—but only looked like—a bad fall.

I did exactly what he said. My agent did not know that I had worked with Paul. "They are killing my singer!" he fretted silently from the audience the next night.

I was Paul's cover for that Timur role, and he was my cover on the days I sang the role. My performances went well for another reason: Teresa Stratas, the magnificent soprano who sang the role of the devoted slave girl Liu. She was such a great singing actress that by her side I truly became a sightless king wandering in a foreign land in search of my son—I was so thoroughly into the role that I forgot I was onstage. She brought me to a higher artistic level, as did Renée Fleming in 2005 the first time I sang with her. The opera was Jules Massenet's *Manon*, and I sang the role of Count des Grieux, the father of the tragic heroine's lover. We had not had a chance to rehearse together before I stepped into the role, and yet Fleming as Manon brought me so naturally and skillfully into it that our duet became one of the most unforgettable singing experiences of my career.

Only major opera houses in the world can afford to pay singers to stand by, so that the show can go on no matter who backs out at the last minute. Sometimes even the cover has a cover. Of course, I, too, have covers for my roles. One time when I was singing the king of Egypt in *Aida*, I suddenly came down with the flu. I had never canceled a performance in my career, but this time I was in really bad shape and decided that I had better alert the artistic department, so they could at least warn my cover. They called me right back and said that he was sick, too. So I phoned him and he said, "Oh Tian, I am so sick," and he coughed three times.

I said, "Oh, brother, I am so, *so* sick," and I coughed four times.

We went back and forth a few more times until he won the cough contest, my heart went out to him, and I went on that night.

There is no reason why opera cannot be accessible to more people and more cultures. Everybody has stories that could be set to music, and everybody, I'll wager—even in Chinatown in Buenos Aires—has considered selling his or her soul for some price.

We always locate the local Chinatown wherever we are, to try the restaurants and find markets where Martha can shop for her ingredients. In the big cities—Paris, London, Amsterdam, San Francisco, Toronto, and even Florence—there are sizable Chinese areas. In Lisbon, it took me five hours, but I found the small Chinatown there. I was happy to find one Chinese grocery store in Bonn. "Are you Chinese?" I asked the proprietor cheerfully. "No, I'm not Chinese," he snapped at me in very good Chinese.

In the small Chinatown in Buenos Aires, we were shocked to discover how cut off they were from mainstream life. Martha and I made many friends in the shops we frequented. When I told them I was singing at Teatro Colón, they looked lost. So it occurred to Martha—why not?—to invite a number of them to the final dress rehearsal of *Faust*. They all worked so hard and deserved to know what went on outside their own lives. More than a dozen restaurant and grocery-store workers showed up in their best clothes, which, of course, were no match for the finery of the Teatro Colón habitués, even for the dress rehearsal. Martha showed them around the elegant opera house, with all of its marble statues and columns, and tried to ease their awkwardness. She explained to them the whole story of the opera. Afterward, she brought them backstage to my dressing room. I could tell from their faces that this was an experience of a lifetime.

I think they could probably tell from mine that this was a great moment of my own life, with my own people, in yet another foreign land.

16

Playing the Devil in China

I BECAME A U.S. citizen in 1995, but I don't think I really felt like an American until September 11, 2001. Along with everyone else in New York, and probably the whole country, I took the horrific attacks and loss of life very personally.

The decision to change my citizenship was both practical and emotional. As an international opera singer, it is far more convenient to travel on a U.S. passport, with which I require few visas and I can get from engagement to engagement with less hassle. For a Chinese citizen to travel from country to country, the paperwork is voluminous, the wait interminable, and in the mid-nineties there was no European Union to simplify the process. As I had learned when I first traveled to Europe for my master class with Carlo Bergonzi, being from a Communist country could grind the process to a halt. Now, although I have to apply for a work permit to sing in Italy and Germany, it's a breeze to travel in and out of the United States—except when I'm traveling to China. Now I, too, require a visa to return to the country of my birth, a procedure that was a lot slower in the mid-nineties than it is now. When I get to China, I have to be admitted as a foreigner, which feels peculiar. Sometimes I think the agents look askance at me when they notice my place of birth on my U.S. passport.

But the day I pledged allegiance to the United States of America and became a naturalized citizen, and later joined with the other new Americans to sing the national anthem, I had such a mix of strong feelings. Talk about the American dream—I have had all my dreams come true in the United States. All that I have seen and experienced and contributed has proved to me that it was good to come, and to stay. I came to this country because of opera. I won Martha because of opera. I have so many friends in the United States and all over the world because of opera. Had I remained in China, would I have entered into the world of opera? Would I have been embraced by it?

But China is my motherland. My parents were born there and their parents before them. Never forget your roots, a Chinese saying goes, and my feelings for the country of my birth were and are just like those for family members, a lineage from which I developed that gave me the base for who I am. It is an ancient culture, and I can never escape from it, even if I wanted to. Every piece of news from China, no matter how good or how bad, lodges in my heart. It always will. I have had such great expectations for China, hoping that it will do so well and contribute to the world. I have these feelings still. And maybe I can help in my way.

In America, though, I have the freedom of expression that I must have as a person and as an artist. I don't have to worry about wiggling my hips. I can create and perform as I please. Criticism comes from critics—whom I can ignore—not from the government.

I am an artist, not a politician. Can artists be above politics? Should they be? Many artists claim that they stand outside politics and maintain their own freedom of thinking, creating, and developing their individual, original point of view. Yet from an opposite perspective, one of my composer friends opined, "Tian, let me tell you: playing music, playing art, it is the same as playing politics. The arts can never be separate from politics."

I don't know. I feel that the arts must always be independent. The arts must speak for themselves—but that very statement would have branded me a counterrevolutionary during the Cultural Revolution.

My one irreversible criterion for myself as an artist and as a person is that I must never do anything against my conscience. Although I became a U.S. citizen in 1995, it never occurred to me to vote (to the dismay of my American friends) until 2004. I had always felt that ultimately, it never really makes a difference which regime is in power. But then came the unconscionable war in Iraq. I think I finally understood that voting against the war was something that I could do for my country and myself. My American friends are always trying to convince me that if everybody voted, things could change.

Violence goes against my conscience. That was the tragedy of June 4, 1989, six years before I became a U.S. citizen, which Americans call the Tiananmen Square massacre and Chinese call the June Fourth Incident—the bloody violence against civilians and soldiers and innocent people on every side.

I had left China during the Anti–Spiritual Pollution campaign in 1983, but the pendulum soon began to swing the other way again. In the mid-eighties, China seemed to be genuinely opening to the world, culturally and economically. More and more foreign companies were launching branches in China; books published there seemed to embrace a wider range of subjects; newspapers actually reported the news. Gone was the single voice, the single tune, the single red color of the Cultural Revolution. It seemed that people could think more independently and exchange opinions to get a broader view of the world. But political movements could spring up suddenly, with or without apparent justification. When the 1989 protests began that led, two months later, to the tragedy that happened in Tiananmen Square, my family and friends inside China were extremely cautious talking on the telephone when I called. Living outside China, I found it difficult to get an accurate understanding of what was going on there.

On the morning of June 4, Martha and I turned on CNN as we sat down to breakfast. We saw the tanks in Tiananmen Square and heard the sounds of gunfire. I threw down my chopsticks and put my head in my hands. How could this be? Our phone started to ring. Everybody had a different opinion about what was happening and why. The news from the official Chinese media and the U.S. media and rumors among Chinese people in the United States and in China were so conflicting. Were hundreds of civilians injured and killed, or was it tens of thousands? I could follow the events only through the Western media, until those sources were no longer permitted to broadcast from China. To me, whatever the specifics were, it was all a horrible tragedy. In Denver, there must have been close to a thousand Chinese people gathered in front of City Hall when Martha and I arrived there later that day, needing to be among our people, all so solemn and sad. Some people hid their faces under their hats, afraid to be recognized. I understood that feeling, having come through the Cultural Revolution. Some people were carrying banners. Just as I had been back in Beijing, because of my loud voice, I was selected to shout slogans, and I believed absolutely in these three: "No violence!" "Peaceful solutions!" "No more tragedies!"

At this gathering I ran into a good friend of mine, a graduate student from Beijing. He held a poster in his hand that said, "Support the Students." I was surprised to find him here because he had become indifferent to politics in China. He and his parents had been treated very badly during the Cultural Revolution. Now he was single-mindedly devoted to his own work and his family. Martha and I drove him home afterward, and he remained silent throughout much of the ride. Then he said, dourly, "I think this is the last time I will take part in any political movement." That statement has been simmering inside me ever since.

A few weeks later, I joined ten thousand people who gathered in San Francisco for a protest concert. When at first I hesitated after the principal organizer asked me to participate, he broke into frustrated tears. "We have pop stars from Taiwan and Hong Kong. Why won't anybody from Mainland China dare to stand up and express his feelings? I just can't understand you!" I was moved by his emotion and promised to sing. But so many of us from the mainland had families back there. What would happen to them if we were recognized? What would happen to us when we returned?

On the plane back to Denver, I wondered whether this was the last time I, too, would take part in a political movement. Politics leaves the bodies of its victims strewn on all sides.

In the aftermath of June 4, 1989, and my change of citizenship, I continue to have a natural emotion for the country I came from. Despite the realities of life under Mao, especially during the Cultural Revolution, I had learned to love life there. I can express these feelings most directly and naturally in the old songs of China, which I love to perform.

Mostly, I just wanted to sing, anywhere, everywhere—and all over China, too. I wanted badly to bring opera to China, but our scheme to help opera in China—specifically, to support the Central Opera in Beijing—backfired on Martha and me.

On a brief trip to Beijing, shortly after we were married in 1991, Martha and I visited the Central Opera House, which had fallen upon hard times. The Central Opera was the first opera house established in Beijing after 1949. It was where my Auntie Fang—the first Chinese soprano to sing the role of the doomed Violetta in Verdi's *La Traviata*—sang throughout her career, and where she was tortured during the Cultural Revolution. Although she never sang again, she ultimately returned there as a director.

When Martha and I visited, we met the opera's principal conductor, Zheng Xiaoyang, who is legendary in my homeland. She had trained in Russia and became the first female conductor ever in China. At a dinner at her home, we were joined by veteran opera singers from the company. All of them told us, so sadly, that opera had no future in China. It wasn't a lack of talent. There was no money. China was undergoing rapid economic reforms, all of which were focused on industry and agriculture. There was hardly any investment in culture. Even the budget they had previously received from the Culture Ministry narrowly covered the overhead. In the newly emerging market economy, where was the market in opera? Without developing their own financing, they would not survive. They could barely produce any operas. All they wanted now was enough money to stage two or three operas, each with two or three performances, in a given year. That was hardly an extravagant wish. It got Martha and me thinking, Could we find a way to provide this financing?

Two years later, early in 1993, when I made my singing debut in Beijing, I saw that there was huge interest in this kind of music—in other words, a potential "market" to be tapped.

It was a triumphal day for me, returning as a full-fledged opera singer to the city from which I had quietly disappeared ten years before. The event was a recital featuring the great baritone Sherrill Milnes and the Central Philharmonic Society—the very same organization with which I had begun my musical career right out of the Beijing Boiler Factory. In front of the packed audience, the TV cameras, and the orchestra players, so many of whom were my friends from long ago, I limped onstage.

I had tumbled down the stairs in the darkened Beijing Music Hall auditorium during rehearsal that morning and spent the afternoon in the hospital with a bunch of bruises and a slight concussion.

Ten years after I left Beijing, I returned to make my singing debut there in a concert featuring the great baritone Sherrill Milnes, who has always referred to me as Mao Zedong. Here we sing a duet. My old Central Philharmonic Society orchestra played. Would you know from this picture that I had spent the morning in the hospital after falling down a flight of stairs during rehearsal?

I was sure I would not be able to sing. Martha, who up to this moment in our years together had never pushed me, changed her style this time. Nothing was broken, and there was nothing wrong with my voice. "It's only pain," Martha scoffed, when I listed my multitudinous aches. "You will never get over the pain you will feel if you miss this opportunity."

I rose to the challenge, and to the spirit of the moment, when I sang "O Tu Palermo," that rousing beauty of an aria from Verdi's *I Vespri Siciliani* that overflows with emotion for the homeland. Then, in Chinese, I sang "My Dear Motherland," with a soprano. I was in musical bliss, raising my voice in song in the city of my birth. My mind was spinning. I felt no pain from the fall (although I had to cancel the first of three subsequent appearances with the Philadelphia Orchestra, to which I flew the next day, and where I couldn't stand up upon arrival).

I had never experienced such a reaction from any audience. After the recital, there was such a roar that we could not even continue our encores. The newspapers raved, and the broadcast kept rerunning on television and radio.

Opera did have a future in China. Martha and I were absolutely certain of that now. It was time to do something for the Central Opera, we agreed. But what?

It seemed meant to be—*yuan*—when a young scientist and his wife soon approached us in New York City with a business proposition. It was an idea, we believed after considerable research and deliberation, that could produce the income necessary to support the Central Opera.

And so our nightmare began.

"Deputy Mayor of Tianjin meets with Dr. Liao Yinghwa [Martha] and Dr. Tian Hao Jiang from America." Again and again, I suffered deep shame when I heard myself described as "Doctor" along with my legitimate PhD wife. Now, in the fall of 1993, I was in China watching the TV newscast of the founding of our Sienna—Xiya, in Chinese—cosmetics factory in Tianjin, a large city southeast of Beijing. Because I had been singing at the Met, I arrived a few days after Martha's foot pushed the spade into the ground to lay the foundation for our joint venture with our Chinese partners. Martha named the company Sienna in part because she had been so struck by the beauty of Siena, Italy, when we visited—a quality the cosmetics we were about to begin manufacturing under her leadership would impart to the women of China, maybe even of the world.

Martha was the chairman of the board of Sienna Biotech Company. I was the vice chairman. Our local partner in Tianjin would not hear of it when I said that he absolutely could not introduce me as "Dr."

"I am just a singer," I protested.

"You *must* be a scientist, because you are the vice chairman of this company," he insisted, as he proceeded to introduce me the way he wanted.

The cornerstone was barely laid, and already things were out of control.

Martha and I had no business experience at all when we first stepped into this three-year venture. And in China, where state-run businesses were converting to private management in a market economy, and entrepreneurs were stepping into a whole new world for them, nobody yet had solid market-economy experience. Our three years in business manufacturing and selling a line of beauty products added up to a lesson in what we should have known in the first place: this is not for us.

The Chinese couple who approached us in New York had been interested in Martha's background in biochemistry and her people skills. Like Martha, Mr. Zhang was a biochemist. Mrs. Zhang had an American graduate business degree, with a specialty in marketing. They had both received undergraduate degrees from Nankai University in Tianjin and had a lot of contacts there. They developed proposals and plans and found a local enterprise with which to partner in Tianjin. Our partners were the farmers from a village outside of Tianjin, which contributed village-owned farmland to this profit-making enterprise, in exchange for 49 percent of the ownership of the company. We and the Zhangs raised the money, which was not difficult, since it seemed that everybody we knew wanted to invest in Chinese enterprises at the time. The Zhangs moved back to China to manage the business. Martha and Mr. Zhang together developed the skin lotions for the product line. The four of us had the factory built, purchased all the equipment and the raw materials in the United States, and even sent over two cars.

When I say "we," I really mean Martha. I was a full-time opera singer. Martha was a genetics journal editor and a startup cosmetics company board chairman who had a husband who traveled around the world singing opera and whom she often accompanied, although more and more of our time together she spent in our lodgings sending faxes. Of course, for a business like this to work, you have to put a hundred percent of your time and energy into it, partners or no partners, and this lesson was among the many we eventually learned. Somehow, though, Martha did manage to oversee the development and the improvement of the products and the design of the packaging. We were quite satisfied with the quality and the aesthetics of the products. Not so with the capability or the honesty of the factory workers or the sales force, or the manner of doing business in China. We were hardly ever there, and from afar we could assert no influence over our hopelessly ineffective local management. Mr. Zhang was a good and honest man, but he and his wife tried to play by the rules of business that they had learned in the West, combined with a very different way of getting things done in China.

As China began its historic, and historically fast, growth spurt, everybody had ideas about how work is done and money is made in a market economy. Commercial and political alliances, often one and the same in China, have never been direct and to the point, as Westerners expect. Developing the relationships comes first, and maintaining face remains uppermost.

Especially in the smaller cities in the countryside or the new enterprise zones, the new "rules," such as they were, could be anything but straightforward. The workers in our factory were the villagers who had previously worked on the farms. They felt free to disappear at any time, and they went home for two hours for lunch. And they helped themselves to the merchandise.

By 1994, we had sales counters set up in top-quality stores in Tianjin, Beijing, and Xi'an. But the salesgirls, we discovered to our dismay, had received no training about the products, how to approach the customers, or how to demonstrate the creams and the lotions. The man we had hired to oversee the training, who talked a good game in the interview, turned out to have no training plan. All the samples that we had sent him ended up locked in his cabinet, where we finally found them when we came over to try to take charge of the chaos.

What he was good at was having relations with the salesgirls he hired.

Our Sienna line of women's skin care products began to appear in high-end Chinese department stores in 1994. Unfortunately, it was not a profit-making business for us, a research geneticist and an opera singer. It was our expensive lesson in learning where we belong.

So Martha, who had never sold a product in her life, took over the training of the salespeople at the counters. I videotaped her at the counter in Tianjin, dressed in her lovely clothes and surrounded by curious customers while she explained the special qualities of the products and with a radiant smile showed people how to apply them. The products flew off the counters as the cash flew into the hands of the sales staff. Yet inexplicably, despite all the practice sessions, no one managed to keep a record of the sales or the products.

There was no accounting at all, at any level, despite the attempts of our company's chief accountant to get control. He instituted a system, and when people refused to follow through, they turned on him and damaged his reputation. He was an honest man, which never worked to his advantage. When we could not get our cars released from customs and officials demanded payment, he complained bitterly about graft and corruption. So one day people from the customs office showed up and announced to one and all, "Someone here is saying that we are taking graft. I am here today to determine who is spreading this rumor. He is breaking the law if we can find no proof of corruption. If he is committing the crime of slander, we will take him away and charge him." Fortunately, somebody stepped up to ask for forgiveness on behalf of the company, and the affront was smoothed over. And the company paid the two thousand yuan, whether it was truly owed or not, to get the cars out of impound.

One day I flew to Tianjin to take part in a ceremony commending our company and nine others as the top ten joint ventures in the municipality. But once I got there, I realized that including Xiya in this list made no sense, since our investment was not so large and the company had not made a profit. It did not take long to find out that somebody from our company had paid money to be included in this group. I was the one who had to go onstage and accept the trophy.

Sometimes the products and the money all disappeared. Once, one of our sales managers left the factory for Xi'an with thousands of jars and bottles of various products and was never seen again. But a couple of weeks later we discovered our cosmetics with different labels appearing all over Xi'an. Apparently, our agent had sold the merchandise to a local enterprise, taken our money, and fled.

Martha had trouble rebuking people so, with my bass voice, I became the heavy, at which I am more effective onstage. One staff member continually altered the receipts for her business trips, so what started off as one hundred yuan ended up as one thousand or ten thousand. We had to fire her, but nobody in the company had ever been fired and no one would do it. Even I ended up confronting her only with, "We hope you leave this company," instead of "You're fired, you snake." On another visit, Martha asked me to deal with some of the workers who were playing cards on company time. Even before I finished, one of the women raised her hand. "Mr. Tian, can you sing a song for us? And please don't be so angry." The rest of them burst into laughter.

Throughout much of this period, I was singing in Bonn and at the Met. I carried my own fax machine with me everywhere. Sometimes there was good news from Tianjin, especially about consumer reaction to our products and to the big stores' desire to stock our products. But mostly it was bad news. In my dreams I can still hear the squeak, squeak, squeak of the old rolls of fax paper scrolling one slow line at a time, each line signaling trouble, trouble, trouble. The other night vision that won't go away is of Martha being surrounded by people saying such sweet words so very courteously, then sneering at her once her back is turned.

We were sheep among wolves.

Still, we thought at the end of two years, we've survived this long; maybe the worst is behind us. We had been talking to another company in Kaifeng, a major city in Henan province that is known for its pharmaceutical industry, both the legitimate and the counterfeit varieties. Mrs. Zhang had made contact with a factory that was undergoing transformation from being a state-run to a privately owned enterprise. They talked about a joint venture in which we would provide the technology and they would provide the factory and the marketing of legitimate pharmaceutical products. Martha went to Kaifeng to discuss how to develop a joint business, but all anyone wanted to do was dine, drink, dance, and sing at karaoke bars. She had to dance with the mayor, sing with the deputy mayor, and drink with the head of economic development and the head of local industry and commerce. But nobody ever wanted to solidify his or her promises. They just wanted to party.

Martha hated it but kept it up for months. Then the mayor of Kaifeng was removed from office for unknown reasons, and the others were transferred or changed jobs. Mrs. Zhang's response was, "We have to go back to Kaifeng and make more friends there."

Martha's response was, "No."

Then Mr. Zhang got arrested, on a grudge.

It all started when Mr. Zhang began to have problems with his assistant, a former classmate of his from Nankai University. Even though the man was at a very high level in the company, in the West it would have been possible for the board of directors or trustees to fire him. But here nobody would do it; this man had too many political connections in Tianjin, and they were afraid of making enemies. The people who reported to this guy refused to do their jobs if he wasn't let go, however. So I did the deed myself, by phone. I deepened my voice and fired him.

A few weeks later the man showed up at the Tianjin office with a bunch of policeman and accused Mr. Zhang of tax evasion. They had no warrant or other documents that would be required in the United States. They took away the office equipment, the files, and Mr. Zhang. From New York, we telephoned all of our connections in Tianjin and Beijing. It took us two days, but they finally released Mr. Zhang without charging him. He left China immediately and returned to the United States (although he's happily back in business in China today).

All production at Sienna-Xiya stopped. Ultimately, we sold the business to the head of the local company, who was decent enough to offer us a small sum of money, although he could have had it for nothing. Throughout the three years, he had tried to do his best as everything spun out of control. We looked on the bright side. We were so relieved to be out of this. Even today, say Xiya or Sienna, and we'll get a headache and then get over it and feel so good that it is gone.

Martha is a scientist-administrator-producer. I'm a singer. People frequently come to us and ask us to invest or go into business in China, but we have learned our lesson. Talk to us about music. Talk nonprofit—a term that is not yet in the Chinese business vocabulary, not even among arts administrators (as we learned a decade later when trying to raise money in China to commission the opera *Poet Li Bai*, our beautiful treasure of a work).

There is an obscure Chinese saying that I recently learned: Southerners don't dream of camels; northerners don't dream of elephants. In other words, a dream needs to be anchored to the realities of time and place. So I will add this: Businessmen don't start a company in order to produce operas. We made not a cent for the Central Opera or for ourselves. The Central Opera is still struggling. In 2003, I gave the new general director this very Western advice: create fund-raising and marketing departments and make their activities primary to your endeavors; raise money in China and around the world. (In the spring of 2007, Peter Gelb, who was just about to take over the reins of the Metropolitan Opera, gave a talk to a packed audience at the Shanghai Conservatory of Music. Gelb was there for the workshop performances of *The First Emperor*, which had been "outsourced" to China. The budding Chinese arts administrators in the audience were interested in how to make a profit staging operas. Even the Met, with thirty-eight hundred seats and ticket prices ranging from fifteen to over five hundred dollars, cannot survive on ticket sales alone, Gelb responded, according to reporters who were present. Chinese arts institutions will need to develop patrons of the arts to provide funding. "As China explores ways to embrace opera and classical music, it is necessary to learn the economics: they're not favorable," he said, with a knowing laugh.)

Yet opera and classical music in China *are* prospering, as is my career there, as long as Martha and I stick to our own business.

*　*　*

Perhaps, for me, the best thing to come out of the Sienna-Xiya years was my first solo CD. *Over the Ocean* was a recording of my favorite Chinese songs that I made with my old friends at the Central Philharmonic Orchestra. I'd been planning this for years, and I finally managed to book the orchestra and a recording studio for four days in May 1994. I arrived from New York and got sick almost immediately, which is always a risk with the physical stress of frequent air travel and jet lag. But the studio had been booked, and this was a very important project for the orchestra. They were counting on me, and we could not reschedule. We were supposed to rehearse and record three songs each on the first two days, and four songs each on the last two days.

In bed in my hotel, I was running a high fever, my joints ached, and I had no energy to move. The recording engineer was my old friend from the Central Philharmonic, an oboist, whom I referred to as Xiao Di, Little Brother. He insisted that Martha get me up and bring me to the studio. He had worked extremely hard to set this up and to work with the musicians on orchestration. I had to show up, he insisted, if only to demonstrate to everybody that I was really sick. Martha was on his side. For the second time, she was heedless of my protestations. If I didn't rise to this occasion, it might never happen again, she told me in no uncertain terms.

The orchestra bided its time while I lay sprawled on a sofa in the waiting room.

After about half an hour, the bassoon player, a qigong practitioner, came in and asked whether he might do some "energy work" on me. I'd never much believed in the Chinese traditional or alternative healing systems, but what was I going to do? So he proceeded, for half an hour, to run his hands slowly above and around my body and to draw away whatever bad energy was afflicting me, which I thought was pure baloney—until I started to feel better again. I tried my voice, and it was sort of there, but I did not want to record in that condition.

Xiao Di and Martha were furious with me. "I'm going to kill you!" said he.

"You have to try!" said she.

It was a plot against me.

The orchestra ran through each song until they were ready. I joined them only on the final take. Martha and Xiao Di, jumping up and down with glee in the control room, gave me a thumbs-up sign.

The second day I was worse than the first. Before dawn, I awoke with my throat swollen closed and my fever registering 102 degrees. We called in an ear, nose, and throat specialist. The diagnosis was tonsillitis. He told me I must not sing for a week. Xiao Di did not believe me when I phoned him. "You told me the same thing yesterday," he said.

"I'll come kill you when all this is over," I rasped.

Even Martha was not convinced that I would be able to sing that day. Finally, the doctor agreed to treat me using ultraviolet lights, a method that is used in China to shrink the tonsils. I could hear the tissues sizzling. Back in the studio, the bassoon player—qigong practitioner took a look at my throat and said he could not help with that, but he could reduce my pain. And, with his hands hovering above my body, he did. We recorded another four songs, the same way— the orchestra rehearsing several times, me singing in one take.

I spent the third day and night in the hospital receiving antibiotics intravenously. I pulled out all the needles on the fourth and last day. "If I die, I'll die in the studio!" I declared operatically. I could see by Martha's big smile that she approved of my attitude. We did seven songs, with me, as usual, performing only one take. Listening to it now, I remain amazed that I could pull this off. The song that most moves me still is "Over the Ocean," the title song. I composed this music to lyrics written by my friend Yu Yanming in 1990, when I was in Denver and longing for the China not of my memory, but the China of my heart.

Hidden among the evening clouds over the golden gate,
My home is on the other side of the ocean.
The bridge over Huangpu, the White Tower of Beihai,

The waves of Yellow River, the Straits of Changjiang,
Standing on this foreign land, I long for my home—
China, where my heart is.
How many times I dreamed of my mother,
Oh, my mother, I want to go home,
How many times I dreamed of my child,
Oh, my child, have you grown taller?
Standing on this foreign land, I long for my home—
China, where my heart is.

Martha believes now that the Sienna-Xiya experience was part of God's plan. He meant for her to save the life of a little boy named Dali.

As we were closing down the business, one of our marketing executives asked Martha for help for his nephew. Dali, a sweet, good-looking, somewhat shy six-year-old, was afflicted with multiple aneurysms, a hereditary condition that could not be treated in China at that time. His parents had no means; his father had borrowed money to buy a taxi after he was laid off from a factory job, and his mother worked for a factory that was not doing well. They did not know where to turn. And thus Martha finally found a nonprofit project in Tianjin that she could fully put her heart into. After much research through her friends in the medical field, she found a doctor at Schneider Children's Hospital, part of the Long Island Jewish Hospital system in New York, which arranged for totally free treatment and hospitalization for the boy. Martha sought donations to bring the boy and his father over and to handle all their expenses. She began a savings account for him as well, which has grown to several thousand dollars over the years.

Dali and his father, who stayed in the Ronald McDonald House, spoke no English but managed to get along with everybody. Dali was nice and polite throughout his painful ordeal. Several aneurysms in his body were removed, but the doctor believed that the one in his brain, still small, was too dangerous to remove at his age. Afterward, Dali tried to comfort his father, holding back his tears and assuring him that he was in no pain.

Dali and his father went back to China after a few months, but Martha continued to worry about the aneurysm in Dali's brain. Two years later, she found a neuroradiologist who specialized in this kind of surgery. He told her that she need not bring the boy back to the United States; there was a Chinese physician whom he had helped to train who had returned to Beijing. But he could not provide the physician's Chinese name, only the English version, through which Martha could not locate her. It seemed to be a dead end until one day when Martha was visiting a colleague at Capital Hospital in Beijing and mentioned her search for the doctor. Her friend said that there was a doctor at that hospital who had trained in the United States. She took her upstairs, and there was Dr. Lin, the very person she had been searching for! She was so moved by Martha's devotion to this boy that she agreed to take care of him almost for free. The story was reported in the newspapers in Beijing.

Dali, now a young man of eighteen, writes to us every year. He is doing well at school.

Faust was the first opera I sang in my native land. It was also the first opera produced in the first modern performing arts complex built in China—the huge, futuristic, French-designed Shanghai Grand Theatre, which opened to great fanfare in 1998. All three performances sold out, although the producer, Bonko Chan, worried at the time that a lot of clever marketing and audience education would be necessary to keep operas onstage in China. An enormously wealthy man in the newly prosperous China, Chan, only thirty-five years old at the time, had fallen in love with opera after hearing his parents' opera recordings as a child. According to one newspaper account, he managed to raise more than a million dollars to produce this French-Chinese collaboration. When he approached my agent about my singing this role, we had to decline since I had previously been contracted to sing with the Baltimore Opera. So the fast-talking producer got right to the point: how much money would it take to get me to Shanghai? He agreed to pay me for the three performances what I would have earned in Baltimore for six. Baltimore graciously let me out of the contract and invited me back for a future production.

The entire creative team was French, including the stage director, who was none other than the former general director at Opéra de Nice, to whom in 1993 I had complained about my treatment by the man who thought I looked "too Chinese." Nobody was saying such a thing now since the entire cast was Chinese, most of them, including everyone in supporting roles, from the Shanghai Opera House. Communication between the creative team and the singers proved difficult, though, since most of the singers spoke neither French nor English and had never sung abroad. Most, too, had never performed any but the most popular operas, such as *La Bohème* and *La Traviata*. So everyone was relieved once the tenor who sang the role of Faust and I arrived. He, too, lived in New York, and because of previously scheduled appearances, both of us got there after rehearsals had already begun.

The local stage crew was not up to international standards.

One scene, in a church, featured a huge cross, twenty-five-feet high, in which I was concealed until the stage lights shined directly on it, revealing a pale devil inside. The cross was raised and lowered with me in it, which always proceeded smoothly when the French stage designer was present. But when he wasn't, being a captive devil inside a cross in a church was truly death defying—especially when the whole thing crashed forward with me inside it. Everybody was screaming so loudly, I was sure I must have died, although I was more scared than hurt. And I was thoroughly frightened every time I had to jump on and off a horse-drawn carriage. The horse wasn't my problem this time. It was the cart, which was rickety and on the verge of collapse. I begged them to fix it. They promised. They didn't. Fortunately for me, it held together, but in every rehearsal and performance I worried and worried.

Then there was the matter of my shoes. Shoes and costumes have to be safe and comfortable onstage. This can be a challenge for designers, who sometimes have the look in mind more than the realities of performing while wearing these creations. Usually, though, the house staff takes these concerns seriously. If my role requires that I fall onstage (and, as this book went to press, as *Poet Li Bai* I'm falling-down drunk from my first moment onstage), you'd better believe I'm wearing knee pads under my costume. The black shoes they provided for this devil in Shanghai were handsome and comfortable, until I tried to move. On the hard leather soles, I slid as if on ice. I knew I'd kill myself with all the running and leaping on things that Mephistopheles had to do. I tried walking on gravel to coarsen the soles, to no avail. I asked three different people, all of whom promised to help me. Ultimately, Martha and I took it upon ourselves to find a pair of black rubber-soled shoes. We searched through the shoe stores of Shanghai, where I put all the shoes I tried on to the test by sliding on bare floors and jumping up and down on the chairs. I appeared mentally disturbed to the salespeople and the customers.

The result?

The devil wore Clarks.

And opera, and this singer, had a future in China.

"Wandering Ch'ing Ling Stream in Nan-Yang"

I hoard the sky a setting sun leaves
and love this cold stream's clarity:
western light follows water away,
rippled current a wanderer's heart.
I sing, watch cloud and moon, empty
song soon long wind through pine.

—Li Bai (701–762), Tang dynasty poet

PART
III

Fishing

17

Millennium

MARTHA DID NOT tell me she'd found a lump in her breast. She tried to protect me. She knows how I count on her for everything. Martha makes my life feasible and easier; she makes it possible for me to sing. Even though she did not share her worry, I wonder how I could have been so blind to what was going on with the most important person in my life.

Opera singers are full of nerves. All the time nerves, more and more nerves. You wake up, and your vocal cords are swollen. You have to give a performance that night, and there's no one covering for you. Onstage, nobody wants to hear one bad sound. There's no mercy. If you don't feel well, if you hit the wrong note, if your voice breaks, nobody feels sorry for you. They'll find someone to replace you. You work so hard, you give an emotionally wrenching performance, yet a critic calls you bland.

"Singers are crazy," I recently overheard Martha telling a friend. "They get very nervous, they get very tense, they get unreasonable, and you have to be there to untie the knots. Otherwise, they will get blocked. They wake up with a headache and think it is all over. I say, 'Go back to sleep. You'll feel better in an hour.' It usually will get better—and I won't have to see that face for another hour! You can't be upset and scream at them because you can't disturb their emotions. If they are not in the right mood, they can't sing."

You have to have a way to let the feelings out. For me, if I have a chance to let go in front of Martha, it's better for me than to hold it in, like my father did. Some singers drink, smoke, take drugs, and even make love between acts.

Martha's sister Diana claims that my only saving grace is that I'm a bass; if I were a tenor, I would be completely insufferable.

Listen to me. All of this about *me*, *my* needs, *my* career, how Martha helped *me*. Where was I for her? Martha waited until February 2000 to tell me about the cancer, three months after she began her lonely journey and two months after my brother's tragic, early death—from liver cancer.

Finally, when I returned home after a performance, Martha told me. The cancer was not confined to the lump. Martha had to have a mastectomy. Diana cried when the doctor told us this news in his office. Martha said, "Okay." Throughout, she was as matter-of-fact and scientific about her illness and recovery as about everything. I was shocked and horrified that I had for so long expected her to absorb all of my operatic angst without thinking what that could be doing to her. I vowed to be there for her then, and always.

I hope I have kept that promise. Opera singers are always worrying about their own health. Every little symptom makes us anxious about our upcoming performance and our future in this business. My doctor, whom I can call from anyplace in the world at any hour, cares for my mind and my worries as much as for my scratchy voice and stomach rumblings. If I would give half this attention to Martha's health—but she does not want this scrutiny. She remains silent about herself. That is her way.

I had thought, after my brother died, that I was as low as I could go. My father and my brother had lost their lives to liver cancer. I had a history of liver disease. What would happen to me? My despair went beyond my concern for my own mortality. I felt guilty. What my brother told me during our final visit had made me rethink my life. It was too late to help him and make up for the years in which I had let him down. But I could be strong for Martha. I had to be.

My brother was six years older and a head taller than me when he left for the navy in 1964. Because he was from a family with impeccable revolutionary credentials, once out of the naval academy he was selected to be one of twenty sailors in an elite unit in Kunming, in the south of China near the Vietnam border. There, he would learn Vietnamese and serve as a military adviser to the North Vietnamese, since China was not officially involved in the conflict over Vietnam. He had not been there long when, through the lens of the Cultural Revolution, our family background turned muddy, and my brother was booted from the career he had always wanted.

I ran to the door and flung it open when I heard his familiar loud and rapid knocking. How shocked I was to find that my brother, as good-looking as ever, was now half a head shorter than me.

Though his given name was Hao Qian, we always called him Tian Mimi. Mimi was a girl's nickname, meaning "Kitty," that my parents gave him before he was born. They were expecting a girl, as they later did with me (and called me, as you might remember, Xiao Lu, "Little Deer").

Tian Mimi came home dressed in his navy uniform but without any official insignia. He was carrying a guitar over his shoulder. I had never seen this "bourgeois" instrument before. I loved it

My brother was my hero when we were small children. He was six years older than me, so we didn't live together much of the time, since he went to boarding school and then joined the navy. When he was around, he protected me from bullies. My mother still refers to him as "the handsomer one."

immediately. Once he got settled in, he played some Vietnamese songs that he had learned from one of his Vietnamese counterparts in Kunming. I loved how soft and light and warm the music sounded—decadent, by Cultural Revolution standards. He gave me a couple of lessons before my parents, my sister, and I had to depart Beijing.

When I returned alone several months later, Tian Mimi was working at a factory on the outskirts of the city and came home only one night a week. That meant once a week I got a good meal; he took me out or we made dumplings with our rationed flour, rice, and meat. When we went out, he ordered hard Chinese liquor—eighty to a hundred proof and made from sorghum, wheat, barley, or millet—and we drank until we were red in the face. My brother was a big drinker and a big smoker, which probably hastened his death. I was too young and self-centered to appreciate the strain he was under in those years. He was forced to resign from the navy, where he had been so happy and on his way to possibly a big career. Now he worked long, hard days in the factory and on his one day off had to see to my welfare. He helped me to clean up my room, wash my clothes, and cook food for the upcoming week, and all this with a cheerful expression, as if things were just fine.

Then my sister, Lin, our Meimei, returned, and he had more chores to do on this one day off. Besides washing her clothes, too, he had to take her to her violin lessons, since she was only eleven and too young to travel about on her own. (She had begun to study the violin because we no longer had a piano.) Then he moved into my tiny room with me and decided it was time that I deal with more chores, like keeping the room clean. He also decided that I should learn how to wash my own clothes. But I was so lazy. I'd drop them into a bucket of soapy water and leave them there most of the week, rinsing them out and hanging them up only hours before he was due back from the factory.

When I was younger, my brother had been tough and protective of me. One time a dozen kids were giving me a hard time at the gate of our complex. I ran inside and told Tian Mimi, who stomped out, kicked open the gate, and growled, "Who wants to fight with my brother?" He looked ferocious. The kids scattered like leaves in a windstorm. Now that I was on my own in Beijing, I did not count on his protection so much. Once he was bicycling past and found me in a fight in the schoolyard, so he got off and offered his help. I said, "Here, hold my glasses," which I whipped off my face and handed to him before returning to the melee. He reminded me of this incident years later since for him it marked a turning point when I no longer needed him.

Once I was out of school and working in the Beijing Boiler Factory, he began to disapprove of me. I wasn't a good worker. I was always playing my accordion or the guitar, which he didn't seem to care about anymore and let me keep. I'd been learning to play the guitar from a Vietnamese translator at my factory. Whenever Tian Mimi came back home, the little room I shared with him was always crammed with my friends, girls included, and everyone was smoking and drinking. "Look at you!" he'd snort with contempt and go into Meimei's room. She wasn't much happier with my lifestyle than he was and preferred to stay alone in her room playing her violin.

My brother was a straightforward person who lived simply, followed the rules, worked hard, never lied, never hurt anybody, and never went beyond the accepted limits. Unlike him, my friends and I were absorbed with literature and poetry, music and arts, things I was sure my brother knew nothing about, and for that I began to look down on him. When my friends and I became enamored of all things Western after the end of the Cultural Revolution, my brother remained locked in the old system, as I saw it. What seemed to make him happiest was reflecting back on his short-lived navy career. Whenever he talked about his ship breaking the ocean waves, his face became radiant. He always had magazines lying around about military weapons and vessels.

In the years after I left for the United States in 1983, my brother was among the many in China who began to talk about going into business. I was all for it. Why should he remain a factory worker? Why didn't he make something of himself in this new world that was opening up for the Chinese? He loved to talk about his elaborate ideas, but he never did anything about them. He spent so much time in fishing-gear stores that an American friend of mine offered to go into business with him in China. My friend sent a lot of material and a proposal to Tian Mimi—who never responded. Then I offered to back the business if he'd run the store. "Let me think about it," he said. And that was the end of it.

For a long time I was so disappointed in my brother. I began to think of him as a *kanye*, a big talker, full of hot air. Sure, he was a sweet guy. But why wouldn't he *do* anything? In truth, I had no idea what he was doing, except that he was now working in the audio-visual department of a cancer research institute, preparing videos for teaching and research. In all the quick trips I made to Beijing between 1991 and 1999, the year my brother was diagnosed, I had spent maybe a total of twenty-four hours with him. We never really talked. He always urged us to come visit, but he didn't have much to offer to the conversation; he was content to watch and listen. I never asked him much since I was always in a hurry, trying to squeeze in visits with him and with our mother. (She was living half the year in Beijing, the other half with my sister and her family in Denver, where they had moved from Hong Kong.)

The year 1999 proved to be the busiest thus far in my career. But three times, when my brother was hospitalized or operated on or moved to a different hospital, Martha and I managed a trip to Beijing, however brief. I felt strongly that I needed to be with him, to leave money for him so that he would see the best doctor, have the best surgeon, whatever he needed. Then we had to rush off for another singing engagement. Martha and I had been planning a longer stay in January 2000, but in November 1999 I got a grim call from my sister-in-law, Jin Dajie (Sister Jin). She began to cry even before she completed her sentence: "The doctor has told me that your brother won't survive more than a month. If you want to see him, you have to come back now."

Jin and my brother loved each other so much. They had been middle-school sweethearts. Then my brother joined the navy; three years later, in 1967, Jin was sent to Inner Mongolia and did not return. She married there, and my brother married as well, fathering a daughter, Hai Di. My parents had been friendly with Jin's parents but had lost touch after they left Beijing. After my father died in 1986, my grieving mother often went out for long, aimless walks throughout Beijing. One day, she realized that she was in Jin's parents' neighborhood, so she walked over to their building and knocked on the door. Jin's mother came to the door, and the two women quickly made up for lost time. Jin's husband had died, and she would soon be moving back to Beijing with her two children, her mother told mine. And my mom confided that Tian Mimi had recently divorced. My mother's head was racing as fast as her feet took her back to her apartment, where she picked up the phone. One thing led to another, and a year later, my brother was married to his beloved Jin.

Throughout the year of my brother's illness, I had been phoning Jin frequently to find out how he was doing. Each call would shake me out of my professional preoccupations, but not for long. Seville, Madrid, Paris, Florence, Frankfurt, Philadelphia, Montreal, New York—it seemed as if I was singing everywhere that year. And in the District of Columbia, as well, where I had scored a great critical success in *Le Cid*, by Jules Massenet, an elaborate opera with Plácido Domingo, who brought this opera—which had not been staged in a century—to the Washington National Opera. (If you've ever seen the movie version of this story, *El Cid*, starring Charlton Heston and Sophia Loren, which won three Academy Awards in 1961, you'll appreciate what a monumental production this opera can be.) My role—as Domingo's father—was big and delicious. Every time I sang the big duet with Domingo, in rehearsals and in performance, I felt that singing opera could not get any better than this. At that moment in the opera, I beseech my son to defend my honor by killing my enemy. How magnificently the great Domingo conveyed his anguish and conflict when I revealed that the man I wanted killed was the father of the woman he secretly loved! My wonderful reviews helped to offset the unpleasant experience I had with the director, Hugo De Ana, one of the most brilliant directors in opera.

During the first two weeks of rehearsal, I had *Lucia di Lammermoor* at the Met, so I was constantly on the train between New York and Washington. Still, my *Le Cid* cover had to take all but four of the early rehearsals. This was a huge, new production, scheduled to be broadcast on PBS, and DeAna was unforgiving. He had no experience with me to reassure him that I was able to learn my role and perform it well with fewer rehearsals, though Domingo tried to reassure him. Still, he wanted to replace me. He refused to speak directly to me; instead, he'd turn to his assistant and say, "Tell Mr. Tian . . . " and I would have to respond, "Tell Mr. De Ana . . . " On opening night he had the good grace to congratulate me. "You were fabulous," he said rather convincingly. I also congratulated him, sincerely. I added that I was glad our war had ended. (This

In Massenet's Le Cid *at Washington National Opera in 1999, I played the nobleman Don Diègue, father of Rodrigue (played by Plácido Domingo). It was a great role. At one point, I had to grab Domingo's shoulder to force him to kill my enemy. In rehearsal, I was afraid of hurting the great Domingo by this action. I overcame my fear when he counseled me that to act the role genuinely was of the utmost importance.*

was fortunate, since De Ana was the director of my first, so-important *Don Carlo* in Genoa a year later; we worked together wonderfully.)

I was on edge professionally that year for another reason: I had parted with my first agent. It was the right step for me to take at that moment in my career but was still upsetting, since Paul Côté had believed in me and helped to get my career off to such a good start. Now I had a full schedule of auditions in Europe at important opera houses set up by my new agents, Bruce Zemsky and Alan Green. My audition at the Royal Opera in London was scheduled for November 29, and it was already the twenty-sixth when Jin called to tell me that my brother's end was near. Martha and I arrived in Beijing the next afternoon, with less than a full day to spend with Tian Mimi before we had to leave for London.

At the hospital, Jin Dajie gently took Martha by the arm and suggested that they go shopping. I remained alone with my brother for the next three hours. For the first and last time in our lives, we opened our hearts to each other.

It was mid-afternoon and the late-fall light came in softly through his window. He was in the best hospital in Beijing, affiliated with the cancer research center where he worked, which rewarded him for his years of service with a *gaogan bingfang*, a VIP suite that is ordinarily reserved for high officials. A provincial governor had been a patient in this very room not long before, Tian Mimi told me proudly. He was sitting up in bed, wearing a sweater over his striped hospital pajamas. His illness had not ravaged his appearance. He was still "the handsomer one," as my mother describes him to this day. His face was vivid with happiness to see me, an expression all the more striking when the sun shifted and illuminated him. Throughout this incredible afternoon and early evening, even as the sun set, his face—his entire demeanor—remained bright. My brother never liked to bring trouble to people, and he wasn't about to do it now.

"Don't worry about me," he said. "I can stand it. I'll get better. Look how strong I am."

It was true, he did look remarkably robust, all things considered. Until he was too sick to work, he continued to ride his bike from home on the eastern side of the city to the institute on the western side, even as people were turning to private cars and motorbikes. (He loved to talk about cars, though; I had offered to teach him how to drive and even to help him get a used car, but, of course, nothing ever came of it.)

For months, I had been thinking about the guitar he had given me way back when. I had never known how he got away with playing such a "degenerate" instrument in the navy.

"I was criticized for it in the navy," he admitted. "But once the Vietnamese guy taught me, I loved playing it." He told me about the worst trouble he got in over it—the night of a national holiday when his ship was in port for the celebrations, and he thought that no one would notice if he stayed on board to play his guitar. He grabbed a bottle of liquor and went up on deck to drink and sing, facing out to sea. "I got caught and was reported," he said, "but I couldn't live without that guitar. Once I got out, I had to have one for myself. I used my demobilization fee, a month's salary."

Then why, if he had gone to such trouble and expense to obtain this guitar that he loved so much to play, did he let me have it?

"I enjoyed so much watching you play and sing. *You* couldn't live without it," he laughed. "You loved that thing."

He let me commandeer his prize possession just like that? He shrugged. "I couldn't very well take it to the factory," he countered lamely.

On reflection, I wasn't convinced of his attachment to that guitar, considering his legendary aversion to music. Probably he was all talk, as usual. Tian Mimi had been the first of the three of us to take piano lessons, but he hated them as much as I did—or so the family story went. Our sister, Meimei, was the one serious musician in the family, although I managed to catch up with her later.

My brother protested. "I loved music and I loved playing the piano. That story is just not true. What happened was that I was a restless kid and was always looking around and outside the window when I was practicing, so they said I was wasting what little time

My brother had given me his guitar when he moved back after his navy career was cut short. Here I am with this "bourgeois" instrument singing "bad" songs during one of my escapes from the factory.

they had free for providing lessons. Mom decided that you should be the future pianist instead of me."

Now I was beginning to understand. My brother had sacrificed his music for me from the beginning. I was not prepared to hear this. It was very painful. I was even less prepared for what came next. "Let me tell you about my band," he said, sitting up straighter in bed.

This supposed no-talent guy had a band? Was this more big talk?

He said that ballroom dancing became very popular throughout Beijing after I left for the United States. Workplaces began to sponsor weekend dance parties for their employees. Tian Mimi was working at the research institute now. "Because I was from a musical family and knew so much about music, they asked me to organize a dance band. We called it Ten-Legged Crab. We had ten players, on piano, saxophone, flute, accordion, and percussion instruments. And, of course, I was the leader. I got all the music, did the arrangements, and copied out the parts for all the instruments."

Wait a minute. My brother knew how to read and write and arrange music and put together a band, and this was common knowledge at his workplace? I was so bewildered.

"Eventually, word got out about us and we started getting invitations to play for big parties at halls and clubs and foreign embassies," he continued. "We performed all kinds of music, even foreign pieces."

"Like what?" I asked skeptically.

"'Red River Valley,' 'Edelweiss,' 'Tennessee Waltz,' Strauss waltzes," he answered proudly. "The last piece was always 'Auld Lang Syne.'"

I could not believe what I was hearing—or seeing. Tian Mimi's gestures became downright musical, as if he were leading the band that he told me about. He spoke of his band as if it were his ten-legged baby. How could I not have known about his gift for music and his knowledge of it? I began to accept what he was telling me. I was mesmerized listening to him—and I blushed with shame at how impatient and dismissive I had been with him over the years.

I don't know quite how it happened, but we started to sing. We had not sung together since he taught me the Vietnamese songs he'd learned in the navy. We started with the Soviet songs that had been popular when we were young. Then we moved on to folk songs, of which he turned out to have an amazing repertoire and a much better memory for the lyrics than I had. We sang dozens of songs with such joy, one after the other, and sometimes in harmony. There was no illness in his beautiful voice, which had such wonderful color, and he was always on pitch. His expression was exuberant; his emotions were expressed in song as naturally as the best performer's. These were skills I had pursued all of my professional life. He was lost in the songs, his eyes closed, his hands waving, as if he were still leading the band. We began a popular song from a famous movie, "Say Good-Bye to the Comrade in Arms." Written to an ethnic melody from Xinjiang, a western province, the song was about soldiers yearning for their lost comrade. I had been humming along since I had forgotten the words, but then I stopped to listen to him. It seemed, as he sang it, that the song had been written just for him, or even by him. He was completely absorbed in the emotion, which he rendered so plaintively. He sang the song again.

As he was singing, I asked myself, Who should be the singer, Tian Mimi or me? My brother had all the talent and the emotions of a born musician. He was the firstborn. I felt so sad that when we were young, no one had recognized him for who he was and what he had to give. After I left China in 1983, and the family came around to my aspirations, it was as if all the family ambitions rested in me. I believed that. So, apparently, did he.

The sun had nearly set by now. We fell silent. I was gripped by a sudden fear that my brother's life would end with the ebbing light.

I asked him why he had never told me about his band.

He responded with genuine surprise. "Why should I bother you with such small things? You are a big opera singer now. We were just amateurs."

"Did you miss your guitar?" I asked him, beginning to understand why the instrument had been lurking in my mind since he had become ill.

"Of course, I missed it," he said. I pictured myself flinging it over my shoulder and boarding the plane for the United States. How he must have needed that instrument to express his own sorrows in the face of the terrible loss of his career. He had had no time to unwind or enjoy himself while he worked so hard to reassure my sister and me that all was well. Like our dad, whom he resembled in appearance, he had kept everything inside. I thanked him now for protecting us back then.

It seemed too unfair to me. I could have and should have helped him to be the best that he could be. He could have traveled the world with me. I could have helped him to be the musician he was meant to be. So my fantasies sped for some moments.

"What about the money?" I asked next.

"Money?"

"How much did your band make for your gigs?"

He laughed. "We never thought about money. We had so much fun playing music together. We all loved music. Maybe sometimes we'd each receive a new shirt or a tie. Sometimes we'd be invited to a dinner after the performance. That's all. We never thought about payment," he said, so amused by the question that I was embarrassed I had asked it. That's when the real question occurred to me: what had happened to *me* in all these years? I had turned against my brother in the arrogance of youth, but then I had assumed that all of my values, including those I had developed along the road to success as an opera singer, should be true for him, too.

He kept on reminiscing. "All of us in the band were in such good moods after rehearsing and playing that we'd work harder. Just thinking that we were getting together to play that day would take our cares away."

I wished fervently that we'd had that old guitar with us that day. I wanted time to move backward to the 1970s and freeze there, and let me walk alongside him with the respect he was always due.

I changed the subject to fishing. No sooner said than he took me on a journey into his imagination. "Here's the place I want to go fishing. It is a deep lake high in the mountains, surrounded by pine trees," he mused, describing the arc of the forest with his hands. "The water is so pure, no pollution has ever reached this place. You can see the pebbles in the water as you wade out into the cold, clear shallows. We will fish for trout here. Do you know how to fish for trout?" he asked me.

I did not tell him that I went fishing for trout every weekend that I could when I lived in Colorado, in places as achingly beautiful as he could only dream of.

He proceeded to share some of his trout-fishing tips with me. He described the choices of lines and hooks, how to cast the fly, and what kind of bait to use. "When the fish first bites, you have to be patient," he instructed. "Walk it, pull it up slowly at an angle." Then he described the various kinds of trout and what they looked like.

I grew confused. Was he telling me about a real place where he actually fished for trout?

He looked at me as if I was a little crazy. "No, he said, "we have mostly grass carp and crucian in Beijing."

I never went fishing with my brother. I had invited him to America, to Colorado, but he never came. Yet he had such a place in his mind. Perhaps he wasn't the *kanye* that I had believed him to be. Perhaps he was a man of great spirit and talent and happiness with a rich and satisfying imagination. A man who was happy to be who he was, with nothing to prove to anyone. A man who could teach me about the meaning of life.

It was so hard to leave him that evening. As I stood up, he patted me on the arm and told me once again that I should not worry about him. Then he tentatively asked whether there was one thing I would do for him. "Sure," I said, surprised. My brother had never asked me for anything, ever.

"If it is possible, can you help Tian Beibei to study abroad?" That was what he called his daughter, Hai Di, who was living with her mother, Tian Mimi's first wife, in Beijing.

I was so happy to be able to do this for him, something he truly wanted from me. (Hai Di graduated from LaSalle College in Montreal in 2004 and now works in design in Beijing.)

Only when he tried to stand up to see me to the door—he insisted on it—did I see how sick he was. He could not stand straight, but he refused to let me to support him.

Tian Mimi died two weeks later.

I had to perform at the Met the night I returned from his memorial in early January. (At my sister-in-law's request, Babaoshan Revolutionary Cemetery played a tape of "Say Good-Bye to the Comrade in Arms," rather than the usual funeral fare.) When I sat down at the piano in my dressing room to warm up, Italian music merged with the songs I had sung with my brother on our last day together. I glanced at myself in the mirror, handsome in my makeup and costume, as I left to go down to the stage. For a moment I thought that I looked like Tian Mimi. I felt that I wanted to say something to him. It was hard to remain focused during the performance. I came back to my dressing room during intermission and continued to play the songs I had sung with my brother.

*   *   *

Thankfully, Martha recovered completely from her mastectomy and reconstructive surgery. She required no further treatment other than a five-year regimen of tamoxifen, which is long ended now. And with her ministering to me, as always, I recovered my spirits. But her silent sacrifices for me during the months of my brother's illness and death, while she was harboring her own deadly illness in secret, will always haunt me—just as my memory of her surgery and recovery will remain with me forever. I pray that I can care for her as well as she cares for me.

For the next year and a half I pursued my career with renewed fervor, in an all-too-modern way. My eyes were on Europe, where I was getting more and more offers, increasing my repertoire— adding five new, heavy, major bass roles—expanding my career, getting great reviews, flying often and everywhere, and taking too little care of my voice.

I arrived back in New York to a fall 2001 schedule at the Met that began as tough and ended as brutal. I was scheduled to cover and sing three operas in the first three months. Two of them, Bellini's *Norma* and Verdi's *Luisa Miller*, were big roles in major operas that were in rehearsal and in performance during the same weeks. I had sung Oroveso in *Norma* before, which took some of the pressure off me, although the role is very difficult. Oroveso is the high priest of the Druids in ancient Gaul, which in 50 BC is occupied by the Romans. His priestess daughter, Norma, has secretly given birth to two children who were fathered by a Roman soldier who has since become unfaithful to her. To sing this role, one must convey the high priest's dignity, depth, and authoritativeness as well as his contradictory feelings as Norma's father.

Singing Count Walter in *Luisa Miller* was even tougher; it's a heavy role with endless arias, duets, and ensembles a cappella—without accompaniment—and I had never sung it before. In this opera, Count Walter has pledged his son to a woman he does not love. As with Oroveso, this father's emotions are complicated. He must sacrifice his son to save his dying kingdom. The director asked me to convey these complex feelings through my voice only, with minimal bodily expression, which made the role that much more challenging as a singing actor. "This is such a thankless role," commented my colleague Paul Plishka, who knew it from experience. For all of Count Walter's singing, the audience doesn't pay as much attention him as to the other characters—unless the bass sings it badly. At the end of this opera, the son and his true love (Luisa Miller) drink poison—which maybe I should have done myself, the way things turned out.

To put a new role in my throat, as we say, I need to leave myself two or three months for learning and practice. But I was so busy traveling around Europe and growing my career that I did not have the time. My throat was tired, and I had laryngitis. I thought I could get through it, though, because mostly I was covering, and other than rehearsals, I did not have that many performances to sing. Then came September 11, 2001.

Such a terrible time it was for all of us in New York City. The only thing that made it bearable, it seemed, was that we were all in it together. Martha and I had lived next to the Twin Towers until 1998. The buildings were an icon for the country and the world, but for us they were symbols of the neighborhood that had nurtured us during the first years of our life in New York. In the building near Lincoln Center where we lived after 1998, our next-door neighbor worked on the seventy-fifth floor of the south tower of the World Trade Center. When the north tower was struck, everyone in her building was told to evacuate the building. She and her colleagues were walking down the stairs when the announcement came for everybody to return to their floors since the building was deemed to be safe. But our neighbor, whose feet hurt and who was now carrying her high heels, decided to continue down to the lobby and take the elevator back up to her office, rather than join her colleagues on the return climb. The second plane hit moments after she stepped down in the lobby; all of her colleagues in the office and the stairwell died. She told us she went to funerals for her colleagues every day for a month.

Everyone in the city had tragic tales to tell, knew people who had died, and traveled down to Ground Zero, sometimes repeatedly, to stand in stunned silence. Everybody smelled that awful, lingering odor of the burning buildings and the dead bodies that lasted for so many months. From our eighteenth-floor apartment, there was no escaping the plumes of smoke as the fire smoldered on and on.

The Metropolitan Opera, like every other institution and business in the city, was in crisis. Performers were canceling—including the bass I was covering for in *Norma* and *Luisa Miller*. That meant I had to take over all performances of both roles, with no cover to back me up. In its current condition, there was no way my voice could manage the combined fifteen performances and all the rehearsals in just over a month's time, including two occurrences where performances fell on consecutive days. Yet how could I say no when they asked me? Everyone was making sacrifices, but this one, I thought, might end up being a sacrifice of my career.

"*Please* don't get sick," Jonathan Friend, the artistic administrator, urged so seriously. "You have no backup. This is a difficult period at the Met. Ask Martha to take special care of you."

"I'll try my best," I said, grimacing inside. What would be the point of telling him that my vocal cords continued to be swollen? It was my duty to pitch in, no matter what. My voice was dull and heavy. I went to my ear, nose, and throat doctor every two to three days. He told me that for my voice to recover, I had to remain absolutely silent for five days. That was impossible. I was rehearsing *Luisa Miller* every day, and I was performing *Norma*. It was like pitching in every game of the playoffs and the World Series with no relief pitcher (I was supposed to have been the relief pitcher!)—and with a sore arm.

I rose to the challenge as best I could. Maestro Jimmy Levine, who was conducting *Luisa Miller*, supported me throughout and did everything he could to avoid adding to the pressure I was under. Still, I was in bad voice on opening night, which the reviews reflected: "Mr. Tian . . . sang fuzzily with . . . errant pitch," wrote a reviewer in the *New York Times* after the October 29 opening. In his review of *Norma* two weeks earlier, another *Times* reviewer had described my voice as "gravelly." I improved in later

I sang the role of the Druid high priest Oroveso in a new production of Bellini's Norma *that opened at the Met in 2001 just after the September 11 attacks. That was such a difficult time for me as a New Yorker, an American, and as a singer, since my vocal cords were swollen and I was singing Count Walter in Verdi's* Luisa Miller, *another new production, at the same time. Truly, it was the roughest moment in my opera career. But New York didn't go down, and neither did I.*

performances of both operas, though there were no reviewers to take note.

Often at intermission during the run of *Luisa Miller*, Maestro Levine called me in my dressing room to cheer me on. "You're doing great, Tian. Keep it up." Paul Plishka helped, too. After watching one of the early rehearsals of *Luisa Miller*, he told me he understood completely what kind of vocal crisis I was in and that, throat problems or not, I had to go on. "I know you are in a very difficult situation," he said. "At this moment you really have to help yourself. Be strong!" he urged. His support and friendship helped me so much. My nerves settled down, and my courage returned.

At least, the Met wanted me to return for *Luisa Miller* when they brought it back the following spring. They could have found somebody else by that time.

Where would I go from here? I felt as if I had fallen from the high point to the low point of my career. And I would turn fifty in just two years.

I was down for a time, but I forced myself to regain my spirit and energy. If Martha could go through her cancer experience with the calm, determined strength that she always exhibited, how could I falter after an unavoidable career mishap? I pulled myself up because of her. After all, I had Martha with me, and I have her still.

My brother remains with me, too, in his way. For years after his death, I had a recurrent dream in which a man and I were fishing at a beautiful mountain lake surrounded by pine trees. The water was so clear, I could see the rocks on the lake bottom. The man and I never spoke or looked at each other, but I knew he was my brother.

18

Where You Come From

TAN DUN LIKES sex. The centerpiece of his opera *The First Emperor* is a long love scene between the emperor's crippled daughter, Princess Yueyang, and the emperor's soon-to-be-former best friend, Gao Jian Li. At the end of the first act, she seduces him, he deflowers her, and she stands up to dance. The emperor, played by Plácido Domingo, is at first thrilled to see her on her feet, until he spots the bloody sheet and sings forth in fatherly wrath. As General Wang, I am devastated, since Yueyang has been promised to me.

How to play this long, lingering love scene was at the heart of the frustration in the rehearsal room the day in 2006 that I sat down to play "The East Is Red" during a break. The first collaboration of the Metropolitan Opera with a Chinese artistic team, *The First Emperor* production was marked by many creative tensions, the usual and the unique, which included trying to translate Chinese cultural forms into Western opera. (How many dinners Martha cooked for us all through these rehearsals, even as she worked night and day on plans for *The First Emperor* gala, for five hundred people!) This day, the Met artistic staff, the performers, and the Chinese directors all had their own ideas about how to proceed, and these viewpoints had to be translated back and forth from Chinese to English to Chinese.

Tan Dun, who served as both the composer and the conductor, was born in China and has lived in New York for two decades. He always has strong ideas about how his works should be staged. He had hoped that this scene would be rendered as erotically as the music he composed for it, but some people on the Chinese team preferred a more restrained, Eastern depiction that employed stylized Eastern gestures. Trying to combine these bodies and body languages was proving to be very difficult for my Western colleagues, who were laboring so hard to master the new musical sounds and actions. At least they didn't have to master the Chinese language since the opera was in English.

Even for the Chinese performers, this music was a challenge. For me, Tan Dun had written music that stretched me to the extremes of my range. Combine these tensions with the cuts and the changes that had been going on for weeks, all of which had to be memorized and rememorized, and I was among the many who were growing frustrated. After changes to some of my music the night before we opened, I kept dreaming that I was singing it the old way, which would wake me up so I'd practice again, only to return to sleep and to the same dream. Everybody was so tired, perhaps director Zhang Yimou most of all. Besides *The First Emperor*, he was also working on his films and projects for the 2008 Beijing Olympics, of which he was in charge of the opening and closing ceremonies. (Throughout the run of this opera, Plácido Domingo was the only person involved whose energy never seemed to flag. He attended all rehearsals and worked with coaches even though, during these same months, he was also conducting *La Bohème* at the Met and *Madama Butterfly* at the Washington National Opera and heading two opera houses.)

I had no part in the love scene—alas, as a bass I never do. But as a Chinese speaker, I was able to help convey the various notions back and forth among the participants.

So there I am, witness to a conversation in my native language about how to have stage-sex at the Met. Then this odd scene shifts slightly, and I'm playing tunes from the Cultural Revolution on the piano in the rehearsal room with colleagues who grew up during that same oppressive period and are now cavorting around the room. Nobody else knows what we are yakking about in our own language, and nobody can figure out why we're so happy after having been so cranky and glum. I must be hallucinating.

Currents change, time and again, on the roaring river. Now the waters are carrying not only me but my illustrious countrymen on a wild ride from Mao to the Met for a new opera headlined by Plácido Domingo. Is this an accident that we have come together here and now? Strange to say, for some of us there was magic under Chairman Mao and Jiang Qing. The creative fire was lit and fed in an environment that was inhospitable to anything but the Party line. We had nothing. There was nothing to have. What was there was ours, a simple song sung in the mountains, a couple of stuffed dumplings, a glass of beer, a line of poetry, a back-and-forth about literature. A hug, a kiss, a dance, if no one was looking. Those who remained outside the radar of politics and who toed the line just enough when all eyes were on us were absolutely free when outside of scrutiny. No parents, no supervision, no structure, just open hearts and natural abilities, soothed by song and poetry. Those songs, those poems, that simplicity is the best of what I had then and what, since my brother's illness and death, I know I have to rediscover. How bizarre that I was rediscovering it all again among my Chinese Cultural Revolution peers in this bastion of high Western culture in twenty-first-century America.

I first met Tan Dun in 1991 at a party at the Chinese consulate for the dozens of Chinese artists living in the New York area at that time. He then invited me to his wild all-night parties at which everybody performed impromptu—or just made noise—as the spirit moved them. The homemade music ranged from pop to jazz to avant garde to folk. Violinists, dancers, pop stars, movie makers, painters, composers, opera singers, videographers. Tan Dun, always drumming and clicking rocks together, was open to anything and anyone, and to any art form.

I always enjoy talking to Tan Dun about contemporary music and arts because concepts develop and change constantly. We have to be open-minded in the arts. Don't judge so fast. Come back and have another try, another listen, a second look. Yes, you were trained in bel canto. Now try something new. Traditional art forms need new concepts. Give them a chance.

*   *   *

I like sex, too.

"Tan Dun, you must do something for me," I pleaded some-
time in the mid-nineties. "Onstage, I am always a high priest, an
old father, a bad person, a devil. I never get a chance to hold
a beautiful woman, to kiss her, to sing a romantic aria. I give you
this responsibility: create a love scene for me."

He promised me he would.

One day at a party not long afterward, he told me excitedly,
"Tian, I am writing a new opera called *Tea* with a fantastic role for
you. You will be the emperor. In the second act, the curtain will open
and you will be naked in a big glass tank onstage filled with tea and
there will be six young naked women in the bath with you. Fantastic!"

*The family gathers to sing Christmas carols at the piano in our New York apartment. At
the time this photo was taken, in 2005, Luke, our Amazon parrot, though in his
twenties, was still a boy. In 2007, a genetic test revealed that Luke is actually a she.
He/she can sing roles from bass to soprano.*

I did eventually sing the role of the emperor in *Tea*, in Lyon, France. No tea bath. No naked ladies. The only relationship I had with a woman was, as usual, with my daughter.

Then the moon rose and everything started to become clear to me. My career had picked up after its 9/11 fiasco, and I was in more demand than ever for wonderful roles, in Japan, Amsterdam, Florence, Verona, Atlanta, Washington, Bilbao, Genoa, and, of course, New York. I was about to record a solo CD of operatic arias for Naxos. Yet if I was ever to find fulfillment in love onstage as great as the true love I have found in life, I would have to create this opportunity for myself. At least, this is my interpretation of the events that have come to pass recently, as I have undergone what amounts to a creative metamorphosis. I never would have expected this at this stage in my career. Now I can say that I have sung a title role in an opera that kept me onstage and singing—and laughing, shouting, gasping, weeping, and falling-down drunk—from beginning to end, when I followed my stage lover into eternity. And I can announce that Martha and I, in an operatic "confluence of East and West," have contributed to "the revitalization of the operatic form," as proclaimed in *Variety*.

After the world premiere of this opera, *Poet Li Bai*, I left the stage in tears, realizing that through Li Bai—his wine, his moon, and his poetry—I came face to face with myself.

It began as a gift. Diana Liao, Martha's sister, wrote an opera libretto about the Chinese poet Li Bai. China is a nation that loves its poets, none more than this eighth-century free spirit who wrote during the High Tang period in which culture flourished. The reverence for Li Bai (also known as Li Po or Li Bo), deemed a Poet Immortal in China, is equivalent to that for Shakespeare in English-speaking countries. He spent most of his life wandering, drinking, and tossing off poems that are direct and simple and deeply imbued with an immediate experience of nature. Needless to say, I learned nothing about ancient poetry when I was in school. I came across Li Bai's work when I was fifteen and just beginning to work in the factory. Some friends and I decided to commit his poems to memory. I think I knew at least thirty of them back then.

Diana insists she did not have me in mind when she wrote the libretto or did not even think that Li Bai might be a bass. She was a United Nations interpreter (soon to become chief of them all), and, in 2000, was swamped with meetings. "The poems of Li Bai, scaling majestic mountains and flying over sparkling lakes, offered delightful relief, as they had done throughout my growing-up years," she said. Encouraged by Chinese playwright Xu Ying, she plotted Li Bai's story. Before sitting down to write, she and Xu Ying journeyed to Sichuan province in central China, where Li Bai lived the longest in his wandering life. (She later joined Martha and me and more than a dozen of our friends from all over the world when we ventured along the Silk Route to Li Bai's birthplace in the summer of 2006.) Diana, now retired from the UN, spends her time writing and translating, often collaborating with the likes of Tan Dun and filmmaker Ang Lee.

She gave the libretto to me as a birthday gift in early September 2001, to do with as I pleased. In a moment of madness, Martha and I later rose to the bait. We would turn this libretto into an opera—a modern Chinese opera, made in China for delivery to the West—with Martha as executive producer.

In some ways we were as naive as we had been when we went into the cosmetics business. But we thought we knew something about the music world, if not the music business, and we wanted so much to foster a new modern Chinese opera to bring to the West. We knew nothing about making a profit, but we need not have worried about that, since there's nothing profitable about making an opera, the most expensive of all art forms to produce. That realization scared off an early backer in China, who wanted to make a killing from it. But we found a generous donor in Hong Kong who was willing to commission a composer, and we convinced Guo Wenjing to write *Poet Li Bai*. Guo, too, is a product of the Cultural Revolution and a classmate of Tan Dun's at the Central Conservatory, as are many of the leading lights in contemporary Chinese music, most of whom now live in the West. But Guo remained in

China and is unfettered by the West's commercialism and, as yet, commercial temptations. Many of his operas, combining the best of Chinese and Western forms in his unique style, have been performed in the West, mostly in Europe, although he is not a familiar name here. The music he wrote for us is classically simple and lyrically beautiful.

Diana's original libretto was in English, so she and Xu Ying, with whom she also collaborated on Tan Dun's *Tea*, created the final Chinese libretto from it and rendered that version into English at the same time, for an unusually beautiful translation that appears for audiences above the stage in the supertitles. But that step remained well ahead of us as we put together the rest of the team, including China's most famous theater director, Lin Zhaohua, and its busiest theater designer, Yi Liming. That was a heady time, flying back and forth to the apartment we had recently bought in Beijing, to meet and ultimately to rehearse with these creative luminaries whom we were so excited to know.

Then the complicated work began, and collaborating with people in the arts on a tight production schedule is not always so easy. Especially those with a creative temperament, and for once I'm not talking about me.

We had a deadline. The Central City Opera—the fifth-oldest opera in the United States, operating out of a once-abandoned nineteenth-century opera house in an old silver-mining town 8,300 feet up in the Rockies outside Denver—was planning its seventy-fifth anniversary season. Martha's organization, Asian Performing Arts of Colorado, was planning its twentieth. The two joined forces to co-commission the production of *Poet Li Bai* for Central City's 2007 summer festival. Opening night was July 7. Rehearsals were set to begin in Denver on June 11. Two weeks before that, everything was ready—the sets, the costumes. Well, not everything. We still didn't have a score.

Martha was fielding dozens of e-mails daily from the Asian Performing Arts of Colorado board about publicity, arrangements for the sold-out opening gala, ticket sales, airline tickets and visas for the performers, and housing arrangements for guests from afar.

And dozens more from Central City Opera about raising funds for the production, set construction, shipping the costumes, the impending rehearsals, and endless other details. She couldn't tell anybody that we did not have a score for the opera and that we were terrified that we would not have one in time. We could not bear to think about the disaster that awaited us.

May 28. I took a taxi to Guo Wenjing's Beijing apartment, where he was holed up to finish writing the opera. We'd already agreed to skip two scenes since there was no time to finish them. But we still did not have the last of what was now a five-scene opera, and we were only two weeks away from first rehearsals in Denver. In my mind I was pointing an imaginary pistol at him, ordering him to finish or else. But one look at him when he opened the door, and I experienced nothing but dismay. He was stripped down to his pants, dripping with sweat. He looked like he had not slept in days. The place was enveloped in cigarette smoke. Without saying hello, he returned to his piano, where he was working. I announced that I would wait for him to finish the final scene. I smoked one for every five of his cigarettes, which added up. I tried reading a book. I listened to him humming and playing. I began to lose patience. "Anything I can do to help?" I intended to say, but it came out as a howl. "Maybe I'll take off my shirt, too!" I added in crazed exasperation.

I did take my shirt off. Both half-naked—me dripping sweat on the piano, Guo nearly collapsing onto it—we began to go over the music together. Four hours later, when he penned the last note onto the score, both of us got so excited. What a stinky, sweaty, sticky, huge relief.

This was our last night in Beijing before we had to return to New York with the complete score and then, soon enough, move to Colorado for the summer to get this opera onstage. At that moment, though, I had to take Guo's music and have a young composer who was working with us create a piano score from it, so that the singers could learn their parts. But the orchestration for the whole last half of the opera had yet to be written. Six weeks to opening night!

When Guo arrived in Colorado on June 15 and we drove up to Central City, he had yet to complete the orchestrations of the final two scenes of the five-scene opera. The first orchestra rehearsal was scheduled for the following week, before which the players had to have the music for their parts! Orchestrating one scene usually took Guo a full week of ten-hour days. Then we still had to get the music to the engraver, the person who would put the whole work on the computer so that we could print it out for the conductor and prepare individual parts for the instrumentalists. But the engraver had already stayed longer than he'd planned to and had to return home to China, so we were in a frenzy to find somebody in Denver to do it.

I could hear every minute ticking by in my head as opening night approached and we still didn't have a finished orchestral score. The four main singers, myself included, and the chorus were already rehearsing our parts from the piano version. But what good would this be without an orchestra? And the conductor, Ed Spanjaard, was about to arrive from Amsterdam. Well, we said to calm ourselves, Ed has worked with Guo before; he must be used to this. But Martha and Diana and I are not used to this kind of stress and tension, and we argued too much with one another and with the director and the designer and cried gallons of tears. Finally, we closed Guo up in his room in the large log cabin that Central City Opera had provided for the singers and the creative team. We kept him on Beijing time so that he did not have to deal with jet lag, only with the agonies of adjusting to this altitude. He worked all night and handed us his finished pages as we awoke, before he went to sleep for the "night."

Yet here we were in this splendid mountain setting working with the calm, easygoing, supportive professionals of Central City Opera, headed by innovative general director Pelham (Pat) Pearce. The company has a history of premiering new operas (including, exactly fifty-one years earlier, to the day, *The Ballad of Baby Doe*, whose title character was sung by Beverly Sills two years later at the New York City Opera), and Pat is keeping the tradition going. (Beverly Sills sang the only *Aida* of her career at Central City; we all mourned her deeply when she died in early July during our stay.)

The sky was blue, the air pure, the mountain lakes full of trout. I promised myself I would go fishing before this three-week opera run was over. The 550-seat opera house, a National Historic Landmark, had been restored to its nineteenth-century charm, but this time with plush seating to replace the hard wooden seats of yore. My family and friends from all over the world who would join us for the gala opening would appreciate that.

Maybe everything would work out.

Or not.

During the stage rehearsal the week before the opening, the motorized stage gave out. The minimalist set consisted mostly of a large platform, which was meant to be a houseboat that was supposed to move as if mimicking the poet's drunkenness and rocking to the waves on the river on which Li Bai has been exiled for the last years of his life. And the designers had not fully comprehended how small this stage was—no bigger, really, than that of an old-fashioned movie house—and some of the design concepts had to be abandoned. Plus, the wigs looked ridiculous on most of us, especially on the chorus, which consisted of thirty students from my alma mater, the University of Denver Lamont School of Music. So we all went with our heads au naturel, except for Chi Liming, the leading tenor from the Shanghai Opera, who sang the role of Wine. The director decided that he should have his head shaved. Communicating with the English-speaking chorus was a challenge, for which Diana was drafted, in addition to her duties working on the edits to the libretto. The soprano Ying Huang, who played Moon and who sings frequently in the United States, was comfortable in both languages. Not so Jiang Qihu, the Peking Opera singer who sang the role of Poetry but who did manage to demonstrate to the chorus how to sit down and stand up in their flowing Chinese robes with a grace that had eluded them through most of the rehearsals.

Then we couldn't find anybody to play the Chinese bamboo flute and finally had to send for a musician from Los Angeles. And Guo Wenjing was in a funk that he didn't have the particular Chinese drum he wanted, so Martha had to drive through the mountains to Boulder to find one.

I sang my first title role in Poet Li Bai *in its world premiere at Central City Opera, one of the oldest opera houses in the United States, 8,300 feet up in the Rockies outside Denver. Martha served as the executive producer. The music, by Guo Wenjing, was not completed until two weeks before the opening. Not having a completed score as the world premiere approached was one of the scariest experiences in my opera career. Happily, this opera was reviewed as "a total success."*

From the rehearsal rooms of the world-class Metropolitan Opera to the stage of the tiny, summer-festival Central City Opera, the week before a brand-new work opens always is always fraught with frenzy and doubt. It's never going to come together! *The First Emperor*, a huge opera, with more than a hundred people onstage in some scenes and an elaborate, thirty-six-level set, did not congeal until the second performance, after the critics had had their say. But audiences went wild for it, with standing ovations at every successive performance, and it went on to become a huge popular success, with every one of the Met's nearly four thousand seats taken for all nine performances. The Met's schedule for the following seasons was immediately readjusted to make room to bring this opera back.

In sleepy Central City we had far fewer pieces to pull together, of course, yet for us it was monumental that our little, experimental, four-character, single-set *Poet Li Bai* proved to be magic from the minute the figurative curtain went up (there was no curtain, actually). Guo Wenjing's music was dreamy and lyrical and as romantic as Li Bai's poetry.

The opera begins with Li Bai waking up from a drunken stupor in the final hours of his life, as he looks back on his life and teases and tussles with his muses, Wine, Poetry, and Moon. There's very little action in this opera—even less so when the stage motor conked out, never to return to motion. It all had to come from my portrayal of the inner and outer life of this complex, gifted, contradictory man, the artist who courted fame and official acceptance at the same time that he flouted convention. He was finally banished from court and exiled to a floating jail.

I am the only character who remains onstage the entire hour and a half. It's all me, in a way I have never sung before. Or acted. It's essentially a one-man show, and this one man had never acted a role with such teeth and meat and carried a whole opera, much less interpreted a brand-new work in its entirety.

Early on, I worried about whether I had the vocal ability to pull this off. But the only way to do it was to abandon my usual concerns, even about color and technique and all the considerations I had been trained for. I had to let my emotions and mood carry me. The director, Lin Zhaohua, gave me all the leeway I needed to be free in my acting. "Go crazy, be free, be yourself," he told me. Whenever I had doubts about my acting, he would say, "Don't act. Be yourself. But don't act like a Western opera singer," by which I think he meant don't just stand there, with one arm out and belting a tune (his notion of what Western opera is all about). And Guo Wenjing's musical ideas, which are free from the pollution of modern life, gave me the inspiration. I would do the whole thing my way—I discovered what that was by doing it—and all in my native language. Certainly, they'd never seen or heard anything like this in Colorado!

Finally, I got to the point where I really could and did let go. I moved beyond my training and looked deep into the character to find myself. My questions in my life were and are the same that Li Bai faced, that we all do: What can I get out of life? What must I give up? What do I want? I got to know myself through this character, and I came to some answers. Onstage, as this poignant character at the end of his life, I sang falsetto, I recited, I laughed hysterically, I cried, I even shouted. Wolves howl, dogs bark, and sometimes we need to shout in our lives, as loudly as we can. And I did, to the limit of my voice, not once worrying about losing it.

The audience—and who knew what to expect of an opera without a sword fight and in Chinese?—got the point. Absent was the restless rustling in the seats that often accompanies a new work; people stayed with me the whole way. So did the reviewers. "His performance, and, indeed, the whole opera, culminates with Li Bai's touching final aria, in which Tian both dramatically and vocally evokes Li Bai's range of emotional states," wrote the *Denver Post* reviewer the day after the opening. According to *Opera News*, "Hao Jiang Tian . . . demonstrated his vocal stature, from Stentorian outbursts to wonderfully deployed falsetto passages."

During the final two of the six performances throughout those weeks, I was not sure whether I was Li Bai or myself. There was no separation. I had no self-consciousness. I did not even know whether my feet were on the ground. This was different from any experience I had had onstage anywhere. Ironically, the smallest stage on which I had ever performed provided unlimited space for me.

This is what made me identify with Li Bai, who at the end of the opera follows Moon, who loves and understands him and whom he loves, into the water. In the legend of the poet's life, that's what he did in the end: got drunk on a boat and tried to follow the moon's reflection in the water, where he drowned. Throughout the opera, Moon keeps repeating, "Why not go home now?" "Why not go home with me now?" "Why not come home now?" In the end he follows Moon home, to go where he came from.

The Chinese expression for these thoughts—*gui qu lai*—really means, as I think more and more about this, the place inside yourself where you are free of worldly cares, a Taoist or Zen state of pure presence inside life, free of yourself, and becoming part of the ongoing process of natural change. This is the place of the greatest creative potential, where you are no longer worrying about the future or fretting about the past. These are the places that Li Bai seeks in his poetry. This is a place I found in the mountains outside Beijing with my friends as we sang and recited poetry beyond the reach of the politics of the Cultural Revolution. This is where I find peace with my brother. This is the place I reached as Li Bai, letting go, singing, and acting, free and following the moon, my muse. Me.

Through Li Bai, a wanderer, as I have been in my own life, I have rediscovered my own humanity. This eighth-century Tang Dynasty drink-loving poet has taught me to perceive a new depth to the characters in the Western opera repertoire whom I portray. The conflicts, the passions, the struggles of life, ancient and modern—I feel them so much more keenly now. King Philip in *Don Carlo*—what anguish he feels over his queen's love for his son. Why can't she love him? He is a king and must maintain his bearing. Without freedom to express himself, such a great inner struggle ensues; trapped inside his human emotions, he loses his way in anger and violence. Oroveso, Mephistopheles, the Grand Inquisitor, new devils and heroes that await me in my path. I feel so much more prepared to give them voice.

I have carved out a career in foreign lands, but in the poetry of my ancient homeland I have found renewed possibilities for dreaming.

"*Poet Li Bai* merits wider exposure," opined the *Opera News* reviewer, and "heralds a prominent international afterlife," claimed another. No matter how long or even whether I sing the role, this opera, our child, will have life beyond Martha and me. And with all the roles I continue to sing, on major stages and small ones, in recitals, in one-man shows of the songs I grew up with, in grand operas and tiny experimental one-acters, I will express the spirit of music that passed between my brother and me the last day I spent with him. This is my goal.

I have a dear friend, John Sie, a cable television pioneer and entrepreneur, who has a big heart and a good head on his shoulders, which helps to balance my operatic temperament when even Martha can't bring me down to earth. John and his wife, Anna, had rented a splendid villa overlooking the Mediterranean on a high cliff in Positano, Italy, and encouraged Martha and me to come stay with them in the fall of 2004. Martha flew down from Berlin, where I was singing in *Aida* at the Berlin Staatsoper. "Tian, you must come down even for a day or two, it is so beautiful here," she phoned to tell me after she arrived there. "You will find this so relaxing and reinvigorating." I had three days between performances. Ordinarily, I will not risk traveling during an opera run, for fear I will not get back in time. But to relax and renew was so tempting. I was so tired. Just this once I decided to take the chance, and I flew to join them for two days and a night.

The splendid view over the Amalfi coast, the bright sun, and the fresh sea air were, as Martha had promised, deeply refreshing. After dinner, John and I stayed out on the terrace as the night grew dark. We began to talk. He asked me what it was I wanted to do in my life now. *Li Bai* was in its earliest stages. What Martha and I dreamed of at that moment, I confided, was some way to help young singers find a future in opera. I became emotional. I wanted to provide the highest level of master classes for them, so that they could learn and carry on the great tradition that I was following. But this was just a fantasy, really, I sighed. John asked what we would need to make such a thing come true. He proceeded to offer organized, clear, logical, step-by-step advice. By the time I had to return to Berlin the next morning, I had in mind what was essentially a business plan to make this dream a reality.

In 2005, Martha and I brought my great teacher Carlo Bergonzi, eighty-two years old, plus two Met coaches to Beijing for two weeks of master classes, funded by Anna and John Sie. It was one of the most satisfying things we have ever undertaken. We held

I love giving master classes and talks in China. Here I am at the Shanghai Conservatory of Music in 2005 with Madame Zhou Xiaoyan, nearing ninety, who has fostered operatic singing in China through great difficulties.

auditions in Beijing for singers from all over China. Eventually, twenty-four singers got to participate, and three hundred more audited the classes each day. Every day I sat in the first row, along with the young aspirants, a little jealous of the level they'd reached in their art at an age when I was still squeezing my accordion in the factory band. Watching the great master work with these gifted singers, I realized that I still could learn from him, and from them.

So many of them asked me about how to make it in opera. I told them that few of them would make it, but all had the right to try. Two of the young singers from this master class, plus one other who won a national audition, came to Central City to perform in supporting roles in *Poet Li Bai* and to participate in the opera's young artist program. At summer's end, the three young singers joined us in New York, where we arranged for additional training. They came to our apartment for lunch the day they arrived in the city. I went to help Martha in the kitchen and returned to find the singers gaping out the window at Lincoln Center across the street. The Met was closed for the summer break, with the season not set to resume for another six weeks, but there was plenty of preseason work underway. I asked whether they would like to go over there with me—right now. "Please!" they cried in unison.

When Martha and I brought them in through the stage door and were greeted by security guards, receptionists, and stagehands, I saw through these young aspirants' eyes what a home I had made for myself in this splendid place. Lighting designers were working onstage for an upcoming production, and I invited the two young men and one woman to walk a few steps onstage for a moment. For two minutes they stared in astonishment at the enormous gilt and burgundy auditorium and the crystal chandeliers.

"Teacher Tian," said the tenor, the most brazen of the three, "can I try my voice here?"

I yanked him off the stage as fast as I could. We weren't supposed to be there. I took them down into the auditorium and invited them to look around. We walked down to the fifth row center, and, as they gazed at the space in wonderment, I suddenly pictured my own face the first day I came to the Met, on my first day in the United States in 1983. I had forgotten what I had seen and felt. Now I remembered sitting in this very row for the second act of *Ernani* the night that Luciano Pavarotti had inspired me to become an opera singer.

Sensing my emotions, the tenor asked me, "Teacher Tian, what was it like for you the first time you came into this hall?" They all gathered around. I told them my story. I saw the same dream I had had then take shape in their eyes now. Perhaps they, too, would sing one day from this stage.

Ten days later, the great Pavarotti died.

Martha's mother used to say, "Be half full. Then you will always have room for more." So I say to these young artists, Dream on. Leave room inside for a cool, clear lake. There you will find your voice. And perhaps your heart's desire.

Come fish with me and my brother. *Gui qu lai.*

"Goodbye at the River"

In this little river town
the autumn rain lets up
the wine's all gone
well then, goodbye!

You stretch out in your boat
the sail fills, you skim home
past islands burning with flowers
banks crowded with willows

what about me? I don't know
I think I'll go sit on that big rock
and fish.

—Li Bai

ACKNOWLEDGMENTS

FROM MAO to the Met, and beyond, is a very long road. This book has been a great experience along this life journey. I am happy and grateful that I have been able to tread these pages with Lois B. Morris. I thank her for her patience, humor, and quick and sharp thinking. Her questions and even our arguments helped to elicit my innermost feelings and to open more doors to my memories.

Grateful thanks to Helen Rees, agent supreme. Introduced to Martha and me by our friend Alice Kandell, Helen made it her years-long mission to get me to tell my stories to a wider audience. After a profile of me appeared in the *New York Times* in late 2002, Helen approached the writers, Robert Lipsyte and Lois B. Morris, to work with me, which resulted in Lois's transformation of my personal opera into suitably dramatic English prose, with Bob advising at every turn. The two have become old China hands and personal friends in the process. Helen, in her wisdom, next led us to another opera fan, our editor, Hana Lane, at John Wiley & Sons, who has firmly guided my life story with sensitivity to music and opera, to the emotional experience of the immigrant, and, not least, to putting it all into memoir form.

So many people have helped in innumerable ways in this journey toward the printed page. A huge thank-you to Stella Xin, for her voluminous and extraordinary translations of everything from musings to poems and songs and for her understanding of my life and experiences. To those who read earlier drafts of the manuscript—including Diana Liao and Genevieve Young—your comments and suggestions have improved this book. Joanna Yuen provided assistance in the final phases of this project, for which we are very grateful.

Grateful thanks to Bei Dao for his permission to use his poem "Huida" ("The Answer") in these pages and to Haun Saussy, for furnishing us his wonderful translation. David S. G. Goodman generously provided his "Trust in the Future" translation of the poem by Shi Zhi. Youqin Wang kindly permitted us to include her translation of the "Song of Ox-Ghosts and Snake Demons" from her article "Student Attacks Against Teachers: The Revolution of 1966."

I am much obliged to my mother, Lu Yuan, and my sister, Meimei (Lam Tin), and my Jiuma in Jincheng for sharing their memories and recollections of their history and our lives in China, especially during the Cultural Revolution. Martha's family, the Liaos, has helped us in critical situations mentioned in the book, in their most inconspicuous and quiet way.

Likewise, to my Denver family of friends, thank you all for the memories, stories, and otherwise forgotten details of those so-important years in my first American city, which will always be the first American city in my heart, no matter where I live. Many of them are board members of Asian Performing Arts of Colorado (APAC), which has supported my career before I even had one. Many of them have traveled to my performances throughout the world and have been present, though unnamed, during many of the events that I recount in these pages. They are Denise Gliwa (the one who sent me to sing in front of the ladies' intimate apparel department at Joslin during the Celebrate China week) and her husband, Kevin; Jan Steinhauser (who chaired Celebrate China and introduced me to matzoh balls) and her husband, Shelly; Celeste Fleming and her late husband, John (who hosted and invited some three hundred friends to our wedding party in their beautiful Japanese garden); Jennifer Heglin (whose dog, Tosca, did get a mention in the book); Lorraine (who chaired the most elaborate Chinese banquet to raise funds for APAC) and Darby Smith; Gayle (always smiling, always helping, always up for a party) and Gary Ray; Jimmy and Linda Yip (hats off to their Nathan Yip Foundation, which gives so many poor kids in China a chance to study); Nancy Elkind; Johnny Hsu; Woon Ki Lau; Paul Ramsey; Lily Shen; Greg

Smith; Julia White; Isabelle Yu; and Ann Walsh and her late husband, Lou.

Not mentioned in the chapter that recounts the creation and production of the opera *Poet Li Bai* is a group of close friends whose generous support has given me the confidence to make a quantum leap in my career. They are Anna and John J. Sie, Betty and Ralph Peterson, Dan Ritchie, and Pat Cortez. I salute and thank them, especially Anna and John, who guaranteed any financial deficit to this production.

I am indebted also to many friends and colleagues who provided invaluable advice at important stages of my career: Shirley Young, Joe Bascetta, David and Cecilia Chang, Wei Christianson, Seiji Ozawa, Lenore Rosenberg, Anita and John Nelson, Tan Dun and Jane Huang, Yu Long, Bonko Chan, Warren Mok, Qian Shijin, Marianne Cornetti, Joan Dornemann, Dennis Giauque, Nico Castel, Denise Massé, Gareth Morrell, Linda Hall, Noriyoshi and Hiroko Horiuchi, Zhou Xiaoyan, Ruth Falcon, Pierre Vallet, Joseph Colaneri, Katherine Chu, Guo Shuzheng, Arthur Levy, Veronica Villarroel, Chiang Ching, Sarina Tang, Wei Fugen, Savio and Emily Woo, Joanna Lee, Ken Smith, Shu Xiao, Cai Lien, Lu Mingsheng, and, of course, my managers, Bruce Zemsky and Alan Green.

Though unseen, others who populate scenes in these chapters include Monica Gancia and Luis Alberto Erize, in Buenos Aires; Hans and Monika Schleuter, in Bonn; and Mary Anne and Fred Whitacre, in Colorado. Their hospitality (for Niu Niu as well) and support, help with managing our lives, merry-making, and now long-lasting friendship add warmth to our existence and spice to these pages.

Others who must be thanked for being with me throughout my wild ride, giving their love and support through all the ups and downs, include Su Xiaoming, Long Shen, Sun Bing, An Ping, Shan Shan and Yeh Qing, Sophie and Sam Chen, Mimi and Eddie Hsiung, Chen Danqing, Liu Dan, Jane Wang, Tony Tan, Sando Xia, Fu Xiaohong and Li-ke Chang, Maggie and Li-kuo Chang, Zhang Zhendi, Han Xiaoming, Terry and Pearl Li, Wang Te, Yu Wenqing, Nie Mengxi, Chen Jixin, Yu Yianming, Helen Mei, Cai Guangyun, Zhang Ningzhou, Yan Gang, Yan Lin, Luan Yi, Liu Shuxin, Chen

Zhongxiang, Su Ying, Theresa and Ling Chen, Sun Xiuwei, Zhou Yibing, Wang Xinming, Zhang Xuan, Zhang Xihai, Rachel Cooper, Sheen and Alan Capalbo, Joseph and Catherine Chi, Lisa Chyn, Lian-Pey Kuo Robins, Sylvie Paulien, Marianne Flettner, Yu Ping, Tian Xiaohui, Zhang Shizheng, Pei Weini, and Jin Peilu. To Kathy Sun, my former colleague at the Central Philharmonic Society, heartfelt thanks for taking care of our pets, Niu Niu and Luke, while we are away.

Clara DeOrsay, whom we call Aunt Clara, is our American mother. At age ninety-nine, she continues to guide us with her wisdom in every step we take. I want to thank her also for her lakeside cottage in Maine, which provides me peace and relaxation while I fish.

I am indebted to all the extraordinarily talented people at the Metropolitan Opera who, since 1991, have provided opportunities, experience, advice, direction, and tales to tell. I thank everyone at that remarkable place, from top management, all music and staging staff, my singing colleagues, chorus members, stage managers, makeup and wardrobe staff, supers, and dancers to those who labor behind the scenes: you have provided an operatic home, without which there would have been plenty of Mao but no Met.

Finally, I am forever obliged to my wife, Martha. The two years during which Lois and I wrote this book were an incredibly busy time for Martha as she tirelessly and successfully produced *Poet Li Bai*. She is a major character in this book and an astute reader of all drafts as well. As she has always done throughout my opera career, of which she is so much a part, she is my most honest audience. Without Martha, there would not be a book.

—Hao Jiang Tian

Above all, I wish to thank Hao Jiang Tian and Martha Liao for allowing me and my husband, Robert Lipsyte, to stick our noses into every corner of their lives, past and present, in our most un-Chinese way. Their collegiality is on a level with their generosity and hospitality, not to mention their sense of adventure and fun.

I will always be grateful to and awed by Tian, for his willingness to go deeper and deeper into his thoughts, memories, and sometimes conflicting feelings—and for uncovering for me and Bob a very foreign, very beautiful, often puzzling, always human culture. This collaboration has been the most colorful and exotic of my career, accompanied by staggeringly beautiful music.

I am indebted to Hana Lane and her extraordinary team at Wiley who labored to get this book into such good form, in particular senior production editor Lisa Burstiner and copy editor Patti Waldygo.

Thanks to Itzhak and Toby Perlman and the Perlman Music Program for luring Bob and me from Shelter Island to Shanghai, where we chanced upon Tian and Martha and began the many adventures that have resulted in this book. We are both grateful to Joan Dornemann, Paul Nadler, and Hemdi Kfar, who first invited us to peek behind the scenes into the world of opera and to see for ourselves how complicated and difficult it is to survive, let alone succeed, there. Peter Gelb, Sarah Billinghurst, Joe Clark, Jonathan Friend, and Elena Clark gave us their time and unfettered access to the Metropolitan Opera for our series on Tan Dun and *The First Emperor* that ran in the *New York Times*, which ultimately provided so much of the background for the opera and opera-making expertise that has gone into this book.

I am obliged to Zhai Zhenhua for writing *Red Flower of China*, the Cultural Revolution memoir that, in all its pain, enabled me to comprehend how and why some of the Red Guards went to their extremes—and, who, as she did, went on to lead an exemplary life. And thanks to the Melbourne City Opera's Web site (Melbournecityopera.com.au) for its entertaining and quotable glossary, which I recommend to everyone.

To Beverley Zabriskie, I am ever so grateful for her insights into psyches East and West. Thanks, too, to Barbara Lowenstein for her able representation.

Xie xie to all the people in China I have met on the three trips that have been devoted to this book—they have shared their experiences of life in that country under Mao and afterward, including

Long Shen, who provided his insights and personal history on the long and malodorous train ride from Jincheng to Beijing. Thanks to the Du family for their hospitality, including Du Yawen, the charming young woman who was seated next to me because she's studying English and I desperately needed somebody to talk to.

My deepest thanks and love go to my husband, "BoBo," for his encouragement and help and his willingness to do without me when I trekked around with Tian and Martha on my own.

—Lois B. Morris

INDEX

Page numbers in *italics* refer to illustrations.